MONEY, INCENTIVES, AND EFFICIENCY IN THE HUNGARIAN ECONOMIC REFORM

MONEY, INCENTIVES, AND EFFICIENCY IN THE HUNGARIAN ECONOMIC REFORM

Edited by
JOSEF C. BRADA and
ISTVÁN DOBOZI

M. E. Sharpe, Inc.
Armonk, New York
London, England

Published simultaneously as Vol. 28, Nos. 1 and 2 of *Eastern European Economics*.

Library of Congress Cataloging-in-Publication Data

Money, incentives, and efficiency in the Hungarian economic reform.

Includes bibliographical references.
1. Hungary—Economic policy—1968–   . 2. Monetary policy—Hungary.
3. Banks and banking—Hungary. 4. Efficiency,
Industrial—Hungary. 6. Incentives in industry—Hungary.
I. Brada, Josef C., 1942–   . II. Dobozi, István.
HC300.28.M66   1990   338.9439   89-24210
ISBN 0-87332-566-4

Printed in the United States of America.

∞

MA   10 9 8 7 6 5 4 3 2 1

Contents

PART II. **THE EFFICIENCY ALLOCATION OF RESOURCES—WHAT HAS REFORM ACHIEVED?**

Illustrations

FIGURES

TABLES

Editors and Contributors

Josef C. Brada

Professor of Economics, Arizona State University; editor of *Journal of Comparative Economics* and co-editor of *Soviet and Eastern European Foreign Trade*.

István Dobozi

Department Head, Research Institute for the World Economy, Hungarian Academy of Sciences.

Tamás Bácskai

Professor and Head of the Department of Finance and Banking, Karl Marx University of Economics; Adviser to the President of the National Bank of Hungary.

Béla Balassa

Professor of Political Economy, Johns Hopkins University and Consultant to the World Bank.

Péter Ákos Bod

Research Fellow at the Research Institute for Economic Planning of the National Planning Office, Budapest.

János Gács

Senior Researcher at the Institute for Economic and Market Research, Budapest.

Aladár Sipos

Director, Research Institute for Economics, Hungarian Academy of Sciences.

Catherine M. Sokil

Assistant Professor of Economics, Middlebury College.

Márton Tardos   Department Head, Research Institute for Economics, Hungarian Academy of Sciences.

János Timár   Professor of Labor Economics, Karl Marx University.

Robert S. Whitesell   Assistant Professor of Economics, Williams College.

MONEY, INCENTIVES, AND EFFICIENCY IN THE HUNGARIAN ECONOMIC REFORM

Economic Reform in Hungary

An Overview and Assessment

JOSEF C. BRADA AND ISTVÁN DOBOZI

Slightly more than two decades have elapsed since Hungary embarked upon a major reform of its Soviet-type economic system of directive central planning, a system that saddled the economy with growing inefficiency and declining welfare. A strong need was felt to make the economic system more flexible and efficient.

The thrust of the 1968 reform, the so-called New Economic Mechanism (NEM), was the abandonment of central planning in favor of an organic combination of the self-regulating market mechanism and central control exercised through indirect, market-compatible fiscal and monetary instruments. The reform blueprint envisaged autonomous, profit-maximizing state enterprises operating in a competitive environment of market-clearing prices, and a close interaction between domestic and world market conditions. The role of the government was conceived as that of a macroeconomic regulator to keep enterprise activities within bounds acceptable to policy makers, and of a shaper of the long-term directions of economic change.

There is no doubt that during the NEM period the Hungarian economy has undergone a considerable transformation, one unparalleled among the socialist systems of Eastern Europe. The reform, unlike several similar efforts in Eastern Europe and the Soviet Union, represents more than a "flash in the pan" and, in fact, remains the longest lasting effort to transcend the basic structure of the traditional Soviet-type economic system.

The first decade of reform

By now it is clear that the NEM process has not been a linear progression toward market-based socialism; rather it has experienced alternating swings. The two-decade old reform process can be roughly divided into two ten-year subperiods, the first covering evolution up to the late 1970s and the second period since then. It was the achievements of the first period that, in the eyes of many Eastern and Western observers, made Hungary a different socialist economy, one that seemed to work. Although in this stage Hungary did not at all become a super-performer in terms of conventional growth indicators—in fact, in this regard it exhibited a substandard performance compared to most of the unreformed socialist econo- mies—the distinctiveness of the effects of the Hungarian mechanism were well perceived. This shift in perception was caused mainly by the change in the position of the Hungarian consumer in the economic system. The consumer market became manifestly better balanced; planners' preferences were less dominant over those of consumers; the influence of the consumer over the producer increased, resulting in a better match between products produced and consumed; and, in addition to the strong growth of the supply of consumer goods, consumers perceived improve- ments in product quality, assortment and similar benefits that are statistically invisible. As a result, the Hungary of the 1970s became an appealing model and a strong bargaining chip for would-be reformers in other socialist countries from Warsaw to Beijing to Moscow.

The economic reality that emerged in Hungary during the first decade of the NEM proved to be a puzzle for analysts both in Hungary and in the West. Though there was a consensus view that the Hungarian economy had become different from the traditional planned economy, opinions diverged on the degree of its differenti- ation, more specifically on whether the changes amounted to a real change in the economic system or merely to a series of sensible policy measures resulting in streamlined, better managed central planning. The different labels then applied to the Hungarian economy aptly reflect the diversity of perspectives concerning the nature of changes under the NEM: "socialist mixed economy," "market social- ism," "modified centrally planned economy," "neither planning nor market," not to mention such popular labels as "refrigerator socialism" or "goulash communism" preferred by Western journalists.

The divergent assessments implicit in these labels reflect, on the one hand, the controversial outcome of the NEM, visible improvements in some areas coexisting with little progress in others, and the persistence of certain undesirable character- istics of the pre-1968 regime, and on the other, the inherent difficulty of separating out the effects of changes in the economic system, in policy, and in the international economic environment. This difficulty was considerably magnified by the drastic shifts in domestic economic policies and the external economic environment that were characteristic of the 1970s.

While the extent of effective, as opposed to formal, changes in the Hungarian economic system remains an open question, it would be hard to deny that the reform brought some institutional and behavioral changes to the economy. It may well be that economic reform in a formerly centralized system must pass through an "extensive" and an "intensive" stage, popular categories in the literature of the socialist countries to describe different phases of the growth process according to the relative weights of quantitative versus qualitative sources of growth. The reform efforts of the first, extensive, decade might have contributed to greater allocative efficiency and improved overall economic performance simply by removing or diminishing some of the most undesirable efficiency-inhibiting characteristics of directive planning, such as directive controls over resource allocation, rigid price controls, excessive central interference in microeconomic decisions, etc. It was a sort of negative reform and certainly the scope for improvement was considerable with its application.

This period, however, did not see simultaneous efforts toward the introduction of elements of a positive reform such as market-based prices, well-functioning factor market mechanisms, and proper micro-incentives—necessary preconditions for altering the fundamental dynamic deficiencies of central planning such as the bias against technological innovation, poor adjustment to changing market conditions, and lack of pressure to minimize costs. It was an illusion on the part of the authorities to believe that the abandonment of the key elements of directive central planning would almost automatically lead to the emergence of effective market forces and market-oriented firm behavior.

The second decade of reform

The second decade of the NEM could well have been the intensive stage of the reform, carrying the country toward the completion of the 1968 blueprint through the introduction of a positive, market-building and efficiency-oriented set of arrangements. In a formal sense, this decade has given the impression of extending the reform in that direction. This period has seen several waves of new reform measures formally moving the economy closer to the original design of NEM: new rules for ''competitive pricing'' were introduced to connect most producer prices directly to foreign trade prices; consumer prices were to be directly tied to producer prices through a uniform turnover tax; multiple exchange rates were replaced by a unified rate in an attempt to bring the forint in line with world currencies and prepare it for later convertibility. In an effort to free enterprises from undesirable central interference, industrial branch ministries were eliminated in favor of a single Ministry of Industry; in order to strengthen competition, efforts were made toward the proliferation of small-scale private and cooperative enterprises; for stimulating competition, a number of monopolistic state trusts were broken up. To improve the labor market mechanism, contract work associations were allowed to operate within enterprises, allowing groups of workers to subcontract their services to their own enterprises, and in an effort to enhance enterprise autonomy and worker self-management, a substantial part of the property rights were transferred to enterprise councils with the right to select managers. Significant liberalization occurred in the wage system with the aim to establish a better linkage between wages and enterprise performance. To promote a more flexible adjustment to world market requirements, autonomous foreign trading rights were given to a large number of producer enterprises. More recently, in a move toward competitive banking, the centralized monobank structure was altered with the creation of autonomous, profit-seeking commercial banks, and some measures were taken toward a limited capital market with the introduction of new financial instruments such as bonds that allow some nonstate-intermediated flows of funds among enterprises and from the household to the enterprise sector. To encourage inter-enterprise resource flows, a limited stock exchange began to operate, and a bankruptcy law was passed under which unprofitable firms may be rehabilitated or closed down. In 1988 the old tax system, riddled with all kinds of *ad hoc* exceptions, was replaced by a new regime based on value-added taxes and a personal income tax.

Though it would be too early to expect positive results from the most recently adopted measures, nevertheless it is paradoxical that the various rounds of institutional and regulatory reforms introduced in the last decade have failed to improve the performance of the economy. As a matter of fact, the opposite happened; the overall economic performance, as well as the internal and external equilibrium of the economy, have deteriorated to such an extent that, at the end of the 1980s, Hungary faces a deep-seated economic crisis of major proportions that has begun to erode the very foundations of the prevailing political structure. A sort of socialist stagflation has set in with the virtually stagnant economy experiencing severe inflationary pressures and growing underutilization of productive capacity. The excessive reliance on foreign borrowing as the main policy response to external shocks affecting the country since the mid-1970s, along with consistently declining export market shares, have led to a persistent and largely intractable debt crisis. Imbalances in the domestic economy have grown considerably; the fiscal deficit has increased, and shortages have reappeared in markets where reasonable balance existed before. Most important, under the balance-of-payments oriented, deflationary, macroeconomic policies pursued during most of the past decade, Hungary's consumer revolution has come to a halt. Particularly in recent years, the population has been forced to bear a progressively greater brunt of adjustment, as possibilities in foreign borrowing and the reduction of domestic absorption through cuts in investment have been exhausted. Real wages and living standard have shown a steady pattern of decline for a large part of the population. Poverty is rapidly rising and today about one-fifth of the population has fallen below the official poverty line, including some strata that previously belonged to Hungary's middle class.

Assessing NEM's achievements and prospects

In the light of the disappointing economic results of the NEM's second decade, when one wave of reform measures was followed by another, the single most important question to pose is: What went wrong with the reforms? Is the NEM-type reform scheme a viable alternative to transcend traditional central planning? What lessons can be learned from the Hungarian experience? Why do economic reforms fail? What are the obstacles? What are the prospects for successful reforms in

Hungary, which today is making desperate efforts at a radical overhaul of its political and economic fabric?

These were the questions to which a group of Hungarian and American economists addressed itself at the Eleventh US-Hungarian Economic Roundtable at Bloomington, Indiana during October 29-November 2, 1987. A number of papers from this Roundtable have been revised and updated for publication in this volume. They focus on two areas: factor market mechanisms and financial regulation, commonly believed to constitute the two weak points of the reform process.

The overall picture emerging from these studies portrays an economy that, after two decades of reform, seems caught in an in-between stage; it has moved away from directive central planning without simultaneously creating a market-driven socialist economy. The studies offer a multiplicity of reasons why the original, basically correct, NEM blueprint has not been fully implemented, thus keeping the Hungarian economy in a half-reformed status beset by the simultaneous existence of weak market mechanisms and ineffective central direction of the economy. Some of these reasons can be summarized as follows:

—The NEM has not been complemented by a depoliticization of economic life. Particularly, fears of unemployment, inflation, and income inequality placed restrictions on the reform mechanism. To varying degrees, the NEM has faced political opposition, usually disguised under a veil of ideological or distributive social justice objections.

—There have been difficulties in extending the reform effort in the midst of serious macroeconomic disequilibrium. The mechanism-distorting feedback effects of grave errors in economic policy have been poorly understood and largely ignored. On several occasions, large macroeconomic imbalances, caused by misguided policies, led to re-centralization or manual guidance with disruptive effects on various elements of the reform mechanism. Such policies included the over-ambitious 1976-80 Five-Year Plan, which generated an overheated economy in the face of an adverse external economic environment and resulted in imprudent foreign borrowing and severe balance-of-payments difficulties. Another policy error was the gross overvaluation of the forint, which necessitated a widespread use of firm-specific export subsidies and the related overtaxation of the best-performing enterprises.

—There is a lack of a truly competitive environment in many product markets due to the failure to establish the institutional preconditions of a market mechanism through an extensive reduction of monopolistic and oligopolistic concentration in industry, and an increase of import competition by the adoption of a more liberal import regime. Despite some progress in breaking up large trusts and creating small enterprises, competition remained limited, especially in the face of protracted balance-of-payments difficulties. The factor market mechanisms have functioned particularly poorly throughout, due to the absence of the appropriate institutional preconditions and continued central interference. The excessive reliance on fiscal redistribution acted as a poor surrogate for real capital market mechanisms. Factor prices remained distorted, with labor undervalued and capital overvalued.

—Effective enterprise autonomy has remained circumscribed. The NEM has not succeeded in cutting the enterprises loose from the tutelage of central authorities. The form of central direction did change, with directive control replaced by a predominantly informal control that included central expectations and guidelines, consultations and bargaining over enterprise plans, particularly those involving large investments. In addition, discriminatory firm-specific credit and fiscal instruments continued to preserve the micro-involvement of the center.

—Profit has not become the expected true indicator of enterprise efficiency. The excessive central intervention in the profit formation process via differentiated taxes and subsidies as well as administrative pricing rules generates substantial divergence between true, intervention-free, and reported, post-intervention profitability which, consequently, weakens the profit incentive.

—In a number of ways, the soft enterprise budget syndrome survived in the NEM. Punishment for inefficiency has largely been absent throughout the reform period as a result of the authorities' refusal to bankrupt losing enterprises. During most of the last decade, subsidization accounted for as much as one-third of total fiscal expenditures, a practice that is contrary to the logic of NEM. This behavior of the center, along with the lack of competitive domestic environment, contributed importantly to the preservation of weak cost-sensitivity and poor adjustment of output patterns to domestic and external changes in demand conditions.

—There is a "regulation illusion" of the central authorities, who usually overestimated their capability to create or, rather, to simulate competitive market conditions and enterprise behavior. The excessive number of changes in the complicated legal rules and regulations imposed a short-run outlook on enterprises. Besides, the regulatory system has become an arena for heavy bargaining between the center and the big enterprises. To a large extent, regulatory bargaining has been substituted for plan bargaining.

—The insulation of the microeconomic sphere from the world market has not diminished sufficiently. The long-standing contradiction between the macro-openness and micro-closedness of the Hungarian economy has not ceased because of the maintenance of a complex web of subsidies, taxes, and disequilibrium exchange rates. These mechanisms continued to prevent the world market from sending appropriate signals for market-oriented adjustment to changes in the external market.

—The price system still suffers from all kinds of distortions and, as a result, is constrained in its ability to send the appropriate market signals. Price controls continued on a wide range of products, and the experiments with administrative pricing schemes, such as competitive pricing, failed to bring about the desired simulation of a competitive environment.

—The piecemeal nature of the reforms limited their impact. Hungarian leaders were late in recognizing the fact that the positive effects of partial reforms reach their limits relatively soon without parallel reform measures in other related areas.

The studies gathered together here tell us, in some detail, a great deal about the achievements and shortcomings of the NEM, as well as the obstacles it faced and the cycles in which reform efforts were followed by retreat. The papers differ in some interesting ways according to the special interest and background of their American or Hungarian authors, and these differences add an important variety and richness to the analyses.

Based on a major multi-year research project conducted at the Hungarian Institute of Economics, Aladár Sipos and Márton Tardos, leaders of the project, offer a comprehensive review of the organizational evolution of the Hungarian economy under the NEM. In this critical appraisal two points come across particularly sharply: first, it has been far more difficult to substitute a regulated market for directive central planning than was generally imagined two decades ago; and, second, the NEM has not been radical and consistent enough to alter the basic deficiencies of the previous system. The paper provides evidence on how the promulgation of market-oriented reforms has repeatedly come into conflict with established practices, and how the authorities, referring to the national economic interest, have continued to control the firms formally or informally. The authors reserve especially harsh criticism for financial regulation, which, despite all efforts, has failed to create a growing role for money. Instead, it has achieved something inconsistent with the logic of the NEM: it has provided assurance of survival for practically every firm.

The need for improving the operation of factor markets is the central concern of the paper by Béla Balassa. He calls for modifying the currently distorted relative prices of capital and labor in favor of the latter. In regard to labor markets, the paper recommends measures to encourage geographical and occupational labor mobility, while avoiding excessive wage increases—a major threat following wage deregulation—by a hardening of the enterprise budget constraint. A variety of measures is proposed to increase capital availability and to ensure the more efficient use of capital, including the broadening of the scope for the direct flow of financial resources among firms through the bond market and the commercial banking sector. Balassa argues that closing down inefficient firms would free resources for more efficient uses elsewhere, but cautions against rehabilitating such firms at the expense of efficient enterprises.

Catherine M. Sokil continues the discussion of financial and labor market reforms from the point of view of whether the preconditions for the operation of a market mechanism have been developed in these fields. Her answers are mixed. Despite some recent positive institutional developments, truly competitive capital market conditions have not yet been created. Better conditions prevail in the labor market, as a result of limited central intervention, some upward wage flexibility, freedom of workers to choose and change jobs, and the very significant opportunities in the second economy. Sokil portrays the Hungarian economy as a dual system, made up of a first and a second economy, with an "unequal playing field" for the two sets of players. Large state firms have a competitive edge in the capital market, while the small private and cooperative firms have an edge in the labor market. The author concludes that the discriminatory policies and regulators underlying these unequal conditions tend to preclude competition in factor markets and to weaken the profit incentive.

The excessive reliance on fiscal redistribution has long been singled out by Hungarian economists as an anti-reform device that weakens the profit incentive and contributes to the preservation of the soft budget syndrome. Recent proposals advocate a more balanced fiscal-monetary mix by significantly strengthening the relative importance of monetary regulation. It is against this background that Márton Tardos asks: Can monetary policy succeed in Hungary? This question has become particularly relevant with the 1987 introduction of a two-tier banking system. The suggested answer is yes, provided some present deficiencies are removed. Among these Tardos refers, for instance, to the problem that the central budget's financing requirements have not been well integrated into the banking system and, as a consequence, the credit supply of the commercial banks must be unilaterally adjusted to the financing needs of the budget. What Tardos describes appears to be the crowding-out effect familiar to Western economists: the need to finance the fiscal deficit induces the central bank to restrict the lending activities of the commercial banks. Under these circumstances, even efficient enterprises might fear that the commercial banks will be unable to meet their borrowing requirements. Tardos outlines a desirable monetary policy that does not extend beyond coordinating the volume of money supply with the economy's productive capacity and fine-tuning the monetary processes in line with central preferences to counteract small changes in economic outcomes.

Following a *tour de horizon* of the historical evolution of Hungary's banking system, Tamás Bácskai offers an insider's view of the recent reorganization of this system. As a former top executive of the Hungarian National Bank (HNB), he was directly involved in designing the bank reforms. He asserts that, apart from the most recently introduced changes, the centralized monobank structure was very little altered under the NEM, and the HNB continued to act more like a central institution of control and a basic safeguard for predominantly centralized investment decisions than as a commercially oriented bank. For a long time many reform-minded economists viewed the HNB as one of the serious institutional roadblocks to the comprehensive marketization of the economy. In recent years, the HNB has been willing to begin surrendering parts of its monopolistic power, albeit with great reluctance. In January 1987, five commercial banks were established. While suggesting that the banking system is moving in the right direction, Bácskai finds changes incomplete and argues that further reform efforts toward truly competitive banking mechanisms are necessary.

A key objective of the economic reform is to increase the efficiency of resource allocation. How successful has the NEM been in this regard? Robert S. Whitesell offers an empirical evaluation of this performance dimension of NEM. Using production function analysis, he finds that the Hungarian economy is much less allocatively efficient than the West German economy. He rationalizes this result by the weakness of horizontal input allocations, the lack of market-clearing prices, and improper economic incentives in Hungary. While this finding does not strike the reader as unexpected, another result of the study is both striking and disappointing: up to 1984, the last year of the analysis, the NEM did not generate any improvement in resource allocation. Indeed, the degree of inefficiency appears to be increasing over time. This finding, especially if confirmed by alternative methodological approaches, lends support to those observers who contend that Hungary's economic reform has not been radical enough to alter the fundamental deficiencies of the previous system.

János Gács carries on the empirical examination of the achievements of the NEM by focusing on the second decade, which basically was a period of austerity prompted by balance-of-payments difficulties. He takes a look at the changes in the structure of industrial production and foreign trade during this period. While the chronic problems of the external imbalance and the long-term modernization requirements would have necessitated an accelerated transformation of the composition of output and export, the facts presented reveal a pattern of structural immobility in most areas. The short-term balance-of-payments oriented policies and the weakness of micro-incentives act in unison to conserve the existing pattern, which in turn leads to further losses in export market shares and perpetuates the balance-of-payments difficulties. Reducing the scope of central interference and adopting effective market instruments are recommended for accelerating the modernization of output and export patterns and for facilitating faster adjustment to shifts in external market conditions.

An important aim of the original blueprint of the NEM was to greatly enhance enterprise adaptation to changes in the economic environment as a basic imperative to maximize profit. Drawing on extensive firm-level surveys, Péter Ákos Bod examines the achievements of the NEM from this angle. While crediting it with certain progress, he depicts an attenuated micro-responsiveness to environmental changes, particularly to world market changes. The country's falling export shares over the course of the NEM are taken as an indicator of inadequate adaptation. Bod finds the underlying reasons for the lack of export competitiveness in the continued strong influence of the center on enterprise decisions; in the highly concentrated domestic market structure, which breeds monopolistic behavior; in the lack of strategic thinking on the part of enterprises resulting, in no small measure, from the equally short horizon taken by the government itself; and from the frequently redefined rules of the game. To achieve a better adaptation to the environment, Bod pins his hopes on the most recently introduced reform package, which may create a clearer demarcation between the enterprise and the state.

As in other centrally planned economies, employment practices in pre-NEM Hungary exhibited the paradoxical simultaneous existence of a labor shortage and of an underutilization of labor. Under the NEM, cost-minimizing enterprises were expected to eliminate this paradox by using labor more efficiently. But the very fact that, even in recent years, the government has been engaged in a campaign for the defense of worktime, indicates that progress in this area proved to be slower than hoped for. János Timár's study on worktime utilization estimates that today not more than 70-75 percent of the time base available is utilized in Hungary's industrial state sector, with the balance lost as a result of full-day absences and leaves taken during the working day, as well as of underutilization due to short-comings in inter-enterprise cooperation, shortages of materials and tools, failures of equipment, etc. He estimates the mobilizable manpower reserve at 8-10 percent of the labor time available. Timár believes that direct actions aiming at worktime losses can be effective only if they form an integral part of a market-oriented modernization of the entire economic system.

Looking to the future

Since the landmark Party Conference of May 1988, when János Kádár was effectively relieved of his party leadership, social changes in Hungary burst forth in ways dizzying to everyone. As a direct consequence of the intractable economic crisis, failed government policies and unfulfilled promises, the legitimacy of the socialist political system is on the line.

Earlier pleas by reform economists for the reaffirmation of the original objectives of the NEM appear today as falling short of what needs to be, and should be, done. The rapidly unfolding liberalization drive now points far beyond the objectives of 1968 in at least two main respects. First, radical political liberalization is considered as a prerequisite for the full-scale implementation of the radical market-oriented economic reforms. Replacement of the discredited one-party pluralism by a multiparty political system is under way. In an effort to depoliticize the economy, the alternative political forces must push for the elimination of the Communist party's role as a parallel network of economic command that frequently overrides the signals given by the market. Second, restructuring the ownership pattern is now viewed as a fundamental prerequisite to overhauling the economic system. A variety of new ownership patterns is being considered, and the partial implementation of some of them is under way. The thrust of the ownership reform is to reduce state ownership in favor of alternative schemes, such as joint stock companies, cooperatives, stock ownership by employees, fully privatized firms, etc., with the aim of creating, as Márton Tardos puts it in this volume, "real owners" in place of the present quasi-owners, to instill entrepreneurial flair in factory managers and workers.

Following the failure of the government's stabilization program pursued since 1987, liberalization, deregulation, and supply-side economics have become the buzz-words of government economic programs. At this juncture, the summer of 1989, given large uncertainties, it is not possible to predict how far and quickly Hungary can proceed with the new round of radical-sounding reform measures. The only thing we can predict with certainty is that they will be implemented under very unfavorable conditions and will encounter grave difficulties. To be sure, a number of hard questions will have to be tackled:

—How can the reform effort be greatly extended in new directions under severe internal and external economic imbalances? The fact that the country will be under a forced foreign debt-service regime for several years to come seems to allow only a relatively narrow scope for all-out liberalization, particularly in imports.

—How can the potentially inflation-generating effects of several important elements—wages, prices, subsidies, imports, etc.—of the liberalization package be held within tolerable limits, when inflation is already at a two-digit level, without keeping the economy stagnant through deflationary policies, thus conserving the obsolete pattern of output?

—How will the emerging pluralistic political system, including a Communist party beset by a deep rift, affect the effectiveness of government policies and reform measures? There are indications that the independent political and social organizations show greater concern about redistributing the economic pie than about its increase. How can these pressures for redistribution be handled without the danger of inflationary "over-distribution" forced upon a government that is steadily losing authority, and whose ability and competence in steering the economy is being questioned following a recent series of confused and erroneous decisions? How will this government be able to carry out the tough marketization and deregulation program that would be a tall order even for a strong leadership commanding public confidence?

—What is the incentive for workers to support the liberalization reform and policies if these potentially involve, even temporarily, further cuts in wages, faster inflation, and the possibility of unemployment? Will the social safety net be put in place in time to deal with the unavoidable social effects of market liberalization when the government is pulling out from more and more areas of traditional social services? There are signs that the earlier pro-reform consensus is rapidly eroding as a growing part of the population finds the greater burden imposed on it a senseless sacrifice. Any major social reform is, in a certain sense, a matter of trust, a belief that things will be better in the not too distant future. Will such a trust be there?

—Will the ownership reform bring about the expected radical changes in managerial and worker behavior or, instead, will it remain at the level of formal changes like several earlier efforts of a similar kind? Is it well understood by the policy makers that the economics of privatization, and the ownership reform in general, cannot be separated from the economics of competition and regulation, since they are interrelated determinants of enterprise incentives and behavior? Will an effective framework of competition and regulation be in place in due time for the desired benefits of ownership reform to materialize?

How successful Hungary will be in finding right answers to these and many other thorny questions will determine, in a large part, whether the unfolding wave of new reform efforts will be able to carry the country beyond the within-system changes of two decades of the New Economic Mechanism.

PART I

MONEY, BANKING, AND REGULATION IN THE HUNGARIAN REFORM

Economic Control and the Structural Interdependence of Organizations in Hungary at the End of the Second Reform Decade

ALADÁR SIPOS AND MÁRTON TARDOS

In 1981 a major research project was launched by the Institute of Economics of the Hungarian Academy of Sciences to study the organizational system of the economy. In this paper the two leaders of the project report on the results, relying on several hundred analyses and case studies as well as on a debate on the findings conducted within the Institute.

The grave functional disturbances of the Hungarian economy, recurring from time to time, indicated already in the 1960s that the socialist transformation, nationalization, and the collectivization of agriculture, as well as the planned economy based on the former had led to such obsolete and bureaucratic management as to put a brake on Hungarian economic development and hinder its catching up with the more advanced countries. The reform of the Hungarian system of economic control and management, proclaimed in 1966, sought to assist in solving this problem. The two decades since then have supplied important evidence about the opportunities that socialist ownership of the means of production provides for substituting the exclusive role of governmental administration in economic control with a planned regulated market, and about the difficulties arising in such a process.

**Structural interdependence of organizations in the economy
after introduction of the New Economic Mechanism**

The policy program of moving toward a regulated market, approved in 1966, set the aim not only of abandoning the practice of directive planning and the central allocation of materials, but also of making cooperative ownership equal to state property, and of opening the way for private initiatives. The program wished to transcend the system of central state administration; of centralized control and direct checking by party organizations; of subordination of monetary processes to the national economic plan; as well as the extensive limitations on the economic freedom of citizens.

In the course of its development between 1968-1984, despite fluctuations, the Hungarian economy was capable of raising the efficiency of management by resolving the internal inconsistencies of the directive planning system, of securing for its citizens, as producers, a growing freedom in choosing jobs and creative opportunities, and of moving closer to the goal of consumer sovereignty.

It also became clear that the hierarchically organized state and cooperative enterprises necessary for market conditions could not obtain their autonomy through decrees and declarations. The actual evolution of enterprise autonomy is hindered by:

—the almost confused dependence of the firms on the territorial, functional, and branch administration, and on the institutions of the Party. Such dependence exists in both formal and informal systems of relations;

—the large number of financial prescriptions which provide opportunities for the control agencies to prevent firms from freely using their funds, and to restrict the use of enterprise incomes for paying wages (earnings) and financing investments; the price regulations that set the price formation rules of the so-called free-priced products also belong here;

—finally, the lack of capital and labor markets. Thus one firm may not have access to resources even for the most profitable investments, while another can use its own resources and even obtain credit for loss-making investment projects.

Thus it may be stated that the changes implemented between 1966-1968 started a process toward a planned regulated market, in the course of which no adequate requirements were raised for the improvement of efficiency. This was due to inconsistencies in the implementation of the program, to conservative political forces, and to some problems that had not been thoroughly considered and thus remained unsolved. Within the framework of centrally determined financial regulators, the firms could make their own decisions on matters of production, procurement, sales, and even investment. But if their financial results deviated from the planned targets, and if their profits did not increase monotonically, their autonomy became restricted by state intervention. As a matter of fact, owing to unforeseen developments in domestic or external markets, or to deviations in their performances from what was planned, the results of firms frequently fell beyond the narrow path deemed acceptable by the authorities. In such cases, when the income of the firm was higher than expected, the central agencies collected the firm's profits, while when income conditions were unfavorable, the firms concerned were at the mercy of the central agencies who could reduce taxes or even grant subsidies. The authorities, because of the large number of firms in distress, came to the rescue, thus undermining their own previously issued rules.

The structural interdependence of organizations, even under the conditions of the NEM, was determined by the simple functional system that had developed after nationalization. Such a system created an easy means for the control of enterprise

wages, and investments. This is aimed at bringing about competition among firms, including the use of market methods of regrouping incomes among firms by issuing of bonds, the foundation of joint enterprises, etc.

Problems of the enterprise structure

One of the questions of major portent, unsolved to this day, is enterprise structure, especially the dominance of big firms and the lack of small and medium ones. Several debates were conducted about a desirable enterprise structure. The period of success for those who advocated the dominance of big firms was between 1962-63 and 1975-77 when the number of economic entities clearly diminished. The opposite tendencies could be observed between 1968 and 1970 and after 1979.

Those participating in the discussions knew well that the concentration of production entails savings in unit costs, and that efficient management demands definite sizes of establishments and firms. They also knew that adjustment to the changing, ever diversifying economic needs would be helped in general, and in the branches not characterized by capital concentration in particular, by competition among firms and by the appearance of new firms.

From the background of the debate, which was partly ideological, the following actual problems should be underlined:

The strong enterprise concentration, developed since 1950, has in most cases not brought about firms that could be viewed as big by international standards, or ones whose activities would have produced significant savings in unit costs. In those branches where international practice is characterized by strong concentration, Hungarian firms are, in general, not big. Still, in Hungary there are relatively many enterprises that are regarded as big, but are squeezed out from the international competition. They are not sufficiently specialized, and thus only suffer from the disadvantages deriving from being big: slow changes in the product mix, clumsiness, and the concomitant high unit costs of production. The unchanged survival of unsuccessful firms is in the interest of many people who spare no pains to argue about the efficiency of scale with general statements, without analyzing these concrete cases. For this they also exploit the natural political reluctance stemming from the social problems brought to the surface by the losses of the major firms. The lack of small and medium firms is most efficient in those branches of the Hungarian economy where technical progress demands a division of labor on the market and cooperation among diversified smaller productive units, as well as a fast modification of production patterns. These characteristics are evident in light industry, services, agriculture, fine chemicals, certain branches of engineering, etc. The creation of firms big in their own area by international comparison, though insignificant relative to the biggest mass-producing concerns, can be deduced from the internal logic of mandatory planning and from the efforts of direct control aiming at transparency. This logic was further supported, even after the proclamation of the economic reform, by two major factors. First, the markedly delimited production lines and the resulting specialization of enterprises allowed firms to be accountable not only, and not primarily, for their profitability, but also, and more importantly, for their quantitatively measurable domestic and foreign deliveries, that is, for commodity supply. Secondly, the post-reform Hungarian economy accepted and strengthened the big firms even where their economic advantages were ambiguous, because, as has been mentioned, Hungarian firms can operate without government support only if their actual results do not show too large a discrepancy from the one taken into account when the regulators were "calibrated." In reality, the bigger and the more diversified a firm, the more likely it is that the deviations from the expected conditions will level out, and thus the planned and actual results will not show any significant differences, either. The trend observable all over the world, that the raising of the volume of output through diversification reduces uncertainties in the results of enterprise management, holds true *a fortiori* under Hungarian conditions. It follows that if, with the regulation of demand and investment valid since 1968, there had been smaller, specialized firms operating, the individual subsidies and tax reductions could have been less easily avoided. All this makes it understandable, although not excusable, that the supreme authorities and firms did not abandon their earlier efforts at concentration, and that the post-1979 organizational efforts aimed at stimulating competition have not led to a great success.

Nevertheless, from 1979 on, significant changes took place. The decline in the number of state and cooperative firms has stopped and even perhaps reversed. The biggest changes occurred in the food processing industry and in some services. Although progress in the breaking up of large organizations has not reached the planned extent, the results are worthy of attention. Even more significant is the formation of subsidiaries and so-called enterprise and cooperative small ventures. Parallel to these, new forms of enterprise also appeared, including economic work teams, civil law associations, specialized cooperative groups, etc., and economic work teams also began to spread within the enterprises. As regards the work teams, actually the most widespread of these new forms, they have not become new forms of enterprise in reality; we cannot regard them to be anything else than work brigades, operating under dependency relations to the enterprise, while enjoying autonomy only in the selection of members and income distribution. This development, not free of contradictions, resulted in a significant number of economic organizations with more or less autonomy not only in agriculture, also considering household plots and complementary farming by employees with main jobs in other branches, but also in industry, construction, trade, and services.

But the strict division of labor between big firms and their subsidiaries, and the avoidance and lack of competition essentially remained the same. Several of our case studies indicate that state and cooperative big and small organizations, primarily in industry, construction, and catering, all reacted to declining demand and sharpening competition by reducing supply, instead of increasing their efforts. Similar phenomena could be observed in the activities of the already existing smaller ventures, as well as among the small service firms of the state and cooperative sectors. Later, in the context of the general regulation of earnings, we shall return to the question of how the defensive behavior of new and old small enterprise organizations became possible, and why they were not forced to compete to meet market demands.

The behavior of state and cooperative firms, particularly that of the new small enterprises and cooperatives, is determined by the activity expected by the center, which may, with some simplification, be called the supply task. If the profitability of this activity was not satisfactory, the meeting of these output goals was supported by individual subsidies and tax reductions. This situation did not change even after the reduction of subsidies and moderation of tax facilities for those firms with deteriorating results. While their staff was diminishing, they reacted with price increases and used their depreciation allowances to cover current costs. Some of the workers withheld performance within the firm during the legal worktime, but they were able to get extra income through overtime premiums, enterprise work-teams, small ventures outside the firm, and illegal work.

Among private activities, the most successful ones have been the farming of family household plots by employees of state firms. The value of output from these small farms exceeds one third of the gross output of agriculture, in animal husbandry it is 40 percent, and for the net output of agriculture it is more than half. Small-scale production secures a considerable additional income for people living in the country-side, admittedly at the price of much extra work. However, in regard to the future, small-scale agricultural production can hardly grow and keep pace with the require-ments for greater efficiency without adequate mechanization and modernization. Thus food supply and agricultural exports may become uncertain. In addition, lacking domestic and imported supply, there is no opportunity for adequate mechanization in small-scale production, and thus capital must be replaced by so much labor that its economic rationality is already questionable. The country is not technically prepared for mechanizing small-scale agricultural production.

The security of agricultural producers continues to require substantial state procurement actions. At the same time, it is a task of procurements to better stimulate farmers to grow products that can be efficiently sold on the world market.

The problems of private activities are different in the other sectors of the economy, and the picture is highly differentiated. In the traditional artisan trades low mechanization and the administrative restriction on the number of employees is coupled with difficult living conditions and the extinction of many trades. In other fields, however, the situation is different. While in the state and cooperative sectors firms are generally forced to restrict earnings, and are sometimes even incapable of paying the wages absolutely necessary for solving their tasks, private activities sometimes result in very high personal incomes. A considerable part of those performing private activities in the new small organizations are not full-time employees. They consider the entrepreneurial activity not as a means of livelihood for their whole lifetime, but rather as a transitory state lasting for some longer or shorter period of time, which they maintain only as long as they can earn significantly more than their full-time labor income, even if complemented perhaps by tips or through other possibly illegal activities. This is remarkable not because some people may, through small-scale entrepreneurial activity, earn essentially more than the employees of big organizations, but because, unlike in capitalist countries, small entrepreneurs across a wide scale of industrial, construction, commercial, catering, and transporting activities consider such a high income as normal, and if they cannot get it, they abandon such entrepreneurial activity.

All this shows that the rather radical transformation of the concentrated enterprise structure in the 1980s entailed contradictory consequences. On the one hand, the organizational structure that has emerged continues to be polarized, although it brought many changes in the size of organizations. Medium-sized firms are invariably missing, leaving only large and small ones. On the other hand, this change in production structure, even if it has improved the range of supply, has approximated an equilibrium relying on competition only in some markets, e.g., those for bread and taxicabs, but it has not resulted in a general breakthrough toward a buyers' market. In general, small entrepreneurs need not take any particular risk when they shift from their employee status to the entrepreneurial one. Apart from a few exceptions, they are forced only to make either small or easily mobilizable investments, and thus they can abandon the activity in question without any risk and can return to their employee status without losses or, and this is even more characteristic, they can look for a new business.

Reorganization of branch control

In the course of the economic changes following 1978, economic policy unambiguously sought to alter the much criticized situation in which, against the spirit of the reform, the autonomy of the profit-oriented firms was restricted by the exercise of supervisory rights of ownership by the branch ministries.

In harmony with this criticism, a delayed element of the reform ideas of the 1960s again came to the fore. This was the amalgamation of the branch ministries and the formulation of a qualitatively new control function. As in the earlier history of the reform, the starting point was the transformation of the control of industry. On January 1, 1971, the Ministry of Industry was formed.

In principle, the new ministry could not determine the tasks of industrial firms and, as distinct from its forerunners, it had no authority over trade in the means of production, nor was it to be a price-setting authority. Thus, according to the approved resolutions, its function was restricted to elaborating the development concepts of the industry, including the central development programs, and providing help in the acceleration of technological development. In a complementary capacity, it was to participate in the organization of technical and economic cooperation with CMEA countries, of product and production cooperation and specialization. Finally, its scope of authority included the supervision of enterprises, extending to the foundation, liquidation, and separation of firms, and the appointment of the higher enterprise executives.

The internal organization of the new ministry was built up to reflect these goals and, by reducing the staff of the control apparatus, it was hoped to forestall interference with the life of enterprises. This was reinforced by the provision that the functional control activity was separated within the ministry from the supervisory function lest the free decisions of firms be restricted by abuse of the latter.

Practice proved to be a sharp contradiction to the accepted principles and ideas about control. The ministry had to choose daily whether to answer the system of general requirements set by the government administration for the Ministry of Industry, or to respond to repeated expectations of the economic control bodies such as the Council of Ministers, the State Planning Commission, and the Economic Commission demanding operative measures, and thus to accede to the pressures demanding individual regulations for firms. It was pushed towards the latter option by its own apparatus, which was formed from the three predeceeding ministries, the staff of which knew from earlier experience that strengthing the position of the ministry crisis-averting interference was more advantageous than were the principles approved when the ministry was founded.

Thus, from 1982 on, the main activity of the ministry was to stimulate exports with the aid of wage preferences and performance premiums granted individually to firms, as well as to regulate imports so that the supply of the domestic market should not deteriorate excessively. The new organization of the ministry did not provide an adequate framework for managing the situation. Therefore, in 1984 when important personal changes were made in the leadership of the ministry, although certainly for reasons beyond the viewpoints on ministerial control, work also started to newly define the tasks of the Ministry of Industry. Together with these changes, the program for the reorganization of branch control beyond industry was struck from the agenda or was essentially modified.

Changes in the financial system

It was the financial regulations that had to struggle with the largest number of internal contradictions. After 1978, both the documents determining monetary policy, and those of fiscal policy, and even those establishing the framework of price and earnings regulations, proclaimed the idea of a competitive economy. It was then that the idea of a competitive price system, adjusting to world market prices, appeared and the idea of a uniform, normative regulation, not differentiated by firms, was emphasized more than ever. Later, in order to mitigate the negative consequences of the rigid regulation of earnings and prices, an experimental regulation of earnings was introduced that applied to efficient firms, and a wage and price club was brought into being for them. For the efficient firms the rigid prescriptions were relaxed under special forms of government administrative control. The principle of price calculations, which prescribed that the depreciation allowance should be obligatorily accounted among costs, was abolished. Thus a possibility was created for the utilization of unexploited capacities in cases where this would help to reduce losses. To facilitate a rational reallocation of capital, the market instruments of capital regroupment among firms was given a role.

The promulgation of market-oriented measures came into complete conflict with established practices. Referring to economic difficulties, the central agencies continued to control firms directly with formal and informal tools. Thus the new market methods, introduced with great emphasis, mostly remained empty forms. The changes of free prices were linked to previously announced obligations; the firms were organized into the regularly changed forms of the competitive price system and wage regulation by official measures, thus restricting their freedom of decision. These measures caused difficulties mainly for the large firms. Many of them could continue to operate only by getting financial facilities, usually tax remissions, and by becoming indebted to other firms. The financial difficulties of the medium and small firms were usually not solved with the aid of discriminatory financial measures. The cause of the difference is not that they are more efficient than the big ones, but the fact that their management is less visible to the central agencies because of the many details that the center seeks to control, and thus their position is more advantageous in the "regulation bargaining" with the center. In the final analysis, the fiscal and credit institutions, as well as the price control agencies, continued to apply discriminatory measures essentially to keep alive all firms, or to prevent their incomes from exceeding planned outlays. In the interest of the survival of the indebted, mostly large, firms, taxes were remitted, and credit repayments were rescheduled. The overwhelming majority of small and medium firms could acquire the means necessary for survival through price bargaining conducted with the authorities.

The large number of changes facilitating capital movements did not affect the major proportions of capital allocation and did not amount to a substantial change towards the market. Rather, their function was to solve investment problems in harmony with central objectives and to support the market slogans.

The budget revenues and the possibilities for money creation proved to be insufficient for covering the budget subsidies and other budget expenditures as well as the burdens of international debt service. Thus a general tapping of incomes originating in the enterprise sphere also became necessary. Enterprises were prohibited from using their reserve funds, part of which was taxed away, the credit amortization payments of firms with liquid monetary reserves were accelerated, and increased burdens were put on investments by cancelling valid delivery and construction agreements.

The fiscal and credit policy measures, combined with export-import regulations and steps taken in the field of economic diplomacy, proved to be sufficient, while some world economic circumstances were advantageous for avoiding international insolvency; as opposed to the earlier targets, however, they did not lead to improved economic efficiency and even prevented realization of the economic policy slogan of a new growth path.

Weakness of the economic restrictions between 1979 and 1984

Between 1979 and 1984 the danger of international insolvency was averted through the strong reduction of investment and real wages and at the price of some deterioration in domestic commodity supply. This could not, however, bring any substantial improvement in the efficiency of state and cooperative enterprises.

This restrictive economic policy could not bring a major success that would have allowed avoidance of the payment crisis and that also would have provided foundations for further progress. This was because, under the pressure of having to reduce debts, the central economic leadership preferred administrative measures to curb aggregate demand, rather than to moderate the administrative interference that permeated every field of management. Under such conditions the halt of economic growth entailed neither a change in management behavior, nor the beginning of a substantial transformation of the production structure. The performance of the economy did not improve, and firms continued to remain indifferent to consumers' needs and to changes in demand and supply. It was only the activity of the small economic entities, falling beyond the main scope of economic regulation, that became livelier.

State-owned and cooperative enterprises were neither pressed for, nor were they capable of, raising the incomes of their employees or members. The population tolerated the fall of real wages and of the real value of social benefits without major objections. Many people were able to compensate for falling incomes from first-economy jobs by increasing their participation in the second economy.

To avoid all these problems, a general regulation of aggregate demand would have been needed instead of the administrative measures chosen in 1979. The general regulation of demand, instead of administrative regulation, means that the state, in harmony with the production potential of the country, determines effective demand and controls it through the budget and through credit emission. The survival and growth of firms operating under strict financial limits depends on whether the income earned from sales of their products and services covers their costs and allows them to grow. Entrepreneurial activity also has institutional preconditions. It suffices to refer to the transformation of the property rights of enterprises that enables them to the viewpoints of capital owners, to the newly-created possibility of bankruptcy, to the substantial relaxation of the rigidities of price regulation and control of incomes, as well as to the development of the protection of interests of various strata.

The general regulation of aggregate demand also entails a greater differentiation of enterprise incomes than the present practice. The regulated money supply forces business units to produce efficiently, to adjust to demand and supply, and to minimize costs. Only economic coercion can produce efficient enterprise management, entrepreneurial spirit, and pressure towards an efficient production structure. Under such pressure state and cooperative firms will respond more effectively to lack of labor effort, to the lack of discipline, to the private work done during the legal worktime, and to the use of enterprise assets for private purposes. All this may also help repress illegal elements and illegal incomes in the entire economy. In order that firms should be forced to pay attention to demand, and that they be at the same time able to adjust to these pressures, their operation must be freed from price, wage, and investment restrictions.

The elimination of such restrictions would, no doubt, entail unfavorable side effects, lasting for some time. The curbing of aggregate demand, without the compensation of enterprise incomes, might even force the closing down of workshops, establishments, and even enterprises unable to manage financially. Such a structural change of the economy would put an end to job safety. Dismissals necessary for the transformation of the production structure, and the handling of the ensuing, even if transitory, unemployment demand serious government measures, among them support of self-employment. Owing to the growing role of free prices, the rate of inflation is not likely to decrease even with a successful monetary policy, and it is more difficult to prepare the population for price rises that would not be preceded by central administrative measures.

Changes entailing unfavorable consequences requires political will. But without political determination the economy is incapable of emerging from the gradually deteriorating situation.

Impact of the 1984 resolution of the Central Committee of the HSWP and of its measures taken in 1985

After long preparation, the Central Committee of the Hungarian Socialist Workers' Party adopted a resolution in April 1984 on the streamlining of economic control. The resolution and the measures following it wrought major changes in the institutional foundation of the autonomy of firms, the development of the financial regulations, and the methods of market surveillance.

Steps toward enterprise autonomy

The property rights of most state-owned firms were taken out of the hands of government administration. Only public utilities and some firms in exceptional positions found their property rights unchanged; in their case the supervision of the owner continued to be exercised by the branch ministries and the local councils. A great part of the property rights of the market-oriented firms was transferred to the enterprise council, or the meeting of delegates, or the general assembly of employees. It is these organs that, in agreement with the local and branch agencies, elect the manager and that decide on essential questions of enterprise development.

The new forms of enterprise control were based on three concepts: self-management, which wanted to place total control over enterprise management in the hands of the employees; the corporative solution, in which the enterprise council consists of three parts: representatives of the state, representatives of the employees, and management; and finally, one in which the property rights were given to several competing, profit-oriented state holding companies seeking to maximize the return to capital.

The present solution, chosen instead of experimenting with the three different concepts, approximates the system of self-management in its principles. It transforms the enterprise supervision rights of the branch ministries and the local councils into the right to inspect the firm's behavior for legality. In principle, this restricts the right of supervisory organs to check whether the laws have been observed. There remain several loopholes through which the central bodies can formally or informally interfere with enterprise decisions. A further weakness of the new practice is that it has not provided a way to resolve conflicts between enterprise collectives and government regulations. A source of even greater problems is that the property rights of the working collectives, formally quite extensive, have not been adequately clarified. This is evident in the fact that the enterprise's interest in maintaining and increasing the value of its assets failed to materialize. This question was not meant to be on the agenda until 1986. Thus there was no clarification, how an enterprise collective, on the basis of its property rights, can become interested in taking decisions for actions, at doing more than producing a short-term increase in its income. For example, how will it react to possibilities for increasing its long-term profitability while ensuring the long-term safety of the working collective? Is the enterprise council or general assembly capable and willing to counter unreasonable claims to wage increases, and if so, on the basis of what considerations? The difficulty of the problem is evident in the fact that the viewpoint of the return to enterprise capital does not always coincide with the long-term interests of the enterprise collective. The utilization of enterprise assets demands considering issues, such as what should be done with assets that cannot be efficiently exploited, from time to time from the viewpoint of the given collective. In addition, not only the collective but also the society outside the enterprise has short and long-term interests attached to the wealth of the enterprise. It has not been adequately clarified whether a representation of these interests is necessary and feasible and who should exercise that task.

An example of the problems than can arise is the result of a new regulation that permits wage increases at the expense of depreciation allowance. In such cases a conflict appears between the short-term incomes of the enterprise collective and the interest in the increase of the value of the enterprises assets. Thus, from the aspect of the short-term interests of the whole enterprise collective, or even more from that of the older workers, it may be advantageous to turn the depreciation allowance into personal income. At the same time, from the aspect of the long-term interests of the younger members of the collective, it may be more advantageous to provide for the safety of current production to reconstruct assets and, for citizens outside the enterprise, it may be more advantageous to close down the firm and sell its assets. In such cases the interests of the enterprise collective exercising the rights of the owner may be divided and/or may come into conflict with the efficient utilization of enterprise assets. The latter criterion may entail a reduction of the income of those producing the obsolete products, perhaps a reduction of staff and/or a change in the structure of the labor force.

The above also indicates that the new way of exercising the state property rights has not solved the basic problem: the regulation of personal incomes and investments. After the changes, the enterprise management and the body checking it do not comprise forces in whose interest it is to raise their voices against the further operation of inefficient firms. Nor do the bodies controlling the enterprise comprise such forces that, on the basis of their interests, would advocate the breaking up of large organizations if this were demanded by efficiency.

The multitude of unsolved problems might easily lead to the new system of enterprise control becoming formal. Already the danger is felt that, following the transitory shock accompanying the formation of new leading bodies and the election of managers, a situation is developing with which everybody is dissatisfied.

The enterprise managers are not satisfied because, amidst the essentially invariable regulations and expectations restricting their scope of movement, they also have to try to come to terms with the enterprise council or general assembly. Therefore, many managers feel that, instead of facilitating their work, the introduction of the new forms of management has made it more difficult. At the same time, the expansion of workers' rights was not unexpected by workers. Earlier, they did not demand the introduction of self-management, and their demands included, at most, participation in decisions affecting income relations and working conditions. Now, under the new conditions, perhaps an increasing number of them will learn the tasks to be done and will like it. But the fear is quite justified that in practice, under the impact of the likely central manipulations, the opportunity offered by self-management will not fully evolve and employees will grow skeptical toward the new forms.

Financial policy

In 1985 the system of regulators was transformed, and the system of taxation was rationalized. The profit tax was reduced. In the interest of enforcing the efficiency requirements the role of taxes on inputs increased; thus a tax on enterprise property was introduced and the wage tax increased. These changes are of doubtful value. For example, with reference to the difficulties of the economy, a tax on investment was introduced which hinders development and is economically unjustified. In all, the changes as a whole rather increased than diminished the extent of income centralization, and the system of enterprise subsidies and tax reductions did not disappear.

Gradual abolition of administrative price formation rules in manufacturing, more flexible price formation in agriculture and trade, accompanied by abolition of the notions of unfair profit and unfair prices, held great promise for improvement in the price mechanism. According to the new rules only a price higher than that of competitors counts as unfair. In price control, the price limitation linked to the rate of profit was eliminated. Thus, in principle, a contradiction that caused problems in earlier periods was overcome. This problem was that, although increased profits were considered to be the goal of firms, when prices were officially checked it was considered harmful, or at least a suspicious phenomenon, when the price calculation of some products, or that of a whole company, yielded a higher than usual rate of profit. Also the prescriptions about the obligatory adjustment to changes in world market prices were to be abolished gradually and in a widening scope.

The changes pointing toward a regulated market did not exert their effect in reality. Fearing an unexpected and strong increase as prices were freed, the evolution of the substantial impacts of the price mechanism was braked by the imposition of an early warning system.

The rigid regulations affecting the raising of incomes of enterprise executives and employees were mitigated by the introduction of various forms of less rigid ones and, within them, by relating the level of earnings to profits. The latter, particularly if working without the simultaneously introduced brakes, abolishes the distinction between wage increment and wage cost, which is harmful from the point of view of economic efficiency. But a more rational regulation of earnings leads to increasing efficiency only if firms are unambiguously interested in profit and in increasing the value of assets. If there is no change in the latter respect, and the firm continues to operate as an economic entity fulfilling supply and export tasks, it will subordinate its strategy and tactics to this goal in other fields of management as well. Thus, in the interest of higher profit it will not risk its relations with its employees, and it will not spare costs, including wage costs.

It may be thus established that the firms' behavior was logical from their own point of view when they exploited the diversity of the wage regulation to find the means for paying high wages. The new form of the regulation of earnings that came to the fore in 1985 favored those firms that attain a high rate of profit and that, in the long run, can bear the burden that the high wage-tax of the new regulation puts on their costs. Thus it cannot be considered a mere chance that the development of enterprise revenues and of wages was not synchronous in either 1985 or 1986.

Also, the new forms of capital allocation were consolidated: associations, the issuing of bonds and shares, the formation of financial institutions, etc. But the dominant forms of capital allocations are and will remain the same in the foreseeable future. Therefore, the previously discussed contradictions related to investment financing will continue to assert themselves. The firm investing a considerable sum relative to its own capital will be forced to resort to credit, not being capable of relying only on its own resources, and thus its success will not depend on the success of the investment project, but instead on the conditions negotiated in its credit agreement. The firm implementing small investments relative to its own capital can remain profitable even if the profitability of the development does not attain the desirable level.

The most ambiguous case of changes is the bankruptcy of loss-making firms and activities and the accompanying dismissals. The long-delayed bankruptcy law has been put into force in such a way that the creditor, finding his interests endangered, can initiate the liquidation procedure, thus forcing the debtor, through an accelerated court procedure, to sell his assets and indemnify the lender only in agreement with the state administration. It is also to be feared that the simultaneously introduced changes will not force the liquidation of low-efficiency workshops and factories either. A direct consequence of both actions, according to earlier plans, would have been the discontinuation of jobs. The original ideas gradually lost ground in practice. This is evident not only in that, owing to the continued strong centralization of free incomes, the purchase of failing establishments and factories under market forms, i.e., the free exchange of properties without central decisions, remains impossible. Moreover, "the reorganization of the wealth of inadequately managed economic entities to be liquidated" is expected from the decisions and organizational activity of state organs. The weakening of efforts at closing down inefficient workshops is almost indicated by the fact that, in spite of the strong excess demand on the labor market, the institutional preparations for the amelioration of unemployment is progressing slowly.

The contradictions of the financial changes implemented in 1985 are mainly rooted in the fact that the system of money emission has hardly been affected. Although the program of bank reform has been approved with great delay, and no resistance has developed against forced interfirm credits, a strict regulation of the money supply is still missing. Instead of a program for regulating aggregate demand, the banking system continues to make it difficult for efficient firms to raise credit and does not, indeed cannot, stop granting credit to low-efficiency firms. Moreover, it does interfere in order to limit the heavy indebtedness of firms to each other.

The way in which the money supply was developed has not restricted aggregate demand, but it has essentially secured the survival of every firm. This practice brings about a particular situation. Excess capacities coexist with shortages on the market for goods and services and with excess demand on the labor market.

The easy supply of money to state and cooperative firms, bearing little relation to their results, has brought about an infernal chain of complicated interrelations. On the one hand, not even the almost insolvent state and cooperative firms are forced to withstand the price-raising efforts of their partners, to dismiss superfluous staff, to reduce wages. They solve the difficult production tasks, not through internal reorganization, but rather by means of overtime, enterprise economic workteams, orders given to expensive suppliers, etc. Nor do they stop supplying their buyers in default of payment. On the other hand, as a natural concomitant of all the above, the just reviewed changes in market-oriented price and wage regulations have not entailed a growing role for money. Instead they have loosened the financial conditions of management. In this case the economic leadership of the country can protect itself from runaway inflation only by means of methods discarded in its declarations. Finally, the unfavorable phenomena observed in the scope of state and cooperative enterprises also loosen the management conditions of small ventures.

The development of trade

The movement toward a market system raised strict requirements for trade as well. The economic reform demanded a multi-channel, diversified trade system, which has not been brought about to this day. The declared free choice of partners cannot assert itself in most cases, as there are not several partners from whom to choose. More firms competing with each other would be needed, but the chances for founding firms are restricted even more in trade than in production.

In the 1980s, and particularly after 1985, efforts were made to change this situation. The firms, first of all the productive ones, obtained new possibilities also in the trade for raw materials, capital goods and consumer goods, and even in foreign trade. Also, organizations were transformed, which increased the number of retail firms, and the number of firms with rights to trade abroad suddenly increased. Still, except for the appearance of private retail shops, the changes do not point unambiguously toward the desired objective. Competition among retail firms is still in an embryonic stage, a consequence of price margins insufficient to cover trading risks, and of the large financial commitments entailed by trading rights.

The government entrusted the market surveillance organization to bring about diversified commercial relations, to organize and control markets. This institution is one of the most controversial elements of today's economic control. Namely, a multi-channel market can only come about by changes in the general conditions, which the market surveillance can help but cannot bring about with its organizing activity. Therefore, it is still the "trouble averting" activity that is preponderant, rather than the tasks of market organization. It is still far from reality that the free market areas should be unambiguously delimited from the trading areas belonging to the scope of market surveillance, and that even the latter should be interfered with only by exploiting the incentive role of the funds made available for this special purpose. Instead, the situations have persisted, and their number even increased in 1986, where the market forces have not solved market shortages, and the measures of government agencies moving between unambiguous legal limits have also been weak. It is with growing frequency that branch organizations, councils, and territorial party organs try to settle social conflicts, such as commodity shortages, spontaneous price rises, dismissals, etc., with the means available to them. In this way, however, only short-term tensions can be relieved. But the local interferences do not point in the direction to be followed in the long run. Instead, they weaken the desirable behavior of economic entities that should be based on enterprise interest and autonomy.

Next Steps in the Hungarian Economic Reform

BÉLA BALASSA

Introduction

Following a review of the macroeconomic situation in Hungary, this paper will analyze the policies that may be employed to ameliorate the performance of the Hungarian economy. After indicating the need for a restrictive macroeconomic policy and for the efficient promotion of exports, the paper will concentrate on the conditions existing in factor markets. Recommendations will be made for modifying the relative prices of labor and capital and for improving the operation of markets for these productive factors in Hungary.

The macroeconomic situation

In response to the external shocks, the slowdown in external demand, and the deterioration in the terms of trade, of the 1974-78 period, Hungary borrowed extensively abroad with a view to ensuring continued rapid increases in domestic consumption and investment. Owing to the deterioration of export performance and the virtual lack of import substitution (Balassa, 1983), foreign borrowing led to the accumulation of a substantial convertible currency debt. Thus, apart from Poland, Hungary's per capita debt surpassed that of any other socialist or developing country in 1978.[1] In order to improve the situation, the authorities set out to eliminate Hungary's $1.2 billion annual deficit in convertible currency trade. This objective, attained in 1981, was transformed to a goal of a $500-600 million trade surplus in convertible currencies, to permit financing interest payments on the debt, in the aftermath of the Polish debt crisis. In fact, Hungary's trade surplus in convertible currencies came to exceed $0.5 billion in 1982 and $0.7 billion two years later.[2] The burden of the adjustment was borne by gross domestic investment, which fell by 31 percent between 1978 and 1984 while domestic consumption rose by 9 percent, only slightly less than the 11 percent increase in the gross domestic product during the period.

The improvement in the balance of trade between 1978 and 1984 did not reflect increased export competitiveness, as Hungary's export market shares declined to a considerable extent during the period (Balassa, 1985a). Rather, it reflected decreases in imports, brought about by cuts in investment activity and by increasingly severe import restrictions. As the adverse economic effects of these restrictions, inter alia on exports, came to be recognized, steps were taken toward the liberalization of imports. The partial release of pent-up import demand, accompanied by expansionary monetary and fiscal policies, contributed to a deterioration of Hungary's balance of trade in convertible currencies with the trade surplus declining to $0.3 billion in 1985.

As to the expansionary measures applied, the National Bank of Hungary provided increased working capital to firms that raised wages over and above the rise in prices, as well as credits to the government that augmented its producer and consumer subsidies, thereby adding to the budget deficit. Correspondingly, domestic consumption rose by 2 percent in 1985, notwithstanding a slight decline in GDP, whereas gross domestic investment decreased by an additional 3 percent.

Hungary's trade balance deteriorated again in 1986 as a 2 to 3 percent rise in consumption, associated with increases in real wages and other incomes, was accompanied by little change in investment, raising the growth of aggregate expenditure above that of GDP, 1.5 percent, by a substantial margin. The doubling of the budget deficit, exceeding 4 percent of GDP, and an accommodating monetary policy importantly contributed to these results, and Hungary incurred a $0.2 billion deficit in convertible currency trade.

The decrease in the volume of convertible currency exports between 1984 and 1986, in the face of increases in the total imports of Hungary's main trading partners among private market economies, was an important factor in the deterioration of the trade balance. Hungary's continued poor export performance, in turn, was the result of a variety of influences.[3] To begin with, Hungary's export competitiveness deteriorated to a considerable extent. Calculated by the use of export weights, between 1978 and 1985 the forint appreciated in real terms by 18 percent if the exchange rates are adjusted for changes in wholesale prices, and by 22 percent if the adjustment is made by the use of consumer prices indices.[4] Furthermore, the fall in investment, accompanied by a substantial decline in the investment share of industries in which Hungary has a comparative advantage (see below), has not permitted the transformation of the structure of exports and the upgrading of their technological level.[5] The higher profitability and the lower risk of sales in domestic and in CMEA markets, and the uncertainties associated with increased reliance on case-by-case interventions by the authorities, have further discouraged exports.[6]

Yet, increases in exports are a necessary condition for renewed economic growth in Hungary. Possibilities for efficient import substitution have been well-nigh exhausted in Hungary's small domestic market. Thus, while economizing on

Table 1

Real Exchange Rate in Hungary, 1970-August 1986
(1976-78 = 100)

	1970	1971	1972	1973	1974	1975	1976	1977
Bilateral real exchange rates, adjusted by								
WPI								
Austria	83.8	89.5	91.0	93.7	104.4	101.3	94.1	101.6
Germany	85.1	90.6	92.3	101.1	109.4	102.4	93.8	100.9
Italy	99.2	100.8	101.1	101.8	118.7	109.2	95.8	101.8
USA	111.3	112.0	106.0	103.3	113.4	105.3	99.6	102.1
Yugoslavia	108.9	103.0	90.8	92.5	113.3	107.4	98.6	103.7
CPI								
Austria	72.8	77.3	80.5	87.6	94.2	99.3	93.2	101.2
Germany	79.7	85.7	89.7	98.1	101.7	102.6	94.2	100.4
Italy	110.4	113.7	115.8	110.0	110.2	116.3	96.0	100.4
USA	118.9	120.9	113.2	103.0	107.2	106.0	101.0	102.0
Yugoslavia	89.2	84.4	77.8	83.3	97.4	99.8	95.4	103.0
Real effective exchange rates								
Export and import weights								
WPI	91.6	94.7	94.6	99.5	111.1	104.4	95.5	101.2
CPI	84.9	89.0	90.8	94.4	99.6	103.7	95.2	100.5
Export weights								
WPI	92.0	94.8	94.2	99.1	111.5	104.9	95.6	101.3
CPI	85.3	88.9	90.3	94.3	99.9	104.2	95.1	100.6

	1978	1979	1980	1981	1982	1983	1984	1985
Bilateral real exchange rates, adjusted by								
WPI								
Austria	104.3	108.4	96.4	84.0	82.5	87.0	87.5	86.1
Germany	105.3	111.0	95.5	82.2	82.6	87.9	87.7	86.0
Italy	102.4	110.9	102.5	89.3	87.2	94.0	96.9	94.9
USA	98.3	101.5	91.9	99.5	103.5	115.6	127.9	126.2
Yugoslavia	97.7	99.7	78.4	78.6	69.6	55.1	57.1	53.6

	1978	1979	1980	1981	1982	1983	1984	1985
CPI								
Austria	105.6	102.4	94.4	82.6	81.1	86.4	85.3	83.0
Germany	105.5	103.7	92.4	79.7	78.0	83.1	79.4	76.5
Italy	103.6	104.7	103.1	92.3	90.2	100.0	99.6	97.6
USA	97.1	93.1	88.5	98.6	104.5	117.0	126.9	128.1
Yugoslavia	101.6	104.3	87.5	86.8	80.1	65.6	64.4	61.9

Real effective exchange rates

Export and import weights							
WPI	103.3	108.5	94.9	86.2	84.3	86.7	89.1	87.3
CPI	104.4	102.6	93.7	86.2	83.6	86.0	84.3	82.2

Export weights							
WPI	103.1	108.7	94.8	85.5	83.1	84.6	86.5	84.5
CPI	104.3	103.5	94.8	86.4	83.5	85.5	83.7	81.5

	1986	1986	July	Aug.

Bilateral real exchange rates, adjusted by

WPI				
Austria	91.5	96.9	99.7	99.5
Germany	92.3	98.4	102.1	102.6
Italy	98.7	104.3	108.3	108.5
USA	107.6	109.4	109.4	105.5
Yugoslavia	60.2	63.6	61.6	64.6

CPI				
Austria	93.5	97.0	98.6	99.8
Germany	85.0	88.1	89.1	89.7
Italy	107.6	110.7	111.4	111.8
USA	115.0	114.2	111.6	108.1
Yugoslavia	69.6	73.1	70.6	75.4

Real effective exchange rates

Export and import weights				
WPI	90.8	96.2	98.7	98.7
CPI	89.3	92.5	92.7	93.1

Export weights				
WPI	88.7	94.1	96.4	96.8
CPI	89.2	92.6	92.7	93.5

Source: World Bank data base.

---

raw materials, particularly energy, would bring import savings, economic growth will require the increased availability of foreign exchange through exports, as Hungary cannot continue borrowing abroad. Several measures were taken to promote exports to private market economies in 1986. They include the deprecia- tion of the export exchange rate by 15 percent in real terms between 1985 and August 1986, irrespective of whether the wholesale or the consumer price index is used as deflator (Table 1); the establishment of four trading houses, together with the elimination of restrictions on the export profile of thirty-eight foreign trade enterprises and the simplification of procedures for obtaining trading rights by industrial firms; increases in profit tax rebates for export-oriented investments from 33 to 50 percent; the elimination of the 15-percent accumulation tax on export-oriented investments, and the concentration of medium-term credits in export-oriented investments; reduced interest rates on short-term export credits; wage preferences to firms increasing their exports; and, last but not least, moral suasion.

Incentives to export to private market economies are warranted as long as import protection and trade arrangements with socialist countries raise the profitability of sales in domestic and in CMEA markets above that obtainable in these exports. But the preferential treatment of increments in exports, calculated annually, may discourage exports in years when increases cannot be achieved, so as to show a larger rise afterwards. There have also been reports that products that are exported in response to government pressure are imported by other firms at higher prices (*Figyelő*, September 25, 1986). Furthermore, it is feared that firms will be artificially maintained by subsidies in order to avoid a decline in exports, and that the exclusive concentration on export-oriented investments will not ensure the efficient allocation of investment funds.[7] At the same time, the provision of credits for export-oriented investments involves a bargaining process as to the amount of exports pledged for a five-year period, and there is uncertainty as to the exports actually undertaken. The bargaining extends to firm-specific measures aimed to maintain and to expand exports with little regard to cost.

The efficient way to promote exports involves establishing an equilibrium exchange rate that provides incentives to exports across the board and permits the elimination of measures that safeguard and extend high-cost exports. Furthermore, in raising import prices, the devaluation will serve as a restraint on purchases from private market economies. It would be desirable to establish the new exchange rate instantaneously, so as to reduce the uncertainty that led to postponing exports in the past. In setting the new rate, account should be taken of the fact that the exchange rate for exports, adjusted for changes in wholesale prices, in August 1986 represented a 7 percent appreciation in real terms compared with 1978, 10 percent if adjusted by the consumer price index, despite the fact that the shift from borrowing abroad to servicing the external debt would have required a devaluation. Moreover, although the forint was devalued by 8 percent against a basket of currencies in September 1986, the need to eliminate firm-specific export support measures further strengthens the need for an exchange rate change.

A customary objection to devaluation in Hungary is its inflationary impact. Yet, such a price increase is necessary in order to offset increases in real incomes in 1985 and 1986 that were not commensurate with changes in domestic production and led to higher imports. Nevertheless, measures would need to be taken to limit the inflationary effect of an once-for-all devaluation and to avoid it giving rise to an inflationary spiral.

On the example of the September 1986 devaluation, firms operating under the so-called competitive price system should not be allowed to raise prices on domestic sales in proportion with the rise in export prices that would result from an once-for-all devaluation; nor should prices be adjusted on CMEA sales. Apart from reducing its inflationary effects, this is necessary to enhance the effectiveness of the devaluation that requires increasing the profitability of sales in Western, as against domestic and CMEA, markets through changes in relative prices. And, most importantly, the government should reverse the expansionary monetary and fiscal policies followed in 1985 and in 1986.

The system of incentives

A more general issue concerns the deterioration of the efficiency of Hungarian industry. While total factor productivity, expressing changes in the combined produc-tivity of labor and capital, increased at an average annual rate of 2.8 percent between 1968 and 1978, it fell by 0.6 percent a year between 1969 and 1982 and showed only small improvements in subsequent years (Csernensky-Demeter, 1986, p. 3).

The increased use of firm-specific interventions after 1978 contributed to the deterioration of efficiency in Hungarian industry. Poorly performing enterprises received government support in the form of reductions in taxes, easing of credit conditions, price increases, preferential wage arrangements, and straight subsidies, while good performance often led to additional charges. In order to improve the operation of the market mechanism in Hungary and to enhance the effectiveness of the devaluation, it would be necessary to narrow the scope of firm-specific measures, with a view to their elimination over time, thereby hardening the budget constraint for the firm. It has been suggested that, under present conditions, the removal of firm-specific support would result in the bankruptcy of 40-50 percent of Hungarian firms. This has been said to be the case because of the lack of effective labor and capital markets in Hungary (Tardos, 1985, pp. 1290-92). The statement assumes that firms could not improve the use of their existing resources through increased operational efficiency or through the utilization of internal reserves, according to the Hungarian terminology. Such is hardly the case, given the low productivity of labor and capital in Hungarian industry that is linked in part to poor work performance and in part to excess labor, hired because of the fear of labor shortages, and the application of a wage system that encouraged lowering average wages through the employment of low-skill labor in the past. At the same time, the soft budget constraint for the firm did not provide a penalty for excessive hiring.

There are examples of substantial improvements in operational efficiency even in private market economies, for example, Fiat in Italy and Chrysler in the United States, where efficiency levels are relatively high. There have also been cases where improvements have occurred in Hungarian firms in response to the threat of closing down. This has happened in the Hungarian Cable Works, although not in Kontakta, a producer of parts and components, where continued firm-specific support has limited the incentives to do so (*Figyelő* August 21, 1986, p. 6, and December 5, 1985, p. 4). Unless possibilities exist for increasing production, which may not be the case in poorly performing firms, improvements in operational efficiency will entail reducing the firm's labor force. This should not be considered undesirable to the extent that the firm sheds labor whose productivity is below its cost. The workers thus freed would be available for other activities where labor shortages exist.

An additional consideration is that the relative prices of labor and capital are distorted in Hungary. The introduction of the 10 percent tax on labor in 1985 provides only a partial offset for the cost of social benefits financed from the government budget. In turn, the cost of capital is augmented by high real interest rates and the price-raising effects of high customs duties on imported machinery, with the accumulation tax further increasing the cost of new investment. According to one calculation, the profitability of new investments fell from over 30 percent in 1969 to 10 percent in the late 1970s and to nil in 1980-81, with a slight increase to 2 percent in 1982-83 (Kunvári, 1986, p. 828). The low profitability of new investments, in turn, entailed a decline in the average profitability of capital in Hungarian industry from over 20 percent to below 15 percent during this period (ibid), with after-tax profits amounting only to 4 percent of gross value added in 1985 (Erdős, 1985, p. 3).

In view of the declining profitability of investments, it may come as a surprise to outside observers that there has been excess demand for investment funds in Hungary throughout the period. The solution to this puzzle lies in the existence of a soft budget constraint. Firms have correctly anticipated that they can have recourse to price increases and various other forms of government support to compensate for the low and even negative profitability of their investments. There is thus need to harden the budget constraint firms face. Also, the relative prices of labor and capital would need to be adjusted. This may be accomplished through changes in the tax system. For one thing, taxes on labor would have to be raised to finance the social benefits provided by the government; for another thing, it would be desirable to reduce duties on capital goods and to eliminate the accumulation tax.

Further changes in the existing regulations would be necessary in order to ensure the adequate operation of labor and capital markets in Hungary. Orderly adjustment requires improvements in the operation of labor markets, while capital markets need to provide funds for those firms that can sufficiently upgrade their operations to become profitable. Labor and capital markets have the additional function of ensuring the flow of resources from low profitability to high profitability activities. The measures that may be taken to improve the operation of these markets will be considered in the following sections.

Labor markets

Since the mid-1970s the wage bill of Hungarian enterprises in the material-producing sectors has increased substantially relative to profits, with the differences rising to a considerable extent after 1978. Thus, while in 1975 the wage bill approximately equalled profits, the former exceeded the latter by about 40 percent in 1984 (Kunvári, 1986, p. 832). This result may be explained by pressures to raise wages as a result of the excess demand for labor under the soft budget constraint. The hardening of the budget constraint would reduce the labor needs of those firms able to improve their operations, and labor would also be released by those firms unable to make the necessary improvements and forced to close down. One should not fear, however, that these changes would lead to wholesale unemployment.

There are several reasons for advocating these policy changes. Unfilled vacancies exceed 50,000, compared with a loss of altogether 15,000 jobs in 1985. The intervention of the official labor placement bureau to find jobs for the displaced workers was necessary in only 700 cases (Gulyás, 1986). At the same time, the number of unfilled vacancies is understated in Hungary, as only a minority of firms utilizes the services of a labor placement bureau, the others preferring the use of informal channels. Furthermore, there is a tendency to underestimate labor mobility by focusing on job opportunities in a particular geographical location and in a particular occupation. Thus, one should encourage geographical as well as occupational labor mobility. As to the former, there is need to reduce the cost of movement just as the cost of migration is partly financed by the state in certain private market economies through tax allowances. As to the latter, budgetary contributions to the cost of training should be accompanied by assistance to firms that undertake on-the-job training.

Small private firms could also create considerable employment if the conditions for their operation and, in particular, the regulations on the number of workers they can hire, are liberalized. These firms can importantly contribute to providing for the needs of the population and increase competition in Hungarian industry.

The introduction of a six-month period of wage payment in the event of the loss of a job, compared with the regular period of one month, and the payment of unemployment compensation for an additional six months by firms that close down some or all of their operations, will ease the transition for workers who have become superfluous. But, notwithstanding the conditions contained in the relevant regulations, there is the danger that the payment of 100 percent of wages for six months, 75 percent for the next three months, and 60 percent for the last three months will induce people to postpone taking a job while working in the second economy as has been the case in West European countries.

The hardening of the budget constraint would provide further inducement to firms to resist claims for large wage increases. It should also limit wage demands in firms making profits, thereby alleviating the disparities that have arisen, as such firms may have raised wages by as much as 18 percent in 1985 and 1986 combined, whereas increases were as little as 2-3 percent in firms making losses that are under central wage determination (Révész, 1985, p. 915). In this connection, it should be emphasized that in private market economies wages do not depend on the profitability of the firm. While there may be differences in wages in accordance with differences in labor efficiency, wages tend to be equalized for equivalent work through the operation of the labor market. This would also happen in a socialist market economy under a hard budget constraint, where profit maximization is the objective of the firm and there is an effective labor and capital market. Under these conditions, there would be a tendency toward the equalization of wages, as firms would not wish to pay higher wages for equivalent work than others. At the same time, firms that are unprofitable at the going wage would cease their operations.

One would, then, have a situation approaching that of the VGMs, the acronym for a workers' collective in the firm that undertakes certain tasks after hours for the payment of a fixed sum. More generally, the principle of compensation for work actually performed, applied in the VGMs, could find application to work done during regular working hours. In this way, one could ensure the profitability of the firm while paying higher wages for more efficient work as is done in the VGMs.[8]

The introduction of income taxes paid on all personal incomes, irrespective of source, enacted in January 1988, will entail partially replacing existing taxes on wages at the firm level. Tax rates would need to be set so as to establish macroeconomic balance in consumer goods markets, which was to have been accomplished so far largely through the taxation of wages at the firm level, and with limited results because the regulations could not be made watertight.

The situation is complicated by reason of the fact that in most firms management is responsible to the workers' collective in Hungary. Now, the danger of excessive wage increases exists in firms making high profits, as workers will wish to share in these profits. At the same time, paying dividends to workers may be objected to on the grounds that they are not the owners of the firm. Correspondingly, for the time being, the application of some rules limiting wage increases may be necessary.[9]

The volume of investment and its allocation

The discussion of capital markets may be prefaced by reference to the availability of investment funds and their allocation in Hungary. The volume of gross domestic investment fell by one-third between 1978 and 1985, with gross fixed investment declining by one-fifth as a considerable decumulation of inventories occurred. However, there was a much larger decline in net investment, i.e., after allowance is made for depreciation. Net investment did not reach one-third of the 1978 level and hardly exceeded six-tenths of the 1970 level in 1985. Industry's share of gross fixed investment fell between 1978 and 1985 from 36.9 to 33.2 percent, expressed in terms of constant prices, while the share of agriculture declined from 13.4 to 11.0 percent and that of transportation and communication decreased from 11.6 to 11.3 percent. In the same period, the share of public and private investment in housing rose from 15.9 to 19.2 percent.

Within industry, substantial increases occurred in the investment shares of mining, chiefly coal, and electrical energy, with the former rising from 10.5 to 22.2 percent and the latter from 14.6 to 20.6 percent between 1978 and 1985. As the steel and chemical industries approximately maintained their share in industrial investment, 23.6 percent in 1978 and 23.1 percent in 1985, the declines were concentrated in the industries of transformation, in particular engineering from 18.6 to 12.1 percent, and in light industry from 10.1 to 6.1 percent. By comparison, production shares in 1985 were 12.8 percent for mining and electrical energy, 29.0 percent for steel and chemicals, and 40.8 percent for engineering and light industry. Yet, it is in the engineering and light industries where Hungary has a comparative advantage, by reason of the availability of relatively low-cost skilled and technical labor.[10] These industries have also experienced increases in total factor productivity in the 1980-84 period while total factor productivity fell in the production of coal, electrical energy, and steel (Csernenszky-Demeter, 1986, p. 3).

The described pattern of investment allocation has thus contributed to the deterioration of the efficiency of Hungarian industry noted above. Together with the reduction in total industrial investment and the limitations imposed on the importation of machinery from developed countries, it has also led to a decline in the technological level of the Hungarian engineering and light industries vis-à-vis private market economies. In this connection, two examples may be of interest. In contrast to the rapid developments that occurred in private market economies, the growth in the use of numerically-controlled machine tools slowed down to a considerable extent in Hungary after 1980. Also, the competitiveness of Hungarian industry has suffered as, owing to the limited and uncertain availability of investment funds and foreign exchange, "with few exceptions, it has not been possible to establish flexible machinery complexes, due to the purchase of numerically controlled machine tools at different times, with different technical levels, programming requirements, and completeness and from different countries and firms, and of different types" (Nádudvari, 1986, p. 7). In the textile industry the average age of Hungarian machinery has been rising, and it much exceeds that observed in private market economies. Also, the constraints imposed on new investment and, in particular, on the importation of foreign machinery, has not permitted the vertical integration of operations required by modern production. Correspondingly, labor productivity in the Hungarian textile industry does not reach one-seventh of labor productivity in the developed countries (*Figyelő*, October 2, 1986).

For the period of the Seventh Five-Year Plan (1986-90), the combined investment share of mining and electrical energy is projected at 42 percent. This compares with relative shares of 27 percent in the 1976-80, and 38 percent in the 1981-85 periods of the Sixth and Fifth Five-Year Plans, respectively, expressed in terms of current prices.[11] In the case of coal, three alternatives have been put forward, involving prospective annual production volumes of 29, 24, and 17 million tons, compared with 26 million tons in 1985. Even the second alternative would necessitate substantial investments, however, owing to the need for mechanization, as there are few miners to replace those who retire, and Hungary has had to import miners from Poland whose number has reached 6-7,000. At the same time, domestic production costs exceed the price at which coal can be obtained from West Germany by 50-60 percent; they reportedly are about 80 percent above the domestic price of coal in Hungary.[12]

The decline in the price of petroleum to $16-18 per barrel on the world market further points to the need for reducing the investment allocation of Hungarian coal industry. In this connection note that, after having raised the production target to 20 million tons immediately following the May 1981 elections, the French socialist government reduced this target to 11-12 million tons at a time when the oil price was $28 per barrel (Balassa, 1985b). Apart from lowering the investment allocation of the coal industry, the adoption of the 17 million ton production target would permit closing down several high-cost mines in the northern part of Hungary. Even if the present oil price will not last beyond 4-5 years, nuclear capacity may be brought on stream in the meantime, while further efforts to lower energy requirements can be made. In fact, Hungary's energy use reportedly exceeds that of private market economies by a considerable margin.

Among the sixteen countries for which data are available, in 1983 Hungary led with 49.5 megajoules per dollar of GNP, followed by China, 40.5; Romania, the Soviet Union, and Czechoslovakia, between 30 and 40; East Germany, Poland, and Yugoslavia between 20 and 30; the United States, the United Kingdom, Italy, and West Germany, between 10 and 20; and Japan, Sweden, and France, between 8 and 10 (Chandler, 1986, Table 2). While these comparisons are distorted by the choice of exchange rate conversion ratios, and the use of more realistic conversion ratios puts Hungary below other socialist countries as far as energy consumption is concerned, the high density of population should reduce Hungary's transportation needs below that of most other countries.

Lowering energy use per unit of output would require raising energy prices. Fuel oil prices are between one-half and one-third lower in Hungary than in major Western European countries (ibid., 1986, Table 10), and the consumer prices of household electricity, heating oil, and natural gas are greatly subsidized. At the same time, the latter uses are very responsive to price; thus, for the 1970-84 period, the long-term price elasticities of demand were estimated at 1.6 to 2.0, 0.9 to 1.1, and 4.5 to 5.3 in these three uses, respectively (Dobozi, 1988, Table 8). It would further be necessary to de-emphasize heavy industry, in which Hungary has a comparative disadvantage, owing to the lack of domestic raw materials and the limited availability of capital. Within heavy industry, it would be desirable to reconsider the decision to maintain steel production at present levels, which would involve continued exports at high subsidies. France again provides an example as, following an increase in 1981, production targets were reduced considerably in 1984 (Balassa, 1985b).

In Hungary, this would involve adopting earlier proposals to reduce capacity by closing down a high-cost steel mill. In this connection, note that, with 57 percent of its steel produced by the inefficient open hearth process and only 11 percent by recycling electric arc, the Soviet Union alone among major steel producing countries has more outdated steel plants than Hungary, where these ratios are 51 and 13 percent. The open hearth process is used to produce 29 to 45 percent of steel in other socialist countries and India, which has extensively applied Soviet technology, but accounts for less than 10 percent of output in private market economies. At the same time, the share of the electric arc process ranges from 15 to 31 percent in socialist countries and India, and between 19 and 61 percent in private market economies (Chandler, 1986, Table 3).

It would further be desirable to reduce the investment allocation of the heavy chemical industry, which was excessively promoted in the 1970s, despite its high energy cost. In turn, improvements in the technological level of Hungarian industry and the transformation of its export structure would necessitate increasing investments in the engineering and light industries. Apart from exploiting Hungary's comparative advantage in these industries, the proposed changes in investment allocation would alleviate environmental concerns. Investments would also be needed to upgrade the food industry, where outdated processing facilities, packaging, and canning have adversely affected the competitiveness of Hungarian products in recent years. And, Hungary has considerable possibilities in developing an integrated industry of aluminum and aluminum products.

However, doubts may be expressed about the desirability of establishing a car assembly facility in Hungary. Apart from the fact that the proposed assembly of 100,000 automobiles a year would not provide the economies of scale necessary for international competitiveness, the proposed project would involve the use of scarce foreign exchange without offsetting exports of parts, components, and accessories. Following the example of several other small European countries, a more appropriate solution would be to engage in the production of car parts for assembly abroad, the proceeds from which could be used to purchase automobiles for convertible currencies. And while it has been suggested that the quality of domestic steel is not appropriate for this purpose, high-quality steel could be imported. This would also be necessary for upgrading Hungarian exports of machinery and machine tools. At the same time, it would permit reducing domestic steel production, which not only involves high costs but is very energy intensive, requiring on the margin imports for convertible currencies.

There is further need to improve infrastructure, including transportation facilities and, in particular, communications. While Hungary was one of the pioneers in establishing a telephone network, this is now woefully inadequate for meeting the needs of modern industry. This conclusion applies, *a fortiori*, to the new branches of telecommunications.[13]

The investment needs for modernizing the industries of transformation and providing for the necessary infrastructure may exceed the possible savings attainable in reducing investment plans for basic industries. It would be desirable, therefore, to increase the share of investment in the gross domestic product of Hungary. It may be objected that, despite recent declines, this share is still relatively high, 25 percent, compared with an average of 21 percent in developed countries and 23 percent in developing countries (World Bank, 1986, Table 5). But the Hungarian investment share is overstated, due to the overestimation of the prices of capital goods relative to consumer products and services that are widely subsidized. According to one estimate, the adjusted share of gross domestic investment in GDP is 22-23 percent in Hungary (Barta, 1985, p. 836). Furthermore, according to official data, the share of net investment in national income did not reach 18 percent in 1985 in terms of current prices, and it was only 10 percent in terms of 1980 prices, which still overestimate the share of investment.[14] Whereas the gross investment figure matters for the introduction of new technology, net investment is relevant from the point of view of increases in productive capacity.

The shortage of investment funds, and the lack of possibilities for foreign borrowing, put a premium on foreign direct investment in Hungary. Such investment has the further advantage of bringing technological, managerial, and marketing know-how to Hungarian industry. Also, it is superior to bank loans, as it does not involve a fixed income obligation, and it is preferable to the purchase of licenses, as it ensures the continuous upgrading of technology.

Apart from the two newly-established banks, foreign direct investments totalled only $35 million at the end of 1985, and industrial investments did not exceed $10 million in total. This is explained by the requirements of majority participation of domestic interests, the high rate of taxation, the high duties on imported machinery, the complicated accounting requirements, and the bureaucratic difficulties of granting permission for foreign participation. Also, Hungarian firms that wished to have a foreign partner were reportedly discouraged by the authorities prior to 1986.[15]

The regulations introduced on January 1, 1986, have eased the requirements of majority domestic ownership, reduced the rate of taxation, postponed the payment of duties in imported machinery by five years, strengthened the accounting procedures, and simplified the process of granting permission. Nevertheless, problems remain, including the lack of free utilization of the paid-in foreign exchange contribution of the foreign partner, import licensing, and price control.

Capital markets

The shift of investment activity from heavy industry toward the industries of transformation should entail reducing the directive role of the state in investment decisions, thereby reversing recent tendencies toward centralization. The adverse effects of these tendencies have often been noted in Hungary. In fact, during the 1981-84 period, the state provided 24 percent of investment funds for low profitability firms, which had an average profit rate of 1.2 percent, while providing only 4 percent of investment funds for high profitability firms, which had an average profit rate of 16.3 percent. As a result of government interventions, the rate of investment by the two groups of firms was practically the same, notwithstanding the observed large differences in profitability (Várhegyi, 1986, p. 5).[16]

The decentralization of investment decisions would link investments to firm profitability as envisaged by the November 19-20, 1986, Party resolution referred to earlier. In turn, profits would need to be linked more closely to enterprise performance through changes in exchange rates and the hardening the budget constraint for the firm, as suggested above. It would further be desirable to provide incentives for household savings, to promote the use of these savings in efficient investments, and to ensure the movement of funds from low profitability to high profitability firms.

Interest rates on savings deposits have traditionally been negative in real terms in Hungary. This is not the case for bonds that have recently been issued for purchase households. The tax-free interest rate on bonds is 11 percent, compared with 3 to 7 percent on savings deposits. At the same time, experience indicates that bond purchases by households have not been at the expense of savings deposits that are used essentially as a down payment for housing. In order to step up investment activity, it would be desirable to substantially increase bond issues to households. Bond issues totalled 5.3 billion forints by mid-1986. An expansion of this activity would require facilitating the issue of bonds by individual firms, as well as improving existing procedures for the issue and the trading of bonds.

At present, the government provides a guarantee to bondholders, with identical rates of interest paid on all bonds. Removing the guarantee or, initially, differentiating the guarantee fee, would make the desirability of the bond dependent on the creditworthiness of the issuer, resulting in differences in interest rates depending on risk. Furthermore, there would be need to establish a secondary market for bonds where transactions are executed under an auction system. The newly-established banks could act as brokers in this market, taking positions in bonds for which they served as underwriters.

Bond issues may also provide a vehicle for the movement of funds among firms. By mid-1986, only bonds valued at 2.0 billion forints were subscribed by other firms. Rather, firms tend to use their profits and amortization funds in self-investment, with little regard to yield, as they expect to be bailed out by the government in the event that the investments sour. The taxing of interest paid on bonds, and low interest rates on deposits with the banks, also favor self-investment. The hardening of the budget constraint, together with the elimination of taxes on interest paid on bonds and higher interest rates on bank deposits, would encourage firms with poor investment prospects to lend the funds they have, rather than to invest them. The establishment of an active capital market would thus contribute to the flow of funds from low-productivity to high-productivity uses. It would also permit firms in difficulties to borrow money to improve their operations, provided that they have favorable prospects for the future. In fact, it would be desirable to permit the issue of securities of varying maturities by the firms, with bonds providing for their investment needs, and commercial paper for working capital.[17] In this connection, reference may be made to the experience of China, which has recently allowed the issue of commercial paper by state enterprises.

Beyond their role in the bond market, the newly-established commercial banks would perform important functions of financial intermediation in Hungary. At the same time, for the banking system to operate efficiently, one should ensure that the banks act on the basis of business principles and that there is sufficient competition among them. Various measures would need to be taken in order to establish the conditions for the pursuit of these objectives. To begin with, the banks should be free to decide on their lending operations, thus limiting the role of plan priorities and central guidelines. This suggests the need to increasingly regulate bank lending through reserve requirements, with the refinancing by the National Bank envisaged at present as assuming a subsidiary role. Also, the banks should be given the right to collect time and savings deposits, which is not actually the case. Furthermore, the banks should be made fully responsible for profits and losses in their operations, and their profits should be subject to taxes at the same rate as the profits of industrial enterprises. These measures would aim at providing them with incentives to maximize profits. Finally, competition would need to be ensured by reducing size differences among the commercial banks and avoiding specialization according to industries and regions. For the same reason, it would be desirable to establish additional commercial banks, including those with foreign participation. It would further be desirable to increase the autonomy of the five financial institutions that have been created to foster innovation in Hungary. These institutions should be provided with their own funds and their decision-making power over centrally-allocated funds increased.

The next question concerns the practical application of the bankruptcy law, under which firms may be rehabilitated or closed down as conditions warrant. Apart from the liquidation during the 1970s of the Hungarian hat-making factory, the products of which ceased to be demanded, there are only two recent cases where a state enterprise has been closed down in Hungary. And, while forty-seven firms are under review in the application of the new bankruptcy law, which became effective on September 1, 1986, these are mostly small firms and cooperatives (*Figyelő*, September 18, 1986). Yet the problems have been concentrated in large state enterprises. In 1982, eleven large firms accounted for 80 percent of accumulated losses of state enterprises and in 1984 there were eleven large enterprises—the two lists overlap to a considerable extent—that experienced losses over several years (Lamberger, Szalai, and Voszka, 1986, p. 27). This is hardly surprising, given that the establishment of large firms in Hungary did not respond to economic imperatives, but was the result of industrial concentration undertaken on non-economic grounds prior to, as well as following, the implementation of the 1968 reforms.

In recent years, steps have been taken to break up large firms that had a quasi-monopoly position. But the government has continued to favor large firms of low profitability with investment funds. Thus, in the 1982-84 period, the seventy-three largest firms had an average profit rate of 5.4 percent but, with the government providing 37 percent of their investment funds, they had a higher rate of investment than the next group of large firms, which had an average profit rate of 7.2 percent and received 17 percent of their investment funds from the state, and small and medium-size firms, which had an average profit rate of 8.1 percent and received 9.5 percent of their investment funds from the state. As a result, the rate of investment of the seventy-three largest firms exceeded that of the other two groups (Várhegyi, 1986, p. 5).

Breaking up large firms would permit separating well-operating units from those that cannot be made profitable. At the same time, in limiting closings to certain units within individual firms, one can avoid the political dilemma involved in the bankruptcy of large enterprises.

Much attention has been given recently to the rehabilitation of firms that are in difficulties. In this connection, it should be noted that in the past such efforts have remained temporary and the problems have re-emerged soon afterwards (Laki, 1985). At the same time, the budgetary cost has been substantial, amounting to over Ft 10 billion a year. As noted by Gyula Csáki, a deputy finance minister, these unfavorable results find their origin in the emphasis on financial rescue operations, generally subject to bargaining between the firms and the government without an overall plan for the rehabilitation of the firms' productive activity (*Figyelő*, September 11, p. 1).

The new bankruptcy law provides for the preparation of overall plans to rehabilitate firms in difficulties. Nevertheless, as an informed observer noted, the danger exists that rehabilitation becomes a slogan that is invoked by every firm in difficulty in order to obtain financing, thereby imposing a large burden on the government budget and on the national economy (Varga, 1986, p. 3). Yet, in view of Hungary's overall financial limitations, there is a choice between making financing available for the development of efficient enterprises, and for trying to save inefficient ones. Correspondingly, emphasis would need to be given to the use of the firm's own resources in effecting improvements in its operations.

An additional consideration is that continuing losses of inefficient enterprises represent a considerable drain on resources. Closing down enterprises would thus contribute to the reallocation of resources to more efficient uses. At the same time, the sale of the assets of closed-down enterprises may not only bring financial returns, but permit a more productive use of these assets. And, once bankruptcy proceedings are initiated, other firms may reinforce their efforts to improve operations and to avoid excessive wage increases.[18] Thus, while it has been suggested that such proceedings be kept *in camera*, there is rather the need to give them considerable publicity, so as to increase their "educational" effect.

Conclusions

This paper has reviewed the macroeconomic situation in Hungary, and made recommendations for a restrictive macroeconomic policy and for the efficient promotion of exports. Note has further been taken of the need to harden the budget constraint facing the firm by limiting, and over time eliminating, firm-specific financial support that is to be replaced by overall macroeconomic policies regulating aggregate demand. This should be accompanied by measures taken to ensure the adequate operation of labor and capital markets while adjusting the relative prices of these factors of production.

In regard to labor markets, emphasis has been given to measures aimed at ensuring labor mobility and avoiding excessive wage increases. In turn, a variety of measures may be used to increase the availability, and to ensure the efficient use, of capital in Hungary.

Investment activity may be stepped up by limiting wage increases, broadening the availability of financial instruments to households, and extending recent measures aimed at attracting foreign direct investments. At the same time, there is need to reorient investment activity from the energy sector and heavy industry toward the industries of transformation, with greater scope given to firm decision making in the process. The efficient allocation of investments would further be promoted by broadening the scope for the flow of financial resources among firms through the bond market and via the banks. At the same time, it should be ensured that the banks act as profit-making institutions and there is sufficient competition among them.

Closing down inefficient firms would also free financial resources for more efficient uses, while care should be taken that the rehabilitation of poorly functioning firms is not done at the expense of efficient enterprises. Rather, the emphasis should be on the use of the firms' own resources in effecting improvements in operations.

Another important issue is the need to establish "property interest," with a view to increasing the value of the firm.[19] This raises the question of valuation by financial markets as well as ownership rights. An analysis of these questions is left for a later occasion.

Notes

The author is Professor of Political Economy at the Johns Hopkins University and Consultant to the World Bank. He is indebted to participants of the Tenth U.S.-Hungarian Economic Roundtable and to Otto Gadó for helpful comments on the earlier version of the paper.

The views expressed herein are those of the author and should not be attributed to the World Bank or to its affiliated organizations. While the findings, interpretations, and conclusions are the results of research supported by the Bank, they do not necessarily represent the official policy of the Bank. The designations employed, the presentation of material, and any maps used in this document are solely for the convenience of the reader and do not imply the expression of any opinion whatsoever on the part of the World Bank or its affiliates concerning the legal status of any country, territory, city, area, or their authorities, or concerning the delimitations of their boundaries, or national affiliation.

1. The relevant figure for Hungary was $545 per head, compared with $571 in Poland, $506 in Yugoslavia, $501 in Mexico, $379 in Brazil, $337 in Argentina, $272 in Turkey, and $232 in Romania. These data derive from international sources and refer to gross public and private debt.

2. Unless otherwise noted, all data originate in official Hungarian sources.

3. In addition to the factors noted below, reference may be made to the loss of food exports due to Chernobyl' that may have amounted to $80 million in 1986.

4. While the results are explained in part by the depreciation of the Yugoslav dinar, the Hungarian forint appreciated to a considerable extent vis-à-vis the German mark and the Austrian schilling as well.

5. In particular, Hungary's market share in the developed countries' imports of machinery and equipment fell from 1.25 percent in 1980 to less than 0.8 percent in 1985 (*Figyelő*, June 26, 1986, p. 9). The same source notes that, owing to the low degree of technical sophistication of Hungary's manufactured exports, average unit values declined while increases were experienced elsewhere.

6. Evidence on the latter point is provided in Balassa (1985a) where note has been taken of several additional factors contributing to losses in export market shares.

7. According to one author, "it is an error to assume that we can increase our export capacity by promoting exclusively export-oriented investments. The experience of the last several years indicated that such actions could help the situation of external equilibrium only for a short time. The permanent improvement of our [competitive] position is possible only

through the *overall improvement* of conditions in our national economy (Barta, 1986, p. 840—italics in the original).

8. This point is made by Pirityi (1986).

9. It is a different matter that one should avoid the error of announcing in advance that, above a certain annual wage increment, the wage tax will become practically prohibitive in the following period, thereby inducing excessive wage increases before the end of the year. This occurred in Hungary, leading to average increases in wage payments of 17.2 percent, including year-end bonuses, in November-December 1985, compared with the corresponding period of the previous year, as against the figure of 9.0 percent a year earlier (*Figyelő*, March 6, 1986).

10. It may be added that, while the Common Market countries limit the importation of textiles and clothing, Hungary has considerable possibilities for upgrading these exports and to export elsewhere.

11. However, according to the figures cited in the Five-Year Plan document, the investment share of mining and electrical energy was 43 percent in terms of 1984 prices in 1981-85.

12. Interview with Ferenc Vissi, the deputy chairman of the Material and Price Board, reported in *Figyelő*, March 6, 1986, p. 3.

13. As stated in a summary of articles dealing with telephones, "a service industry that is one of the most dynamic (if not the most dynamic) in the world has gotten to the brink of bankruptcy in our country in recent years. The neglect of the development of infrastructure over several decades greatly contributed to this desperate situation" (*Figyelő*, August 7, 1986).

14. According to the same author, the 12 percent share of net investment in 1984 in constant prices was only 8 percent if adjustment is made for price distortions (ibid).

15. Interview by Béla Csikós-Nagy in *Figyelő*, January 16, 1986.

16. As discussed further below, this has meant promoting large firms of low profitability.

17. The proposed changes would also permit alleviating the constraints imposed on the firm by the central regulation of working capital that has been justly criticized (Gadó, 1986, p. 3).

18. This will not happen as long as firms can confidently expect government support. Thus, it has been reported that two large firms in difficulties raised wage costs by about 10 percent in 1985 (*Figyelő*, December 5, 1985, p. 4 and September 25, 1986, p. 7).

19. For perceptive analyses, see Tardos, 1985 and Bársony, 1986.

References

Balassa, Béla. "The Hungarian Economic Reform, 1968-82." *Banca Nazionale Del Lavoro Quarterly Review*, June 1983, pp. 163-84. Republished as Essay 12 in Béla Balassa. *Change and Challenge in the World Economy*. London: Macmillan, 1985, pp. 261-81.

Balassa, Béla. "The 'New Growth Path' in Hungary." *Banca Nazionale Del Lavoro, Quarterly Review*, December, 1985a, pp. 347-72.

Balassa, Béla. "La politique industrielle socialiste." *Commentaire*, Summer 1985b, pp. 579-88.

Bársony, Jenő. "A vagyonérdekeltség kialakitásának problémái" [Problems Related to Interest in Enterprise Property]. *Közgazdasági Szemle*, April 1986, pp. 435-53.

Barta, Imre. "A beruházási szféra feloldásra váró ellentmondásai" [The Contradictions of the Investment Sphere Requiring a Solution]. *Közgazdasági Szemle*, July-August 1986, pp. 834-43.

Chandler, William V. "The Changing Role of Market in National Economies." *Worldwatch Paper 72*. Washington, D.C.: Worldwatch Institute, September 1986.

Csernenszky, László and Katalin Demeter. "A struktúra változásaa változás strukturája"

[Transformation of Structure and Structure of Transformation]. *Figyelő*, June 19, 1986, p. 7.

Dobozi, István. "The Responsiveness of the Hungarian Economy to Changes in Energy Prices." In Josef C. Brada and István Dobozi, eds. *The Hungarian Economy in the 1980s: Reforming the System and Adjusting to External Shocks*. Greenwich, CT: JAI Press, 1988, pp. 237-265.

Gadó, Otto. "Meg kell szüntetni a tartós készlet mérési módszerének központi elő irását" [The Need to Abolish the Central Determination of the Measurement of Inventory Needs]. *Figyelő*, October 16, 1986, p. 3.

Gulyás, Károly. "Válás magyar módra" [Divorce Hungarian Style]. *Figyelő*, September 18, 1986, pp. 1, 6.

Kunvári, Arpád. "Miért jutott holtpontra beruházásaink jövedelmezősege?" [Why Has the Profitability of Our Investments Reached the Zero Point?]. *Közgazdasági Szemle*, July-August 1986, pp. 825-33.

Laki, Mihály. "A gazdaságirányitós és a vállalati valság" [The Guidance of the National Economy and Level Crisis]. *Külgazdaság*, May 1985, pp. 41-58.

Lamberger, Galina, Erzsébet Szalai, and Éva Voszka. "Válságkezelés és vállalalatmegszüntetések" [Crisis Management and the Closing Down of Firms]. *Valóság*, August, 1986, pp. 24-31.

Nádudvari, Zoltán. "Számvezérlésü szerszámgépek. Fejlett technika-félállásban" [Numerically-Controlled Machine Tools. Developed Technology-Halfway]. *Figyelő*, October 16, 1986, p. 7.

Pirityi, Otto. "Viszaforditható-e a folyamat?" [Could One Reverse the Tendency?]. *Figyelő*, March 6, 1986, p. 5.

Révész, Gábor. "Bérezés an 1980-as évek Magyarországán" [Wage Setting in the Hungary of the 1980s]. *Közgazdasági Szemle*, July-August 1986, pp. 809-24.

Tardos, Márton. "A szabályozott piac kialakitásának feltételei" [Conditions for the Development of a Regulated Market]. *Közgazdasági Szemle*, November 1985, pp. 1281-98.

Varga, György. "Tiszta vizet a poharba" [Put Clear Water in the Glass]. *Figyelő*, March 20, 1986, p. 3.

Várhegyi, Éva. "Utolso par elore fuss?" [From Last to Be First?]. *Figyelő*, December 4, 1986, p. 5.

World Bank. *World Development Report 1986*. Washington, D.C., 1986.

Hungarian Financial and Labor Market Reforms

Developing Conditions for the Market Mechanism?

CATHERINE M. SOKIL

Introduction

It can be said that markets exist in every economy but simply differ in the degree to which they are controlled.[1] A free market system is simply one in which there is a minimum of controls, or constraints, on individual behavior in markets, and these more often take the form not of constraints but of influences on the incentive structure to which individuals are expected to respond. The approach undertaken here strives to examine the operation and effectiveness of Hungary's developing system of economic "regulators" using the standard tools of neoclassical economic analysis. Given the component parts of the Hungarian economic system—firms, households, markets on which the two interact, and the central authorities or planners, who now are to affect the interaction between the firm and household and the operation of markets via more indirect tools—we seek to show how these are likely to operate in Hungary. As Hungary intends to move toward a freer market system, it is necessary to examine its policies and reform blueprints in the context of how markets work, or are supposed to work, in the free-market system.

Probably the most significant result of the Hungarian reform process has been the change in the scope of planning, from the micro to the macro level, and the change in the instruments of central control, from directives to indirect "regulators," including prices, wage rules, interest rate and credit policy, exchange rates, taxes, and incentives. These are described variously as indirect, macro, and market-type policies. These regulators, interestingly, consist of instruments that are also used in market economies, as well as some instruments that are typically uncontrolled, or market determined, in market economies. In Hungary, regulators are not market determined, although more radical reformers feel they ought to be, but presumably they are influenced by market conditions.[2] All of the regulators, however, are instruments of the central planners that affect the operation of markets in Hungary through their impact on the objectives and constraints of firms and households. Changing incentives affect the objective of the firm and household, and changing controls and rules affect the constraints under which firms and individuals operate. These, in turn, affect the demand and supply of final goods and resources. The economic reforms, then, may be examined by means of a comparison between the theory of the firm and the theory of the household in a market economy, in a traditional centrally planned economy (CPE), and in Hungary.

Given the importance currently assigned to the more efficient use of resources in Hungary, this paper limits itself to those regulators affecting the labor and capital markets most directly, namely, wage rules, taxation, incentives, and interest rate and credit policy, and thereby ignores such crucial issues as prices of final goods. In the process, it asks whether the preconditions for the operation of a market mechanism and the use of indirect macroeconomic policies are being developed in Hungary in the factor markets for labor and financial capital.

One precondition is to create the institutional structures of the market system in factor markets, an acknowledged goal of the Hungarian reforms undertaken in the 1980s. Essentially, this precondition involves the development of competitive conditions. In factor markets, as well as in product markets, conditions for competition include mobility and free entry as well as exit. A way to achieve this goal is to increase the role of the private and cooperative sectors, in which a freer market exists, and to allow them to compete with the state sector. An alternative is simultaneously to increase the autonomy of enterprise managers by making their objectives clearer, and by reducing the constraints, including administrative interventions, imposed on them. In the factor markets, these constraints traditionally take the form of wage controls and restrictions on the use of financial resources of the enterprise.

A second precondition for the operation of a free market mechanism in factor markets is that households as suppliers, and enterprises as final demanders of labor and capital resources interact directly, with minimal central intervention.

Finally, the policy tools that are developed must be indirect tools that affect all competing players uniformly. Discriminatory policies create unequal constraints and objectives, create an unlevel playing field, preclude competition, weaken the role of profit and performance as signals for the efficient allocation of resources, and preclude the effective use of macro policy.

Changing objectives and constraints in the Hungarian enterprise sector

For firms in the private enterprise free-market system, the goal is maximization of the profit. The constraints on the firm are varied, but mostly consist of legal regulations that apply equally to all firms and that are kept to a minimum under the   ideal laissez-faire market system. In the competitive ideal, firms compete on markets for final goods, as well as for factors of production, on the basis of prices that reflect relative scarcities. In contrast, in a CPE the limited discretion managers have over the operation of the enterprise is the result of the imposition of many constraints on the enterprise by the center. Managers are motivated by the managerial reward structure. Because the enterprise lacks a clear long-term goal, and because the nature of the trade-off among competing short-term goals is unclear, the trade-off among objectives is informally communicated to the manager by the bonus system, by party campaigns, by promotion and prestige considerations, and the like. These informal signals are likely to conflict with each other. The reforms in Hungary since the 1968 introduction of the New Economic Mechanism have sought to make enterprises more responsive to prices and profits. Since the abolition of compulsory central planning, the objective function of the Hungarian firm has essentially become an open-ended rather than a fixed-target goal, eliminating the major sources of the incrementalism that characterizes traditional CPEs. In principle, at least, firms are to maximize profit, and indeed, profitability has become an important goal.

At the same time, the 1980s have witnessed the enormous growth of small-scale cooperative and private enterprise in Hungary. Approximately 1.6-1.7 million small-scale organizations complement the productive activity of 7,200 state and cooperative enterprises in Hungary today (Varga, 1988). The forms this burgeoning second economy takes include, but are not limited to, small cooperatives, specialized industrial and service cooperative groups, contract work associations, and enterprise contract work associations.

Generally speaking, as one shifts from the state to cooperative to private sectors, or, from the first to the second economy, one encounters fewer constraints imposed by the center on managerial decision making. Simultaneously, there is a stronger role for market forces, greater labor participation in management, a closer relationship between remuneration and effort, less bureaucratic intervention, and generally smaller size of decision-making units. The result is that there are really two basic theories of the Hungarian firm. One is pertinent for larger state enterprises, whose objectives include profit maximization, but who must also concern themselves with other indicators such as fulfillment of contractual deliveries to the CMEA market, convertible currency export goals, the growth of labor productivity, supplying the domestic market with inexpensive consumer goods, and even decreasing the share of white-collar employees (Bauer, 1982). The autonomy of these enterprises is limited. For example, ministries may retain power over managers of these firms by setting bonus conditions. The constraints on these firms are largely administrative, and as a result the constraints imposed by profit maximization are often "soft."[3] The second theory of the firm applies to the small cooperative and private enterprises in Hungary. These operate very much on the basis of profitability, their objective being to maximize members' earnings. The constraints on these firms are mostly economic and legal, and in most cases they are enforced, making them "hard."

If the enterprise is not profitable, it is dissolved. Members generally assume limited liability for the losses of the enterprise, meaning that they risk their financial contribution, if any, and payment for their labor services.

The differences in constraints imposed on large state enterprises and small-scale private and cooperative enterprises result in unequal competition on factor markets.[4] Varga (1988) points out that the small enterprises have a competitive edge in the labor market, for they are not bound by the wage regulations of the state sector, whereas the large firms have the advantage in the market for capital.[5]

Changing objectives and constraints in the household sector

The theory of the household in the market economy is based on utility maximizing behavior, in which the individual's allocation of time between labor and leisure is influenced by the real wage. Individuals are considered to be free to provide their labor services in the location and in the precise quantities they desire. In the CPE, the individual maximizes utility subject to quantity constraints on consumer goods markets. The resulting rationing of consumer goods leads to forced saving that, in turn, reduces workers' labor effort. Even in a planned economy individuals are considered to be relatively free in their provision of labor services, although limits may be placed on labor mobility and precise wage rates assigned for specific job classifications, regardless of productivity and effort. Households may also face restrictions on second economy participation and on the types of financial instruments which they may purchase.

Excess demand for labor puts the workers in a position of power in a CPE so long as their mobility is not restricted. In Hungary, workers are in a particularly powerful position because labor shortages prevail, and because constraints on the labor supply side are minimal. Individuals have the freedom to choose and to change jobs, and they may work in either the first, socialist, or the legal second economy, or both. The supply of labor, a function of the labor-leisure trade-off, is therefore affected by expected real wages in both the socialist and private/cooperative sectors, as well as by expected regulations on private activity.

The labor market

The Hungarian labor market provides a very clear illustration of the basic thrust of the reform, to substitute indirect instruments, primarily in the taxation system, for direct instruments such as commands from the center. The labor market also illustrates the problems of substituting indirect for direct instruments. Among such problems are the very complicated taxation rules that have resulted, and an environment of uncertainty as these rules are constantly modified. As a result, enterprises receive conflicting signals about their goals and constraints. These conflicting and changing regulations reflect changing priorities of the planners, who weight the desirability of differentiating wages to promote greater effort and to signal where labor is most needed against the principles of income equality and the need to control purchasing power. Perhaps the greatest uncertainty in recent years surrounded the introduction of a personal income tax in January 1988. Another problem is that the rules of taxation lack uniformity across firms, especially between those in the first and those in the second economy.

The firm's demand for labor

In a market economy, the firm's demand for labor is determined by the value of the marginal product of labor, and workers are hired so long as the value of their marginal contribution to output exceeds the wage rate. The enterprise in a traditional CPE tends to hoard all inputs, including labor, due to a reward system based upon firm size and the volume of output rather than on profit. This tendency is exacerbated by the lack of cost consciousness due to the soft budget, and by the underpricing of labor that results from state controls over labor mobility. For this reason, detailed labor directives may be employed by the center, including prescriptions on the number of employees in various categories, on wage rates, on the total wage bill, etc. Nonetheless, whereas the firm must go to the center for capital authorizations, even in the CPE the firm must go to the market for labor and compete with other firms for workers.

In Hungary, the demand for labor is affected by the degree of profit consciousness of the firm, by its tax regulations affecting wage and other payments, and by its ability to lay off workers. The evolution of the Hungarian wage system set the stage for current problems. Historically, firms have paid virtually all wage taxes, including a 40 percent social security contribution. Until recently, Hungarian wage policy was based on very progressive taxation of the increase in the average wage beyond some tax-free limit depending upon profitability, a policy that encouraged firms to stock up on cheaper, less skilled and/or motivated workers.[6] Ironically, the mobility of the labor force encouraged an active market for cheap labor, in which firms turned to non-wage benefits to evade the restrictions on average wages while effectively competing for workers.

Presently, wage regulation takes two basic forms. First, wide ranges of minimum and maximum wages, typically varying from 50-100 percent around the average wage, are defined for different skill categories. The total wage bill, or total wages paid out by the firm, is subject to very progressive taxation that discriminates across firms according to their profit rates, or profit/asset ratio (Marer, 1986). This progressive wage bill taxation does encourage firms to economize on labor. However, regulations and enterprise-level labor union and Party organization pressures make it difficult to lay off workers. The legacy of central planning, then, is that many large state firms are overstocked with unproductive workers who are now hard to lay off. These large firms compete for labor against the small enterprises, who have no such legacy. The large firms are thus less responsive to the real wage rate in their demand for labor and the small firms are more responsive.

The household's supply of labor

Due to wage controls in the state sector, many Hungarians sacrifice leisure-time to supplement their socialist sector income with income from the second economy. Kornai (1986) estimates that one-third of the labor force's total worktime is spent in the second economy. The private sector alone contributed 15-17 percent of national income in 1986 and it is expected that in Hungary official statistics grossly underestimate the extent of the second economy.[7] It is generally thought that a freer wage mechanism, including even greater wage flexibility and free entry and exit in the first economy, would eliminate the associated social problems of overwork and, in some cases, underemployment of labor in the first economy.

There are a number of ways in which workers can increase their labor supply through participation in the second economy. Most numerous, employing the largest number of workers, and most controversial are the contract work associations (CWAs). CWAs are groups of workers who subcontract their services to state enterprises and cooperatives. A special form of a CWA, the Enterprise Contract Work Association (ECWA), is comprised of workers who perform what are essentially overtime duties for the socialist sector firm in which they normally work. The firm originally paid no wage taxes on the remuneration of these workers.[8] Even if they paid 250-300 percent of the normal wage to such workers, firms found it worthwhile to hire them.[9] This is in part because firms hired their best workers via the ECWAs, thereby circumscribing the strict wage regulations that did not allow them to adequately compensate these workers. The ECWA system thus served as proxy, albeit a very imperfect one, for a more flexible wage policy, and so improved the labor market mechanism. Since 1985, however, the functioning of this imperfect system was dampened by the fact that ECWAs have been subjected to taxes, borne in part by the firm and in part by the workers. These include a progressive income tax and a 10 percent surcharge on the payments by the firm to the ECWA. This largely eliminates the cost advantage of these arrangements. In any case, the degree of competition introduced into the economy by the enterprise contract work association form is limited.[10] Essentially, the parent firm is a monopsonist, or the sole purchaser of the services of the ECWA, and has the power to refuse its services. Although the parent firm tries to encourage competition among ECWAs, in many cases the ECWA is the sole seller, creating a bilateral monopoly based on bargaining and wielding of countervailing power.

The majority of people engaged in the second economy retain their jobs in the first economy because there are certain characteristics of first economy jobs that are not available in the second economy, such as access to housing and difficulty in being dismissed for poor work performance. Moreover, first economy employment is a prerequisite for some second economy jobs in ECWAs (Kornai, 1986).

The result, to simplify, is that the firm has two basic types of labor. Wage controls cause productive workers' wages to be below the value of their marginal contribution to the firm's output. The firm provides overtime wages via the ECWA to keep this worker from being bid away. Unproductive workers earn more than their marginal contribution, are a legacy of average wage taxation, and are, by contrast, difficult to fire.

The contemporary Hungarian labor market can be characterized by the lack of central direction intervention; limited upward wage flexibility; excess demand for labor as a whole, although labor surpluses and shortages coexist; freedom on the part of workers to choose and change jobs; and very significant opportunities in the second economy. Wage regulations make it difficult for the state sector to compete for workers and less responsive to real wage rate changes than the second economy. Moreover, the pervasiveness of second economy employment opportunities and their relationship to the first economy detracts further from the effectiveness of the state sector's wage policy.

The market for financial capital

Investment in market economies should occur when the present value of a project's expected future income stream exceeds its cost. The traditional CPE rations investment on the micro level. Enterprise investment activity is strictly controlled by the center, whose priorities may not be dictated by considerations of efficiency. Enterprises that have the financial resources to undertake investments are not free to do so without authorization, nor is there an efficient mechanism to move financial resources to firms that do have profitable investment opportunities. Enterprise managers are rewarded on the basis of the size of their firm, thus providing them with incentives to seek the largest possible level of investment. Such investment hunger results in bargaining between the center and enterprises over investment resources, in which the firm benefits from the existence of the soft budget constraint, the fact that the center is forced to bail out ailing enterprises in the absence of bankruptcy (Hewett, 1981). In this environment the firm's demand for investment resources is obviously quite interest inelastic.

On the other hand, the center possesses very powerful instruments for the control of enterprises' investment funds: it may appropriate the profits of the firm, and it supervises the firm's finances. Investment subsidies from the state budget supplement the enterprise's own investment resources. Furthermore, credit from the central bank is provided for approved projects. In this environment, the interest rate mechanism is virtually irrelevant. The control over enterprises' investment resources effectively means that the financial resources of the state are indistinguishable from those of the enterprise sector. Financial intermediation between the household and enterprise sectors is performed almost completely by the state budget and by wage and price control and the separation of enterprise and household banking.

Under the NEM, the institutions of the capital market were changed, and enterprises' financial autonomy increased only to a very limited extent. The National Bank of Hungary achieved an increasing role in financial management, but still continued to serve more as a central institution of control than a commercial bank. Its decisions were more influenced by central authorities' preferences than by considerations of profitability and the solvency of its clients (Tardos, 1985). The untouched centralized monobank system remained as a safeguard for predominantly centralized investment decisions. Nonetheless, as Bácskai's contribution to this volume shows, meaningful changes took place, including the replacement of grants with loans, more meaningful interest rates, and bank evaluation of credit applications on the basis of expected earnings of the project.

Beginning with the NEM, an enterprise's taxable profit was allocated according to rules to three funds: the sharing fund, for distribution to employees; the development fund, for investment; and the reserve fund, for contingencies. Furthermore, allocations to the various funds were subject to differential taxation. These strict controls on enterprises' financial resources have been progressively weakened. Today, the Hungarian capital market, like the labor market, provides an illustration of the substitution of indirect instruments, particularly tax instruments, for direct instruments of central control. Currently, the major instrument to control the enterprise's use of its financial resources is differential rates of taxation. An enterprise pays an assets tax of 3 percent, in most cases, on the value of its real and financial assets; a 10-percent wage bill tax; and a 45-percent linear profit tax. After-tax discretionary resources may be used for investment, subject to an 18-percent accumulation tax, in most cases; wage increases or profit-sharing that are taxed according to one of several basic schemes; loans to another firm via, for example, the purchase of bonds, subject to the assets tax in the following year; or bank deposits. Not surprisingly, the accumulation tax has evolved into a more effective instrument of investment control than the interest rate mechanism.

Under the reforms of the 1980s, a limited capital market is being developed in the interest of more efficient allocation of capital resources and as an aid in the valuation of the firm. At the same time that enterprises have been granted more autonomy over the use of their after-tax profits, new financial institutions and instruments have been introduced. Enterprise investments are increasingly self-financed, and the development of financial instruments, such as bonds, have allowed some nonintermediated flows of financial resources among enterprises and from the household to the enterprise sector. The monopoly of the national bank has been abolished, with the result that enterprises now have a choice of five commercial banks from which to borrow and with which to maintain their accounts.

However, truly competitive banking conditions have not been created, for enterprise accounts were initially assigned to specific banks on a sectoral basis. Not surprisingly, since these assignments were lifted few enterprises have changed banks. The banks differ significantly in their balance sheets, size, strength, and branch networks. Moreover, regulation by the central bank in the form of refinancing limits, interest rates charged on refinancing credits, and reserve requirements, also differ across banks. In light of these limitations, it is difficult to imagine that bank lending to established clients will indeed become hard, and that a business relationship will automatically develop between banks and firms, the more so as the state continues to provide capital subsidies, mainly to larger firms, via the transformed state development bank, now the State Development Institute.

Small new financial institutions have proliferated. These provide capital for new ventures in the form of credit and/or equity, and are a source of hard financing for some of the new small enterprise forms. These small institutions actively compete with each other, and they have also made major loans through syndication. At the same time, the sources of financing for large firms have also become harder. In addition to an offshore bank, two foreign banks operate in the domestic Hungarian market.

The small-scale enterprises contribute to the development of a capital market only to a limited extent, because member financial contributions so far have been very small, and because many of them (ECWAs) rely on the capital of the parent. Indeed, because they employ the capital of the parent at no cost, they have been charged with wasteful use of capital and a short-term perspective on the goals of the firm (Varga, 1988). Part of the problem is uncertainty about their future taxation. However, in some of the new enterprise forms, there is now an auction market for capital functions; for example, in retail trade, shops are operated by the winner of a competitive bidding process.

Due to legacies of the past, household and enterprise finance remain institutionally separated. Traditionally, households have earned negative real interest rates on deposits that might be tied to the acquisition of consumer durables, and they have obtained housing loans at negative real interest rates from the National Savings Bank. Though mitigated somewhat by the activities of the private sector, the separation of household and enterprise finance is strongly entrenched due to differences in tax systems, interest rate policy, and the pricing system between the enterprise and the household sector. The personal income tax to be introduced in 1988 is being implemented, in part, to correct these distortions.

Conclusions

The Hungarian economy appears to be evolving into a dual economy that can be characterized by two distinct types of firms, two distinct theories of the household, and two parallel labor and capital markets. In such an environment authorities must consider the implications of the second economy for the possibilities to make effective use of more indirect instruments of control in the first economy.

Addressing the four preconditions of a market mechanism developed in the introduction, the current answers in Hungary are mixed.

1) Institutional development of resource markets has come a long way in the 1980s. Questions still remain surrounding the freedom of entry and exit and mobility, particularly in the capital market, but also in the labor market. Autonomy of enterprises in both labor and financial decisions has increased at the same time that the second economy has grown. The two distinct types of firms compete unequally for labor and minimally for capital, due to differences in legacies, in regulation, and in institutional development.

2) Firms and households interact rather directly in the labor market, but their

interaction is limited in the capital market.

3) An unequal playing field is not unique to Hungary and is mitigated by the fact that firms within each group do compete with each other. Competition among firms in the second economy is significant, but is mitigated by the prevalence of ECWAs, whose members may work only for the parent firm.

Many additional questions remain concerning the development of the market mechanism and market-type instruments in Hungary. In particular, the question of creating competitive conditions and an efficient pricing mechanism for intermediate and final goods has not been addressed and is, of course, an important component of the framework that must be developed. Another issue not addressed here is the relative costs of labor and capital and their impact on the firm's substitution of these two factors for material inputs, which also depends upon the tax system.

Notes

1. The disequilibrium literature acknowledges not only that markets exist but may not clear, but also that some markets, including the labor and consumer goods markets, are relatively free even in traditional CPEs.

2. This is similar to, but not quite, the Lange model, and results in substantial "regulator bargaining." See Kornai, 1986, p. 1700.

3. A significant development may, however, be the new bankruptcy law, Decree No. 11 of 1986.

4. According to Varga, the small cooperatives are taxed on gross income rather than profit, originally at a rate of 28 percent, and raised to 35 percent beginning January 1, 1985. Workers' remuneration varies directly with after-tax profits.

5. Competition between the first and second economies on product markets is not dealt with here. For most sectors, the share of private and small cooperative sector output appears to be growing relative to the socialist sector, but it is significant only for a few sectors, including retail trade, construction, computer and other services, and the knitwear industry.

6. The system introduced in 1985 allowed firms to "self-discriminate," i.e., to place themselves into one of three basic categories of wage taxation. These included progressive taxation of individual workers' wages; progressive taxation of average wage increases; and progressive taxation beyond a tax-free limit, respectively. The choice was limited, however, by factors such as the perceived degree of price competition faced by the firm.

7. One reason for such underestimation is that production by enterprise contract work associations is included in statistics for the state and cooperative sectors.

8. Payments to ECWA members were not included in the wage bill, and thus they were not subject to the strict regulations governing wage expenditures, including the flat 10 percent wage bill tax and the 40 percent social security tax.

9. Varga (1988) also provides an interesting comparison of the average cost of a man-hour of labor for a large firm based on whether the worker is a regular employee, an ECWA member, a member of a complementary workshop of a cooperative, a subcontracting firm, or a guest worker—in order of increasing wage.

10. According to Varga, 30 percent of firms have no or only 1-2 small ventures in operation.

References

Bauer, Tamás. "The Hungarian Alternative to Soviet-Type Planning." Paper presented at the US-Hungarian Roundtable, March 21-24, 1982.

Hewett, Edward A. "The Hungarian Economy: Lessons of the 1970s and Prospects for the

1980s." In Joint Economic Committee, United States Congress. *East European Economic Assessment*, February 27, 1981.

Kornai, János. "The Hungarian Reform Process." *Journal of Economic Literature*, vol. 24, no. 4 (December 1986).

Marer, Paul. "Hungary's Price, Wage, Tax and Subsidy Systems and Policies, and Their Effects on Its Economy." Annex 1 to *Stabilization, Growth and Structural Adjustment*, World Bank, Country Economic Memorandum, 1984.

Marer, Paul. *East-West Technology Transfer: Study of Hungary 1968-1984*. Paris: OECD, 1986.

Tardos, Márton. "Question Marks in Hungarian Fiscal and Monetary Policy." *Acta Oeconomica*, vol. 35 (1-2), 1985, pp. 29-52.

Varga, György. "The Role of Small Ventures in the Hungarian Economy." In Josef C. Brada and István Dobozi, eds. *The Hungarian Economy in the 1980s: Reforming the System and Adjusting to External Shocks*. Greenwich, CT: JAI Press, 1988.

Can Hungary's Monetary Policy Succeed?

MÁRTON TARDOS

Early efforts to monetize the economy

The historic, and continuing, fundamental principle of the socialist planned economy was that within a reasonable time it should render the market and money superfluous and replace it with conscious and systematic guidance that would provide a framework for peoples' lives and for the economy, thus leading to the age of man's control over social and economic events. Yet the world, as well as views formed about it, have since radically changed. It became obvious that the period following nationalization, when the role of money was subordinated to the urge to fulfill plans, was not only marked by naiveté but was equally damaging to economic relations. Boosting production often became an end in itself, and as such it did not help meet human needs. Demand frequently remained unsatisfied, and there was nothing to effectively stop the waste of resources and the rapid increase in costs of production. The imbalance of demand and supply also resulted in the decline of creative spirits.

The ensuing situation soon made decision makers realize that the role of money could not be ignored. In its reform efforts, launched in 1954 and continued through 1956-57, the Hungarian economy set itself the political goal of strengthening commodity and financial relations. Later on, in 1966-68 the concept of a market economy, guided by the plan, was proposed. One proof of how substantially our way of thinking has since changed, is that the 1966 decision of the Central Committee of the Hungarian Socialist Workers Party, a basic document of the reform, did not deal with the coordination of a planned central management and the active role of money circulation. This concept was also missing from an address by Rezső Nyers, then economic secretary of the HSWP CC, as well as from guidelines interpreting the decision.[1]

The 1966 decision first and foremost stressed the organic unity of national economic planning and the market. In this sense, it mentioned the growing importance of state-controlled economic competition between profit-oriented companies. It added that "the socialist state would then ensure the implementation of national economic plans, or in a wider sense, the central regulation of economic processes not simply by breaking down global plan figures but instead by exploiting possibilities provided by the commodity conditions, that is, mainly by economic means." Among such economic means mentioned by the resolution were rules of taxation; budget expenditures; government control of wages and prices; setting the foreign exchange and export and import policies.

The decision also referred to an active credit policy toward both investment and the use of current assets. It is known that even the word "market" was avoided during the implementation of the decision in general and in statements formulating the goals of the reform after the suppression of the Prague Spring. From 1972 onward, buffeted by domestic and external confrontations, the practice of Hungary's economic management moved even further away from the acceptance or application of market and money-flow mechanisms.

Such an application of monetary and market mechanisms would have meant the threefold use of money and prices. Money would have served as a measure of value, a medium of exchange, and a form of accumulation to make economic processes easier to survey and calculate. Money circulation and the pricing system would have served as vehicles for implementing goals set by the plan, for helping to stabilize the economy, and for promoting the continuous growth of companies. Finally, it was hoped that money circulation and the pricing system would, provided the above-mentioned requirements were actually met, make executives and employees of companies interested in the fulfillment of the plan in an effective way. The economic policy of the 1970s allowed the mechanism of the monetary system to work only in such a controversial manner. The regulations applied resulted in fiscal and monetary practice that differed among various companies and groups of users. No extensive market automatism came into being; companies were not integrated by money circulation (Tardos, 1985b). Thus the new economic mechanism in Hungary failed to give birth to a market; instead it turned into another version of the traditional Soviet system, combining strict but indirect plan instructions with the self-accounting of companies (Antal, 1985). By curbing the decision-making rights granted enterprises in 1966-68 as well as the freedom of the market, this system diminished the contradiction between the economic mechanism and the functioning of the centralized and hierarchically organized sources of economic policy.[2] Nevertheless, the change in the economic management had positive results. It managed to eliminate the weak points of the traditional plan-instruction system that were rooted in the inherent inconsistency of obligatory instructions and the central distribution function of the material and commodity balances (Tardos, 1985a). However, the indirect planning system was unable to achieve a breakthrough in facilitating an adjustment to varying demands of users and in saving resources. Consequently, not only did the expected improvement of efficiency not come about but, in addition, the country could not meet the challenge of the deterioration of global market conditions. The ensuing difficulties reflected not only the fact that the reform of 1966-68 had improved efficiency only slightly but were also due to a weakening resistance against borrowing from the West.

The period of economic restrictions

The tensions caused by adverse trends in the hard currency situation and the country's balance of payments had at least two consequences by late 1978. On the one hand, the existing practice of economic management was reviewed and new methods sought by which the government hoped to improve economic performance and to obtain the indulgence of the population and of creditors as well. On the other hand, the danger of insolvency justified restrictive measures to cut back incomes. The country's economic institutions were simply not prepared for the implementation of such measures. Because of this, the idea of a regulated market was raised again. Proponents of the regulated market argued that market economies based on the demand-oriented attitude of firms can avoid insolvency by increasing exports, and promoting import substitution by reducing the money supply. For a restrictive policy to properly improve the economy's adaptability and efficiency, a number of prerequisites must be met, the most important of which are perhaps the following:

—it must be capable of limiting effective demand by coordinating fiscal and credit policy;

—it must create an equilibrium exchange rate;

—it must induce companies to react quickly to developments in the money market;

—it must allow the restructuring of production caused by the new situation to be reflected in prices;

—profitable or new activities must obtain money to cover their additional wage, material, and import costs even when money is scarce; capital must be available so that, immediately after the bankruptcy of failing companies, their assets and manpower can be effectively integrated into new companies;

—for persons dismissed because of restricted demand, or adversely affected by a substantial cut-back of real wages, the protection of trade unions or unemployment benefits must be given, and also they must be provided with a choice among the possible responses, such as a change of workplace, setting up their own business, etc.

Neither in 1979, when the restrictive policy was launched, nor in 1982, when, owing to the immediate danger of the country's insolvency, the demand for restrictions grew, was the country prepared to implement monetary restrictions. It was not simply that the wage and pricing system and the credit mechanism were accustomed to bargaining, or that the cost-sensitivity of companies was low, but their legal status, the rules of association for the establishment of new companies, and the law ruling on bankruptcy did not make effective responses possible. The protection of employees and the scope of their freedom of movement, too, left much to be desired. So it was no wonder that, in order to win the confidence of foreign banks, the government— besides some rhetorical praise for the concept of market—attempted little else than trying to dismantle a few big companies and to encourage private enterprise, including measures to drive informal, and thus untaxed, small enterprises within the legal frame-work. Major tools of the eventually successful "staying afloat" policy were import restrictions; individually applied administrative pressure to boost performance; and export promotion. Anything attainable by applying such methods and by economic diplomacy, membership of the IMF, World Bank, etc., has already been attained. It would have been even better if by the time we had exploited the temporary results obtained by using up stocks and hastily mobilizing hidden reserves, that is, by 1984, we would have been able to enter on a new path of development (Antal, 1987; Kornai and Matits, 1987; Sándor, 1987).

Failure of the new path of growth

The package of new and market-oriented economic methods as demanded by the circumstances and also promised by the government had, however, failed to arrive. The fear of radical changes was well demonstrated by the formal debate on whether the reform's reform or the implementation of principles already adopted in 1966 was necessary (Bauer, 1982). Unfortunately, behind tactical issues of wording there were genuine problems. The refusal to consider a radical turn toward the market was also shown by the fact that the relevant complex proposal was adopted no earlier than April 1984, and even then not as a Central Committee decision but as a mere statement. When finally adopted, the package of programs contained quite a few inconsistencies, and it was further weakened in 1985 when, during its introduction, it was widely declared that the seven lean years were over and a new upswing had started.[3] For the purposes of this study, the weakness of the program is best indicated by its soft points in the field of the changes in property rights, i.e., the introduction of new company forms and the development of the money market, in the latter case by having put off the reform of the banking system until 1987.

Political leaders could clearly see that the institutional creation of the autonomy of companies had to be a key element of any change in the economic management. Numerous experts sought and found answers to that question. They wanted to give a clear and favorable signal for a wide range of autonomous companies, i.e., ones picked out from the hierarchy of the administration (Sárközy, 1986). All suggestions were based on the recognition that the owner, the genuine source of economic management, was missing from socialism. Workers and employees did not develop an ownership awareness, not because a petty bourgeois mentality was still lingering there, but because their objective situation was far removed from that of an owner. In reality they do not own the means of production and cannot do other than sign up with state companies or cooperatives on the terms that, in exchange for their work, they get an income sufficient to live on. Company managements, aligned with the state hierarchy, do not represent an owner either; they see their company either from above or in a selfish managerial way. None of the above-mentioned interests is that of an economic unit. Suggestions by the experts were geared toward helping to create a great number of independent economic units. To accomplish this they proposed, besides expanding self-management and private entrepreneurship, to set up state-owned asset centers and to organize corporate forms representing the interest of state and employee alike. Through a maze of esoteric paths, and much to everybody's surprise, there arose a decision, suggested by none, that companies be directed by company councils and members' meetings. The logic of this decision may best be approached by assuming that the method often applied by committees prevailed, that is that, in order to comply with requests advising more caution, passages of the text of the proposal were omitted, as long as this raised no significant objections on the part of the decision makers. Yet the final form makes no one happy and this applies not only to experts but presumably to company managers and employees as well (Tardos, 1987).

There is as yet insufficient experience, but I dare say that the new company forms have only strengthened the time-honored attitude of Hungarian companies that, instead of considering the increase of wages and incomes as a tool of cost-efficient management, they use it to iron out conflicts within the company. Hence the changes implemented failed to spur the responsibility and commitment of either management or employees toward goals such as the preservation of company assets, improving the company's future profit-making potential.

As for financial changes, there has been a lengthy tug-of-war over the banking system. Most experts agreed that cutting back state intervention and strengthening credit ties would be successful only if accompanied by the deregulation of prices, wages, and investments. To push back discriminative individual processes, or to generalize what in Hungary is called normativity, is possible only if effective aggregate demand is strictly limited, that is, if it is coordinated with the economy's productivity. This would call for a banking system where a central bank, publicly controlled by the Parliament, regulates the quantity of money and finances the budget while commercial banks, fully separated from the central bank, grant business loans. Yet this program, too, has been implemented partially and with much controversy. The reform of the banking system was missing from the 1985 package.[4]

Rather than keeping the economy's revenue-producing capacity within reasonable limits by demand management, efficient companies were harmed by the policy of cutting or calling in credits and subsequently raising interest rates. The result was that efficient companies turned their back on the banks and availed themselves of the latters' services only when strictly necessary (Sándor, 1987). At the same time, the fiscal authorities attempted to introduce new taxes and to centralize company profits more than ever before. Unlike previously, they helped companies in trouble more by reducing their taxes and less by giving them subsidies (Kornai and Matits, 1987). Continuing with such tax exemptions was all the more necessary because the bankruptcy law was still in the making.

At this point it is worth looking into the relationship between money emission and inflation. The government considers a certain calculated price increase as a means of income limitation. Only a fraction, 2 to 4 percent per year, of verifiable price increases comes from market processes; the bulk is the result of central price measures. It is remarkable that the swelling of money emission, including credits,

Table 1

Aggregate Economic Data for Hungary, 1979-1986

	GNP		Money supply		Export surplus	Price increase (in %)		
	billion FT	growth in %	billion FT	growth in %	billion Ft	GDP	at state compa- nies and coopera- tives	con- sump- tion goods
1979	1648.9	6.5	342.06	8.3	-23.4	5.6	.	8.9
1980	1879.7	14.0	352.29	10.7	-15.6	5.1	.	9.1
1981	2032.1	9.2	380.20	7.9	-8.2	5.1	6.5	4.6
1982	2214.6	7.9	405.57	6.7	+ 6.8	5.8	4.7	6.9
1983	2367.3	6.9	421.20	3.9	+17.1	5.0	5.3	7.3
1984	2559.7	8.3	443.09	5.2	+30.9	6.3	4.1	8.3
1985	2695.0	5.1	487.77	10.1	+21.4	6.0	4.4	7.0
1986	2845.4	5.6	541.70	11.1	-15.4	3.6	2.0	5.3

Source: Statistical Office (CSO) and National Bank of Hungary, *Statistical Reports.*

short-term ones in particular, did not cause so much a higher-than-planned inflation or rapidly growing shortages in the commodity supply as it did the deterioration of export performance and growing imports, and, as a consequence an exacerbation of the debt situation (see Table 1). From Hungary's experience, it is evident that, when the rate of growth of the money supply is less than the growth rate of GNP, the export surplus grows, and when the rate of money supply expansion exceeds the growth of GNP, net exports fall, as they did in 1986, or the trade balance becomes negative.

The rigid competitive pricing system introduced in 1981 was abolished, yet bureaucratic "harmonization" of supply and demand by so-called "free" prices remained in effect. It was only in the wage system that significant liberalization took place. Restrictions were also reduced as separately administered and regulated company funds, such as the reserve fund, the investment fund, the profit sharing fund, etc., were merged. All these methods have, however, failed. Companies frequently used their growing freedom to make unjustified wage increases that led to a step-by-step return to central income control. These developments resulted in an economy that was neither planned nor market (Bauer, 1982). Thus instructions have been replaced by expectations, and discriminatory financial incentives have been dropped. But the resulting gap has not been filled by the compelling force of money and market. This explains why in 1985-86 the economy's productive capacity diminished in every respect. This, combined with the deterioration of the terms of trade, pushed the economy to the brink of a crisis that was exacerbated by a slump in the agrarian prices, a narrowing supply of raw materials, shrinking export possibilities mainly in the oil derivatives and steel markets, rising standards for manufactured export products, etc. (Table 1).

What can monetary control do?

Prior to the introduction of a two-tier banking system in Hungary, the prerequisite of effective monetary control was not present, and in such situations one must choose between direct but discriminatory methods of management and even-handed indirectness, and it is reasonable to wonder whether monetary restrictions could bring about better results. There is ample room for doubt because some countries, mainly developing ones, with monetary instruments more sophisticated than Hungary's, cannot contain their foreign indebtedness nor can they control high rates of inflation. Also, a successful monetary policy in most industrialized countries has had serious consequences for employment.

I do not think that fears can fully be set at rest. What is clear, is that questions of monetary regulation in industrialized and developing countries are not identical with the ones facing Hungary. Both economists and policy makers in market economies agree that monetary policy must not make effective demand exceed the economy's productive capacity. Also, it is obvious that the circulation of money must not be disrupted by discriminatory interference, especially not by siphoning off revenues from efficient companies in order to keep inefficient ones afloat. Last but not least, everyone agrees that the movement of money incomes among owners, companies, and economic activities must be influenced by prices and interest, the level and movement of which helps achieve a balance of demand and supply nationwide as well as in the individual markets.

Hungarian proponents of monetary regulation are not asking any more of monetary policy than what it has achieved in market economies. Economists in Hungary, as well as in the West, are also aware that a money-regulated economy not only cannot be controlled precisely enough for the restructuring not to create some frictional unemployment, but also that unemployment cannot be avoided during slumps or setbacks. It must also be admitted that economics has not said the last word yet on the test methods of monetary policy, on the most reasonable combination of monetary and fiscal instruments, on the use of monetary instruments, and on the possibilities of the anticyclical policy (Bokros, 1987). All this, however, should not keep us from experimenting with the only means of regulation we know. In this regard we must learn from those countries and monetarist neo- and post-Keynesian economists and experts who have studied the experiences of market economies over the past decades. We ourselves, too, must try to find the solution most suitable for us.

Another group of domestic critics of monetary policy has raised two questions. First, neither the "fine-tuning," so popular in the United States during the 1960s, nor a longer-term monetary control can be successful in the market economies (Szegő and Wiener, 1987). Such critics base their arguments on the theses of

Kalecki (1980) and Péter Erdős (1974), and spice them with a concept drawn from surveys of the attitude of socialist companies, the notion of forced growth. The first statement consists of two elements. First, that in a monopolistic situation, big companies generate their own incomes, thus monetary policy cannot stop the outflow of money. Second, that the regulation of the supply of money cannot be properly controlled by the central bodies. Another argument of the critics is the companies' hunger for investment that, in their opinion, can be stilled by capitalist entrepreneurs (Szegő, 1984).

The debate has raised important questions. It is true that the monetary and fiscal policy of the past decades had not fulfilled the hopes of the leading capitalist countries. As I have mentioned before, it proved unsuitable for a stop-go type of fine-tuning of the economy. Also, it is true that so far no one has succeeded in stilling the hunger of socialist firms for investment. Still it is not quite clear what positive conclusions can be drawn from this. As it is, recognizing the limits of human knowledge and of social insensibility to market signals, respectively, should not lead to total passivity. Moreover, if I accept the statement of the critics of the monetization of the economy, that they do not recommend a return to mandatory planning or even to a modified form of it, then I think that we can only conclude that an efficient market must be created. This, considering our current knowledge, must mean that we must accept that, instead of fully eliminating economic fluctuations, economic policy must focus on accepting some small fluctuations and on enforcing a long-term development tendency, just as is being done in the leading industrialized countries by pragmatically harmonizing their monetary and fiscal policies. On the other hand, efforts must be made to influence the economy's structural evolution and to create a property rights structure that will produce reasonable conditions for efficient development.

In Hungary, just like in capitalist economy, monetary policy must be strengthened to make it capable of enforcing the balance of money supply and demand under any circumstances, of counteracting excessive money creation in the long run, and of providing conditions for the development of economic agents interested in maintaining and adding to their personal or corporate assets. The task of restructuring the structure of socialist property goes beyond the subject-matter of this paper, but, as I have said elsewhere, I think the problem is solvable, and that even a partial solution to this problem is better than nothing (Tardos, 1987).

Hungary's monetary policy after elimination of the monolithic banking system

After a lengthy tug-of-war, on January 1, 1987, a banking system characteristic of market economies was established in Hungary. Market economies require the existence of competition and entrepreneurial activity, and they expect their central banks to control the money circulation and to finance the budget. At the same time, the traditional tasks of a credit bank, the collection of deposits, granting of credits, and maintaining accounts, should be performed by competing banking institutions separated from the central bank. For this purpose in 1987 five large banks were granted licenses to provide a wide range of financial services (Babus, 1987; Fábri, 1987). The only deviation from free market conditions exists with regard to foreign exchange operations and banking transactions on behalf of the population. The former activity remained a monopoly of the central bank, the National Bank of Hungary, while the latter is dealt with by two organizations, OTP, the National Savings Bank, and the cooperative savings banks.

Since June 1987 there has been a free choice of banks, and parallel bank relationships also may exist. Competition has been created because no banking institution may refuse any company wishing to open an account at it, and, except for a few special instances, banks are not bound to grant credits. Credit flows among banks have been unlocked.

The newly established banks are joint stock companies. Four percent of the principal item of their respective balance sheets was allotted as stock capital by the budget (see Table 2). In addition, the banks increased their capital by issuing more shares and thus, besides the budget, many big companies in Hungary nowadays hold a fair number of bank shares. Nevertheless, according to the World Bank, the capital supply of Hungarian banks is still low.

The Hungarian Credit Bank and the National Commercial and Credit Bank were formed from the previous commercial and credit department of the National Bank of Hungary (NBH). The Budapest Development and Credit Bank was established by merging a part of the State Development Bank, the Budapest Credit Bank, and the Pest Country Directorate of the NBH. After some modification of their scope of activity, the Hungarian Foreign Trade Bank Ltd. and the General Assets Trade Bank Ltd., too, are now operating as fully licensed commercial banks. Both their clients and organizational framework come from the division of the NBH, the Budapest Credit Bank and the State Development Bank, respectively. Seven of the NHB's former county directorates belong to the Hungarian Credit Bank and ten to the National Commercial Credit Bank. Both banks have branches in Debrecen. In the future, the NBH will have small offices in every county seat. The Budapest Development and Credit Bank was formed from the Budapest Credit Bank, six NBH branches, and from the Budapest department and country branches of the State Development Bank excluding its State Development Institute.

The state, as a shareholder, is represented by the Ministry of Finance, which holds the majority of shares, and by the Center of Banking Institutions. As is usual with joint stock companies, the founders establish the by-laws of the bank. The bank's highest executive body is the General Assembly, which elects the Board of Directors that directs the day-to-day activities of the bank, and the Board of Supervision that exerts general control over the bank's activity and is made up of financial, accounting, and legal experts.

From another part of the State Development Bank the State Development Institute was formed to perform certain tasks of financing and to "pass on" the

Table 2

The Banking System in Hungary, from January 1, 1987

	Form of property rights	Value of assets, in mil. forints
Central Bank		
National Bank of Hungary	joint stock company	10,000
Commercial banks		
Hungarian Credit Bank	joint stock company	5,500
National Commercial and Credit Bank	joint stock company	5,500
Budapest Development and Credit Bank	joint stock company	2,500
Hungarian Foreign Trade Bank	joint stock company	3,000
General Assets Trade Bank	joint stock company	1,000
Banks for the population		
National Savings Bank (OTP)	state-owned	1,300
Development banks		
State Development Institute	state-owned	
Small financial institutions		
INTERINVEST Foreign Trade Development Association	deposit company	2,000
Construction Industry Innovation Bank	joint stock company	744
TECHNOVA Industrial Innovation Fund	deposit company	424
Agrarian Innovation Bank	deposit company	600
Industrial Coop Bank	deposit company	300
INVESTBANK Development Bank	deposit company	620
General Enterprise Bank	joint stock company	2,200
INNOFINANCE General Innovation Fund	joint stock company	500
Bank for Small Business	subsidiary of OTP	300
Hungarian-foreign joint banks		
Central European International Bank Ltd., Budapest	joint stock company	20 mil. dollar
Citibank, Budapest	joint stock company	20 mil. dollar
UNIC BANK	joint stock company	

expectations of the central structural policy to commercial banks. The Institute will finance central investments, and sign up commercial banks to arrange the relevant financial transactions. Also, it may suggest the terms for granting subsidies and manage the budgetary funds backed by state guarantees.

In addition to the five big banks, two organizations engaged in dealing with banking transactions for the population, and the State Development Institute, there are twelve more specialized banking institutions, two of which are subsidiary banks. These banking institutions were established as limited partnerships and reorganized into limited companies by December 31, 1987. In compliance with the intention of their founders, these are engaged in financing innovative activities but would like to expand into all commercial banking activities. Also, there are two joint venture banks: Citibank Budapest Co., Ltd. and UNIC-BANK Co., Ltd. They enjoy the rights of extra-territoriality and, as such, operate as off-shore banks.

The theoretically unlimited money-creating capacity of the five commercial banks empowered to keep accounts is controlled by the central bank. The array of control instruments includes both fixed and flexible means of influencing bank behavior. In principle, permanent control instruments include the reserves of the central bank, stipulation of the so-called monetary basis, and the refinancing of credits. Reserve requirements determine the percentage of deposits placed at commercial banks that must be kept in the form of cash and of deposits with the central bank. The flexible instruments include interest rate policy, refinancing over and above the normative refinancing funds, and securities transactions. Such a wide range of instruments can be effective in an advanced banking system. But ours is not like that yet.

In my view, it is too early to evaluate and judge the banking reform. This is all the more difficult because the new system has allowed a free choice of banks only since the middle of 1977. Nevertheless, numerous and often contradictory reports in the press and literature, as well as discussions held with experts, prompt us to mediate on several key aspects of the new system.

Originally we assumed that, although the former monolithic banking system was unable to regulate effective demand and supply, the central bank together with the network of commercial banks could do so.

We assumed that a profit-oriented system of commercial banks would be able to eliminate the earmarked nature of various money flows, and stocks would rearrange credit so as to give an impetus to efficient economic activity, resulting in pressure on inefficient activities that ultimately would lead to cut-backs and bankruptcies. In effect, the first year of introduction did yield such results (Bódy, 1987). The money supply of firms and their liquidity have been improved despite the economy's weak overall, and even weaker export, performance. Experts agree that the support of poorly managed companies has not been eliminated, and that there are no signs of an acceleration of the financing of innovative activities begun earlier by small banking institutions. Criticism condemning the lack of positive changes could be rejected as impatience if we could receive optimistic promises from those managing the banking, instead of statistics reflecting inertia. The fact is that, along with cautious, and often apologetic, statements from the government and the National Bank of Hungary, the leaders of new banks report limitations on their scope of action.

The regulation of the money supply is hampered by the budget's money-creating activity, which has not been integrated into the banking system. As a result, the credit supply of the commercial banks must be adjusted unilaterally to the government budget. With regard to the regulation of the budget's money-creating activity, debates in Parliament have brought only slight and insufficient changes. Due to its need to finance the budget deficit of the state, the NBH will be forced to restrict the lending activities of the commercial banks. Thus efficient companies, too, have good reason to fear that banks will be unable continuously to meet their credit requirements. Another weak point of monetary policy is the existing practice of refinancing. It is generally agreed that the reorganization of the banking system was preceded by an unwarranted wave of money-creation in late 1986. The NBH did not prevent lending officers, destined for jobs with commercial banks, from hastily granting new credits to companies that they knew would become their clients in their next job at a commercial bank. In this way officers in their new positions at commercial banks demonstrated their goodwill toward their partners without having to accept the odium for their deeds. On the other hand, by early 1987 the central bank created a difficult situation so that it could prove that it was still "master of the house." In this spirit, the central bank started the year with radical restrictions on the money supply. By means of refinancing quotas, it reduced in two phases the credit stock for circulating assets by a total Ft. 28 billion. As a consequence of this credit contraction, most company managers came to believe that the safety of their companies lay in keeping stocks of material and parts instead of holding liquid money deposits. Therefore the majority of companies continued to minimize ties to banks.

The system of business relationships maintained by commercial banks is not reassuring, either. In this respect, one must consider not only that practically all long-term credits are decided upon by the state, but also that the profitability of banks is controlled by the general assembly of shareholders, and by the Board of Directors and the Board of Supervision, both elected by them. The owners of the bulk of shares, the Ministry of Finance and/or the Center of Banking Institutions, have virtually renounced their rights as shareholders. Thus the board of directors consists more or less of delegates of big companies that have rounded out the capital given to the banks by the Ministry of Finance and/or the Center of Banking Institutions. It is worth mentioning that quite a few companies that purchased bank shares were indebted to the NBH as they are not to its legal successors. The NBH used to regularly revolve the whole or part of this debt. Thus the main interest of shareholders lies not in a safe and profitable placing of bank credits, but in maintaining the practice of revolving credits. In such a situation it is hard to imagine a board of directors that would vigorously encourage the management to call in hopeless loans or, if necessary, to initiate bankruptcy proceedings. The profit interest of commercial banks makes the situation even more complicated. In the course of bankruptcy proceedings, losing a part of actually frozen debts may cause banks to show a loss on operations because, in such cases, the rules do not allow them to raise the nominal income of their employees. This explains why bank managers initiate bankruptcy proceedings in exceptional cases only, since this is something they cannot afford because two to three bankruptcy proceedings may easily ruin them (Babus, 1987).

Having listed the above factors restraining the market behavior of banks, it is perhaps superfluous to add that, in spite of all logical arguments, there are still two different refinancing practices existing, one for fixed and another for circulating assets; that the refinancing of centrally preferred investment credits by the central bank, that is, in some cases the increase of frozen amounts, is automatic because of government decisions. Moreover, to call in credits and to initiate bankruptcy proceedings, even if in principle the economic management expects commercial banks to do so, runs into the savage and relentless opposition of the political bodies, including ministries, county and town councils, and Party committees. It may be enough to cite the confusion caused by the only bankruptcy instituted since the reform of the banking system against a big company, the Veszprém State Building Co., which was initiated by the biggest commercial bank to set an example (for details, see "A VÁÉV helyzete," 1987).

Lessons and possibilities

For some, the uncertain outcome of the bank reform confirmed their previous belief that increasing the efficiency of socialism by market-oriented reforms was hopeless. Others claimed that half-hearted changes led nowhere because money processes controlled from above in every detail neutralized the reforms. As I see it, both standpoints reflect important truths. A substantial change in the management system, and the success of the bank reform in particular, can be hoped for only if and when the political system accepts the fact that the circulation of money is the key regulator of efficient economic operations, and if and when it acknowledges that man is unable to master the circulation of money without breaching the requirements of efficiency. By no means does this mean that the regulation of money and market, or the deliberate economic control of society, are not necessary, and the government must let loose the reins. But, aside from a direct regulation of public services, coordinating the volume of money with the economy's productive capacity and slightly correcting the monetary processes according to state preferences is all that is necessary and possible. As it is, that is all that social power is capable of doing without causing considerable losses in market efficiency. It seems that changes in 1968, 1979, and 1985, and even the bank reform of 1987, have been insufficient to increase the role of money to the extent required by efficiency considerations and radically to transform the status of the center.

Thus experiences indicate that doubts with regard to the creation of an efficient socialist market are not unfounded. This, however, runs counter to a requirement arising from the recent economic situation. As things are, this position has not improved properly precisely because of the weakness of changes introduced. Society has had to pay dearly for this failure to transform the power structure and for the constant undoing of reforms geared to creating a genuine market. If this situation continues, the inherent economic problems and the deterioration of living standards will only worsen. Economic success calls for multiple changes. Prerequisites for an efficient national economy are solving the difficult task of central wage control; coordinating the supply of money with the utilization of resources; and adjusting the budget to the availability of credit. This, however, can be accomplished only if policy does not seek to eliminate the conflicts incident to the circulation of a controlled amount of money; if it enables commercial banks and owners of companies to husband assets they were entrusted with, and expects them to draw the ensuing management and personal conclusions; if it creates a situation in which economic units may acknowledge possible losses, instead of being forced to drag along paper assets like the new, efficiency-oriented commercial banks do in the case of frozen credits. Another important prerequisite is that they should enjoy a much freer hand than they do now in setting prices and wages in the competition for effective demand.

It is up to the government, controlled by Parliament, to provide for the preconditions required for the success of a market-orientated reform. This process has, however, been stunted by further contradictions; first, that changes, essential for an efficient money and market management and implying a self-imposed limitation of power on the government, must imply a one-party system; and, secondly, that the demand in Hungary for further reforms has been raised at a time when the restructuring of the system of economic management has been on the agenda for as many as twenty years, with no spectacular achievements. Also, it ought to be realized that reforms cannot rely on boosts from foreign credits, and that expenses cannot be covered fully or partially by curbing consumption. So the intention to create the efficient market needed for social stability and progress has been confronted with the overriding and short-term interest of citizens and certain social groups seeking to safeguard their political interests. Neither a justified skepticism nor doubts can deter us from stressing again, in the face of our current experiences, the need for a socialist economy ruled by money and market, including an efficient banking system.

Notes

1. For details see Hungarian Socialist Workers' Party (1966, 1968).
2. One sign of the Hungarian economy's domestication was that in the Brezhnev era most of the Soviet Union's economic literature did not even consider Hungary's move to abolish plan instructions as a substantial modification of the system (Golubeva, 1978).
3. One cannot disregard the important fact that the slowdown coincided with the post-Brezhnev transition in the Soviet Union (Andropov's illness and death, and Chernenko's election as CPSU general secretary), which was marked by conservative tendencies that no doubt made themselves felt in Hungary as well.
4. Bankers originally claimed, though this is now mentioned only with regard to maintaining the monopoly of foreign exchange trade, that such changes would involve the risk that creditors would not like the market-oriented measure, but citing changes in the legal status of their debtors, would demand their money back at once (Zdeborski, 1987).

References

"A VÁÉV helyzete" [The Case of VÁÉV]. *Figyelő* 31, 13, March 7, 1987.
Antal, László. *Gazdaságirányítási rendszerünk a reform után*. Budapest: KJK, 1985.
Antal, László, Lajos Bokros, and György Surányi. "Fordulatot a pénzügypolitikában" [Turnover in Fiscal Policy] *Figyelő* 36, September 4, 1986.
Antal, László and Éva Várhegyi. Tőkeáramlás Magyarországon [Capital Allocation in Hungary]. Budapest: KJK, 1987.

Antal, László, Lajos Bokros, László Csillag, László Lengyel, and György Matolcsi. "Fordulat és reform" [Turnover and Reform]. *Közgazdasági Szemle*, vol. 34, no. 6 (1987).

Babus, Endre. "A csődtörvény egy éve" [One Year after the Bankruptcy Law]. *Heti Világgazdaság*, vol. 9, no. 37 (1987).

Bauer, Tamás. "Második gazdasági reform és a tulajdonviszonyok" [Second Economic Reform and the Property Rights]. *Mozgó Világ* 10 (1982).

Bódy, László, "A bankreform félévi mérlege" [Half a Year after the Bank Reform]. *Figyelő* 31, July 30, 1987.

Bokros, Lajos. "Az üzleti viselkedés kibontakozásának feltételei a kétszintű bankrendszerben" [Conditions for Business Behavior in the Two Tier Banking System]. *Külgazdaság*, vol. 31, no. 1 (1987).

Bryant, Ralph. *Controlling Money*. Washington, DC: The Brookings Institution, 1983.

Erdős, Péter. *Adalékok a mai tőkés pénz . . . elmélethez*. [Contributions to the Capitalist Monetary Theory of Our Day]. Budapest: KJK, 1974.

Fábri, Ervin. "Változó váltó helyzet" [The Bill of Exchange]. *Figyelő* 36, April 9, 1987.

Falubíró, Vilmos. "Fizetőképes gazdaságtalanság" [Sound Inefficiency]. *Figyelő* 40, October 1987.

Golubeva, V. I. *Szisztema planirovanie . . . VNR* [System of Planning . . .]. Moscow: Nauka, 1978.

Hungarian Socialist Workers' Party. *A Magyar Szocialista Munkáspárt KB 1966. május 25-27-i ülésének anyaga* [Resolutions and Materials of the Session of the Central Committee of the HSWP, May 25-27, 1966]. Budapest: MSzMP, 1966.

Hungarian Socialist Workers' Party. *A Magyar Szocialista Munkáspárt határozatai és dokumentumai 1963-66* [Resolutions of the HSWP 1963-66]. Budapest: Kossuth, 1968.

Jánossy, Dániel. "Huncut tallérok" [The Funny Money]. *Figyelő* 36, January 15, 1987.

Kalecki, M. *A tőkés gazdaság működéséről* [The Capitalist Economy]. Budapest: KJK, 1980.

Kornai, János and A. Matits. *A vállalatok nyereségének bürokratikus újraelosztása* [Reallocation of Enterprise Profits]. Budapest: KJK, 1987.

Ligeti, Sándor. "A bankrendszer átszervezése" [Reorganization of the Banking System]. *Külgazdaság*, vol. 31, no. 1 (1987).

Radnotzi, János and G. Róbert Rózsa. "Az állami bankfelügyeletről" [State Control of Banking]. *Bankszemle*, vol. 31, no. 4 (1987).

Sándor, László. "Hitelezés üzleti vagy hivatali alapon" [Business or Bureaucratic Credit Launching]. *Figyelő* 36, January, 1987.

Sárközy, Tamás. *Egy gazdasági szervezeti reform sodrában* [In the Current of Economic Organizational Reforms]. Budapest: Magvető Kiadó, 1986.

Szegő, Andrea. "Vita a reform alternatíváiról" [Discussion about Reform Options]. *Kritika* 1984.

Szegő, Andrea and György Wiener. "A nyereségképződés makrogazdasági törvényszerűségei" [Profit Rules in the Economy]. *Pénzügyi Szemle*, vol. 31, no. 1 (1987).

Tardos, Márton. "A szabályozott piac kialakításának feltételei" [Conditions for a Regulated Market]. *Közgazdasági Szemle*, vol. 11, no. 2 (1985a).

Tardos, Márton. "Az infláció sajátosságai és a pénzgazdálkodás fejlesztése Magyarországon" [Inflation and Monetary Policy in Hungary]. *Gazdaság*, 31 (1985b).

Tardos, Márton. "Vállalati tulajdon, vagyonérdekeltség, tőkepiac" [Property Rights, Interestedness, Capital Market]. *Külgazdaság* 31, 3 (1987).

Zdeborszki, Gy. "Devizagazdálkodás és külgazdasági banktevékenység a kétszintű bankrendszerben" [Foreign Exchange in the New Banking System]. *Bankszemle*, vol. 31, no. 2 (1987).

The Reorganization of the Banking System in Hungary

Tamás Bácskai

The pre-socialist banking system in Hungary

The Hungarian banking system developed from the first third of the nineteenth century along the continental path, leading to the predominance of universal banks, the department stores of finance. This system of a large number of small banks with numerous branches, a sizable part of them at county and town levels, was controlled by a handful of big banks that were tightly intertwined with large foreign banks.

This situation created many well-trained and broadly-skilled bank officers because, especially in the provincial banks and in branches with a limited staff, the bank employees had to be "jacks of all trades," mastering all banking and stock exchange operations. Due to the fact that the Association of Banking Employees, a trade-union-like organization, had a strong left-wing audience which had considerable influence among bankers, the higher echelons of banking staffs consisted largely of pro-Allies liberals who had not been associated with Nazism. Thus, to a considerable extent, the new regime was able to draw its banking cadres from professionally well-trained, and politically loyal or neutral people. From 1949 on, even after the filling of the controlling posts with cadres of the labor movement, the lion's share of the former banking staff remained in lower posts as deputies of the new upper-level managerial staff, or in influential advisory jobs. Thus, the correctness and the professionality of banking operations, accounting, calculation, compilation of balance sheets, correspondence, both domestic and foreign, has been maintained at very high standards. Nevertheless, by having eliminated former top-level managers to a large extent, there was and is a scarcity of bankers who are specialists in allocating loans so as to optimize the safety and profitability of a portfolio. This lack was not obvious until the present decentralization because, even after the reform of the economic mechanism in 1968, the autonomy of the banks continued to be severely curtailed. There is a justified hope that Hungary can fill this gap since, from 1951 on, there has been university training for banking, and many of the posts in the banks hitherto not requiring higher education are filled with university graduates. Another factor facilitating the emergence of bankers is the country's strong involvement in foreign trade, handling of World Bank loans, setting up and running joint ventures with foreign equity, etc., which have acquainted hundreds of Hungarian bank employees with foreign banking.

Concerning central banking, Hungary established its own Central Bank rather late, in 1924. Nevertheless, this bank, the National Bank of Hungary, had as its predecessor the Budapest Main office of the former Austro-Hungarian Bank, the central bank of the Austro-Hungarian monarchy. The newly emerged Central Bank operated between 1924-31 under the strong influence of the Bank of England and personally of Montague Norman, later Lord Cobbold, and it excelled especially in keeping the money supply tightly tied to changes in the metal-base through its rediscounting operations. From mid-August 1931, with the suspension of convertibility, the National Bank of Hungary assumed the function of managing and rationing foreign currency for imports and ran scores of bilateral clearing accounts. With the advent of the 1938 armament program, the indirect financing of the budget and direct controls over commercial banks came to the fore and, with these, a bureaucratization of the operations evolved. At the same time, the National Bank of Hungary, with its branches in every district, every county, and with personnel trained in keeping banking accounts, carrying out payment and clearing operations, etc., offered itself naturally as the skeleton of the future banking system.

The banking system in the framework of directive planning

The government that took power in Hungary after World War II made industrialization, full employment, and the establishment of collective farming the principal aims of its economic policy, and government management the means of achieving them. There were several factors that facilitated the latter: a disillusionment with market mechanisms and their consequences among the so-called middle-class and especially among the intelligentsia; the apparatus, instrumentarium, cadres, and legal stipulations inherited from the war economy of 1938-45; and, in the field of foreign currency, from 1934 the terrible shortages to be handled only by rationing and not by market methods. Also contributing was the relative underdevelopment of the country, which required major efforts to redistribute funds from consumption to capital formation and from agriculture to industry.

The nationalization laws of 1948 and 1949 concentrated practically all industry in the hands of central and municipal governments, and the bulk of the land was cultivated by collective farms or state-owned farms. These companies were guided by a central plan. The idea of a national plan was not new in Hungary. In March 1938 the Darányi government had launched a "billion pengoe plan" which envisaged the annual expenditure from budgetary means and bond issues of 200 million pengoes, 8 million pounds sterling at the then prevailing exchange rate, for five years in the form of investment subsidies to heavy industry, transport, and agricultural improvement. It was due to capital formation under this plan that the number of factory workers rose from 289,000 in 1938 to 392,000 in 1943, an effective means for expanding employment. In 1941 Hungary also launched a ten-year investment plan for agriculture. There were, as a result, civil servants for planning, and returning Marxist exiles from the Soviet Union and from the West brought with them generally theoretical, but also practical, planning and implementation experience.

The post-war plans were novel because they were intended to guide productive and distributive activity as an integrated entity and thereby also deeply influence consumption. Another novelty was the detailed planning of production and its distribution in physical units, with some aggregation of those units in money terms, either as a convenient form of representing quantities or where the specification of items in their own physical measures was considered to be superfluous. The technique of the preparation of plans was based on material balances, with a process of bargaining whereby ministers for the industries concerned or other political authorities negotiated for supplies.

Statistics and public administration reflected the delineation of plan targets in physical terms. Industrial enterprises were grouped by product and subordinated to intermediate level central administrations, which were components of an industrial ministry. In this hierarchical system, where decision making was concentrated very close at the top of the pyramid, where targets were formulated in physical terms, and industrial enterprises were directed through administrative orders, where horizontal contacts among enterprises could be made only through mutual superiors, and where the means of production were rationed in kind, there were no choices for enterprises regarding technologies, markets, etc. There were also no choices for banks regarding the allocation of credit because there was no active role for credit and money. There was, alas, a passive role, the role of reflecting or mirroring the fulfillment of the plan by financial control carried out by banks or one bank. The banking system was reorganized in order to fulfill the aforementioned objectives. Banks were nationalized in 1947, nationalization being restricted to Hungarian-owned shares, and reorganized in a way to meet the new requirements.

The execution of every planned movement of goods and services was to be "controlled by the forint," and it had to have a corresponding bank entry. To facilitate this, the National Bank of Hungary became the obligatory center of the accounts for all publicly owned enterprises, including the cooperative sector. The National Bank, in its capacity as a central bank, first managed all government and municipal accounts, later only those of central government agencies. In order to have an adequate movement of goods and of payments for them, the maximum lapse of time between the two was limited to one month. This was also a means of avoiding and outlawing any inter-enterprise credit relationships and of establishing the sole possibility of bank credits, later, for certain purposes or for certain customers of credits of one or other single authorized bank. Control did not mean only the assessing of the flow of goods and services, but also the companies' remaining within the tight constraints of their working capital, wage-bill, allotted capital, manpower, and inventories. Hence, the bank financing current production audited and re-audited balances of the companies, carried out spot checks of inventories, compared planned and actual wage-bills, sanctioned excesses in the latter if not substantiated by an adequate increase in productivity, etc. In scrutinizing credit applications, an inquiry into the solvency and the creditworthiness of the enterprise was not important, as the political guideline of ''money—or the absence of it—cannot hinder planned economic activity'' exempted the banks from such an obligation. They had to find out whether the activity to be backed by a loan was a planned one or not, whether it was covered by physical assets such as inventory, buildings, or machinery or not, and whether the company's own funds and liabilities (wages accounted but not yet paid, debts to suppliers) were insufficient to finance the planned action without recourse to a loan.

The division of labor within one bank, or among banks, was based upon a sectoral specialization for several reasons. The administrative reason for this practice was that a bank, or a directorate or department of the bank, had to have a valid counterpart in the hierarchically construed agencies of control, the branch ministries or departments of the latter, county and district councils, etc. In addition, the supervision of the implementation of company plans, formulated in physical terms, required the specialization of the bank inspector in the peculiarities of specific branches, rather than in comparisons among branches, with a view to opportunity costs and the building up of a portfolio. Last but not least, there was a specialization, formerly completely alien to the universal banks of Hungary, separating current, working capital financing and the collecting of deposits from investment financing. Because, for a long time, investment outlays were non-reimbursable and bore no interest, there was no need for banking expertise except in accounting, there was only a requirement for an inspectorate composed chiefly of technicians. All the banks were large, hierarchically organized entities, with little regard to small ventures. The lack of choices in allocation, and the absence of a material interest in the outcome of their operations, gave rise to bureaucratic tendencies.

Last but not least, the National Bank of Hungary has remained a bank of issue. Being an amalgamate of a bank of issue, a commercial bank, an investment bank for agriculture, the foreign trade bank of the country (the Hungarian Foreign Trade Bank fulfilling only auxiliary lines of business), the central bank and a foreign currency management agency, it grew into a mammoth institution of wide monopolistic competencies with features of an authority manageable only through detailed instructions. This made its decisions on loan applications similar to decisions of public administration, with few traces of businesslike behavior. Within the Bank, the different functions could only be realized at each other's expense, but trade-offs were made without open clashes and compromises of interests and without public control. Thereby the Bank ceased to function as a real bank of issue, and it financed planned targets without a meaningful impact on the deviation of their costs from the planned ones. The bank operated till the mid-1980s without any target figure for the money supply and without regard for the size of its deposits or for their maturity composition. Until the early 1960s it tried to control only the notes and coin in circulation, without controlling their roots, the other monetary aggregates. Commercial banks in its bosom did not have to face liquidity constraints, nor to take into calculation risks, the hedging against risk (except in the term operations in the international money market), nor to build up a portfolio. The narrow specialization according to branches and subbranches of the national economy limited the horizon of the Bank's staff to one company or to a group of similar firms, and led to an unsound identification of the banking employee with the sector financed by him or her.

Banking for the population was restricted to the National Savings Bank, with the unnoticeable competition of isolated, mostly rural, savings cooperatives. Until the late 1980s the Savings Bank hardly had any active operations to serve its depositors, the population.

The reform process of economic policy and the economic control and management system

The reform process started with the revision of economic policy. The first relevant changes came in 1957 when, having reviewed the conditions of both society and the economy, the economic policy—aimed at promoting rapid capital formation to the detriment of living standards, and at investing mainly in heavy industry to the neglect of other sectors, mainly agriculture—was adjusted to political, social, and economic realities. The steady increase in living standards, as well as a balanced development of all branches of the national economy with a view to foreign trade competitiveness, became the new goals. As an important means to achieving these goals, the enhancement of the active participation of procedures, both in industry and agriculture, based on their self-interest and material stimulation was accepted. In agriculture, compulsory deliveries of agricultural produce were abolished and market relations were given greater scope by introducing contractual production and procurement.

Labor incomes in industry were, to a certain extent, linked to enterprise profits through a form of profit sharing. The artificial price and cost system made the judgment about profits difficult, and although the price reform of 1959 reflected costs better than before, pricing remained autarchic, thus reflecting domestic cost levels in the interest of maintaining enterprise activities carried out in Hungary above water. Enterprise-level economic decision making was extended between 1963 and 1965 by a constant reduction of obligatory target figures, by the elimination of medium level administrative agencies in industry, and by granting some major industrial enterprises the right to export and, in extremely few cases, to import.

The cooperative movement, in agriculture, in industry, and in services, acquired a number of efficiency-raising new features. The taxation of gross income (wages plus profits) increased interest in production. The expansion of the production of household plots, owned by cooperative members, was given both central financial and cooperative level impetus. The development of cooperatives helped to elect better prepared, more experienced managerial personnel who had a market orientation. In fact, we may say, the economic reform that preceded the one in industry by a decade, made agriculture the experimental ground for the further implementation of reform in Hungary.

By the mid-1960s, the reserves of extensive development, mainly manpower, were exhausted, and a switch to intensive economic development became necessary. This change demanded a creative, and, as we only later realized, an entrepreneurial attitude from the actors of economic life at every level, but especially among managers. It was of paramount importance to grant more responsibility and scope for action to decision makers. In the early 1980s we had to discover that it is also necessary to make managers able to make good use of their enlarged competencies. This is being achieved by elections of managers by the whole staff in medium sized, and by indirect ballot in big companies.

In 1968 a comprehensive reform of the economic control and management system took place in industry. The reform was preceded by a scientific debate on the nature of the socialist economic mechanism in Hungary, which was based upon empirical studies, economic policy analyses, and influenced by the debate among von Mises, Oskar Lange, and Abba Lerner on rational decision making in a socialist economy, and by Soviet discussions prior to Stalin's ascent power. An invaluable contribution to the debate was made by the Economic Commission, created by the Government in February 1957 for the elaboration of a comprehensive governmental program. It was chaired by Professor István Varga and its Secretary was István Antos, first deputy minister of finance. With the participation of more than two hundred experts from different spheres of economic, political, and intellectual life, and of different political affiliations, the commission worked in an organized, collective, and systematic way and in a constructive, critical, unbiased spirit on a general economic, and hence also social, reform. Both its blueprint and the participation of its members in the preparation for the 1968 reform left an indelible mark on the document of 1968.

In the 1960s, raising the efficiency of economic management had already become a focal point of the further development of the national economy. It had to contribute to the raising of productivity of labor and the efficiency of enterprises through the rational management of resources. Qualitative rather than quantitative aspects of production came to the fore; the returns on investments, the modernity of products and of technology through the implementation of research and development achievements, the international competitivity of the output became the foci of policy makers. These aims required a marked development of socialist production and ownership relations and their actual manifestation: the economic mechanism.

The reformers reinterpreted the concept of central planning and control in the context of an open and sophisticated economy of the late 1960s and came to the conclusion that national economic plans had to concentrate on the major trends of economic development and had to be open to changes based on differences between the assumed and real external and domestic environment during the five-year planning period. As the plan is not spelled out in the form of obligatory target figures for the enterprises, the system of economic regulatory tools or instruments, i.e., making an impact upon enterprise decisions on the basis of collective and individual interestedness, is a bridge between central planners and enterprise managers. The regulatory system envisaged consisted of a small and diminishing number of direct instructions or administrative regulations and a major and growing sphere of indirect instruments transmitting information and impulses from foreign markets through exchange rates, international interest rate levels, loan maturities, etc., providing signals on the state of equilibrium of the different domestic markets, and informing firms of the intentions of economic policy. Thus the plan, economic policy, and the instrumentarium were all meant to reckon with and react to the market.

An important tenet of the reform ideas was a new interpretation of the system and order of social or group interests and conflicts among them, as well as of the bargaining processes aimed at compromises of interests in Hungary's socialist society. The former rigid concept drew up a hierarchy of national, collective, and personal interests with a strict supremacy of the first over all others and the subordination of the third to the preceding ones. The new interpretation acknowledged a much more variegated pattern of interests, embracing also market competition, and, instead of rigid subordination, many other market and non-market forms of interest clashes and harmonization.

It was expected that, as a result of the modernization of the economic system and of the expansion of the scope of the decision making process based on material or rather pecuniary interest, the activity and initiatives of enterprises and their staff would be encouraged, and that this would lead to a rapid improvement in economic performance. Unfortunately, it was also assumed that the driving force of energies released by the reform would also lead to unemployment, inflation or, in the absence of the latter, to shortages, or would deflect commodity flows stipulated in bilateral trade agreements with CMEA counterparts to other markets. Thus too many constraints were put upon economic rationality. No changes were made in Hungarian policy applied to capital inflows, loan capital in the form of loans or joint ventures with foreign equity, either.

Last but not least, institutional changes followed the reform only with a long delay. The general reasons for this phenomenon are explained in Márton Tardos' paper in this volume. The specific reasons for the absence of a banking reform lie, first and foremost, in the aforementioned tight constraints imposed upon economic rationality, which de facto excluded the application of a monetary policy and a businesslike allocation of loans for both working and fixed capital formation.

Manipulated prices and costs are poor guides for allocation decisions based on business considerations. The maintenance of unsuccessful enterprises, and their employment effect, limited possibilities for rejecting credit applications, thereby affecting both the allocation loans and the money supply. Foreign trade quotas limited choices both between inputs of different origins and outputs with different destinations. Beyond these reasons, which emanated from the regulatory environment of the banking activities, there were other sorts of counter-considerations, too. Those who did not support, or only reluctantly supported, the reform process considered the untouched centralized monobank system to be a safeguard of predominantly centralized investment decisions through centrally managed long-term investment loans. The National Bank of Hungary did not easily surrender its monopolistic powers and argued that more banks would cost more but would not increase capital formation; that a "multibank system would not lead to competition when credit is scarce; that a multibank-system with money creation by commercial banks is more inflation-sensitive than a monobank with exclusive rights of money creation; and that compartmentalizing banking would be an obstacle to the full comprehensive view of the economy provided by a monobank."

In his 1985 article on Hungarian fiscal and monetary policy, Márton Tardos made the following, correct, statement: "After 1968, the National Bank of Hungary . . . received an increased role in financial management, beside the National Planning Office, the National Office for Materials and Prices, and the Ministry of Finance. This role has remained, however, much more that of a central institution of control and management than that of a commercial bank. It is characteristic of this situation that it cannot deny loans for development projects supported by Government authorities and cannot stop granting working capital credit to enterprises whose solvency it no longer trusts. . . . The Bank issues a quantity of money corresponding to the planned rate of inflation and reconciles it, not with a safe return of the money placed, but with the financing of economic actions judged to be useful from the national economic aspect. . . . It does not raise the rate of interest to insure against a demand for credit jeopardizing the stability of currency but applies credit quotas."

Nevertheless, meaningful changes occurred within the financial sphere:

—non-reimbursable investment grants were replaced by loans;

—banks were required to evaluate credit applications and pass judgment on the project and on the current and future creditworthiness of the applicant;

—the same screening had to be done, though temporarily without an immediate effect, for loans on working capital;

—interest was paid on medium-term deposits of companies;

—more market-conforming, though not equilibrium, interest rates, based on the cost of the bank's resources, were introduced.

Similarly, significant changes occurred through the legalization of enterprise credit and equity relations, and the establishment of a small but rapidly growing bond market. These measures made the work of the banks more businesslike and offered somewhat greater choices to enterprises seeking sources of finance.

A long way to Tipperary—debates on banking reform

During the drafting of the economic reform, the question of banking reform was the object of heated discussions which were reflected in the economic literature from the late 1960s on. It was pointed out that in a socialist country either a single- (or a double-) level banking system could exist. A single-level banking system exists if the central bank is not solely a bank for banks and a lender of last resort, but rather maintains direct credit ties with the economic units, handles their accounts, and executes their payment orders. A double-level system is one where the central bank operates in the traditional way, indirectly influencing enterprise behavior through commercial and other banks. The monobank system was not embodied in a single bank, either in Hungary, or in most of the other socialist countries. Only in Albania, Cuba, and Mongolia does a single bank carry out all banking functions. In the typical single-level banking systems one usually finds, in addition to a central bank which grants working capital and some investment loans and manges or carries out foreign currency operations, one or more invest-ment/development banks with or without short-term lending operations to the building industry, a foreign trade bank sharing external operations with the central bank, and one or more savings banks. Yet, each of the aforementioned banks is in a monopolistic situation either to a certain group of customers or to certain types of operations.

In the discussions of the future banking system four types of systems were put forward. In his article on this question Sándor Ligeti (1986) summarizes the four types in the following manner: "In principle, the interrelationship of commercial banks in a two or double level banking system may be set up in the following ways. 1. There exists only a single commercial bank beside the central bank. 2. Commer-cial banks are specialized according to branches/subbranches of the national economy. 3. Commercial banks cover certain geographic regions. 4. There is no division of labor among commercial banks, customers may utilize the services of any commercial bank; there is competition among the banks." This latter type of organization is featured in the same issue of *Külgazdaság* in an article written by the outstanding research fellow of the Institute for Financial Research, Lajos Bokros (1986): ". . . in order to arrive at all at a situation of competition, it is necessary to have at least an overlapping of the spheres of customers and types of transactions of the credit banks."

Solution No.1 is only of a technical, or, I may venture to say, a technocratic solution. Technocratic in the sense that there would not be any competition pressure on the single commercial bank. According to Ligeti, it would artificially create a monetary policy impact between the Central and the sole commercial bank and a technical buffer-bank facilitating the rejection of "exaggerated" credit demand at an "outpost" of the central bank. Solutions 2 and 3 are purely the continuations of monopolistic positions in new forms. An additional counter-argument is also mentioned by Ligeti who argues that "these banks may easily become the representatives of particular interests." I think this is true, as branch ministries in the past and counties in the present jealously represent the interests of economic units under their supervision to the detriment of other ministries or counties.

My opinion is that the freedom for the founding of banks by interested state-owned and cooperative enterprises, or of savings banks in the form of cooperatives by the savers if those have the necessary capital and are able to "buy" banking expertise, is most desirable. In this case, one cannot exclude the possibility of banks on a branch, subbranch or a territorial base, but in competition with banks that possess a mixed clientele and with transactions created "from above" in the reorganization process.

From the point of view of monetary policy, banks based on a branch or a territorial base should have individual monetary regulations because of the differences in their deposit-collecting and placing possibilities which would be an obstacle to a general normative monetary policy. It is noteworthy that, for a short period, the GDR and Bulgaria made use of branch commercial banking. The abandonment of that type of banking reflects a disappointment with its results. A similar type of banking was introduced in China on January 1, 1984. A radical change can come about only by having recourse to solution No. 4, the system of competing commercial banks existing in developed market economies and in Yugoslavia.

In the discussions in Hungary ample attention was given to the conditions under which it makes sense to reorganize the banking system, since the minor changes in 1970 did not alter the essentials, but only regrouped certain activities among banks. It was agreed that a further development of the ECMS and of the institutional framework was required for a meaningful banking reform. I have already mentioned the compromises blunting the edge of the reform and the delay in implementing institutional changes. In practice, however, more than the above-mentioned factors put a brake on the application of the reform. These factors were described in the publication *Further Development of the Economic Control and Management System* [ECMS], no. 17, 1984, of the series "Public Finance in Hungary," published by the Ministry of Finance. I will cite these factors here in an abbreviated form: "Initially the consistent practical enforcement of the principles of the economic reform was greatly hindered by the fact that central control could not always meet its functions efficiently enough, and a part of enterprises failed to meet new and higher requirements. Later, the consistent enforcement of the principles of economic reform was hindered by unfavorable changes in the world economy, i.e., the readjustment of relative prices, the world economic recession, the recession of the capitalist economies, their strengthening protectionism." I should add, too, the slowing of growth in the socialist economies, and the unwillingness to change the economic policy in Hungary by restructuring output in view of the cost and demand structure in the world and our investment structure in view of the latter and the newly emerging competition by the so-called Newly Industrialized Countries in commodities and markets of Hungary. All this entailed a growing state subsidy to branches and enterprises that were outdated, and to a growing supremacy of fiscal policy to the detriment of monetary policy and the sound allocations of credit. Instead of taking into account these sources of the shortcomings of central economic policy, the booklet puts the blame on enterprise management, writing: "Inadequacies of management came more and more to the surface." In fact, there was a wide gap between the reform rhetoric and the actions of the government.

The resolution adopted by the Central Committee of the HSWP on December 6, 1978, correctly determined that: "Enterprises, plants which are not profitable, the activities of which are not in harmony with the interests of the national economy and which—among the given investment possibilities—cannot be profitable by means of rationalization might not be maintained, their losses might not be covered by state subsidies. In such case the state organs, helped by Party and social organizations—as a last solution—have to be determined and use their means for partial or total liquidation."

It is a striking feature of the period that these central intentions were frustrated by ill-interpreted social considerations and delayed the adjustment process that should have taken place in a differentiated utilization of capacities, capital and labor flows, etc. Instead, state subsidies were introduced that, in the words of the aforequoted booklet of the Ministry of Finance "were not coupled with the raising of the standards against economic units and their managements in a satisfactory way."

These subsidies affected economic organizations in a differentiated way; thus the normativity of the regulatory system suffered. As a result, the scope of authority of directive and administrative bodies, e.g., of branch ministries, increased to the detriment of enterprise decisions, with unfavorable consequences for businesslike decision making by banks. A high degree of volatility of the regulatory system, especially of taxes, their number and their rates, developed. As the booklet on Further Development of the ECMS justly emphasizes, the stability of the regulatory system ". . . is especially important, so that economic organizations can be in a position to adjust their business policies with the necessary foresight and can be able to undertake obligations related to development or to the raising of personal incomes." This development also did not tally with businesslike banking as, even in cases of the best loan-backed enterprise allocations, changes of taxes or of the exchange rate may have had a disproportionately greater impact on enterprise profits after taxation than any change in the market situation.

Only from the late 1970s on were substantial efforts made to modernize the institutional system of economic control of the enterprises and to correct built-in brakes in the ECMS. These efforts were hindered by subsequent deteriorations of the world economy in 1979 and 1982, giving rise again to direct interference by government agencies in short-term economic processes, phenomena inconsistent with a change in the content and forms of the banking system.

Yet, with all the relapses, there was and is a process of the development of the ECMS. In the field of producer prices, former autarchic price formation was replaced to a great extent by a system where producer prices of industrial goods traded in international markets are adjusted to export or import prices. At the same time the range of administratively determined prices narrowed. This was a major achievement of 1980, completed with the introduction of a uniform exchange rate of convertible currencies on October 1, 1981. Though the tax burden on enterprises increased, the autonomy of enterprises in the utilization of after-tax profits grew. In the financing of investments the share of state grants not subject to repayment decreased considerably. These now affect only investment projects in infrastructure and a small number of particularly large investment projects. Channels for inter-enterprise capital flows as well as population-enterprise flows were opened.

The changes in the institutional and organizational system were of equal importance. In the late 1970s, artificially united large enterprises with monopolistic positions were split into parts, corporations called trusts were not trusted anymore, but rather eradicated and the enterprises controlled by them released to autonomy. In order to promote a more flexible adjustment to market requirements, more than 200 producing and domestic trading enterprises were given an autonomous foreign trading, especially export, right, without interposing a specialized foreign trading company. The specialization, and thereby monopolistic situation, of the latter was abandoned. New legal stipulations permitted the formation of various forms of small-scale ventures in order to encourage individual initiatives and to adjust ownership forms to the scale of activities.

A very important step was the amalgamation of three branch industries into a single Ministry of Industry dealing with industrial policy and not with the exercise of ownership rights. This has developed into a new division of powers between the authorities and enterprise managements concerning ownership rights and the exercise of the rights of the employer. Two new forms of management have emanated: enterprise councils and management by elected managers.

In the banking field, two joint ventures with foreign equity emerged, an off-shore bank, CIB, and a bank functioning under Hungarian regulations in forints, Citibank. A score of so-called developmental financial institutions have been founded, financing primarily innovative investment projects with a quick return both by taking a stake in the capital and by granting credits. Generally, and from the point of view of banking decentralization, the most significant event was the enactment of Decree No. 11 of 1986 about the bankruptcy, euphemistically called "winding-up," of enterprises. It also regulates the economic rehabilitation of enterprises and provides for the creation of an Economic Rehabilitation Fund. These developments created the necessary conditions for the reorganization of the banking system.

The banking system after January 1, 1987

On January 1, 1987, the National Bank was transformed into a classical bank of issue, a bank of banks and the lender of last resort, and a central bank, the bank of the government, retaining temporarily the actual management and not only the regulation of foreign currency operations. There are five commercial banks fully authorized to undertake all operations, except , temporarily, foreign currency operations and accepting deposits from the population. This latter activity will remain the domain of the National Savings Bank and the 260 Savings Cooperatives with their more than 100,000 branches, and, perhaps, that of a Postal Bank, the organization of which is under consideration by the Postmaster General. Initially, the five banks "retain" their original clientele. Within a year clients may switch over to another bank with their account, or they may make use of the services of more than one commercial bank. The banks may also select their customers and reject credit applications; they are only obliged to open an account for the client.

There is a major problem with the initial clientele. As pointed out in the aforementioned article by Bokros "the five commercial banks bear branch features with their initial clientele. The Hungarian Credit Bank (Magyar Hitelbank) has initially a heavy, machine, and building industry bias, the Countrywide Commercial and Credit Bank (Országos Kereskedelmi és Hitelbank) an agricultural, food industry, light, and domestic trade one, the Budapest Development and Credit Bank (Budapesti Fejlesztési és Hitelbank) a broadly defined infrastructural one, the Foreign Trade Bank of Hungary (Magyar Külkereskedelmi Bank) carries—true to its name—a clientele with a marked foreign trading feature. The General Bank for Securities (Általános Értékforgalmi Bank) did not get an initial clientele." Though this statement is relevant only to the headquarters of the mentioned banks, and not, or not to a significant degree, to their branches in the provinces, nevertheless there is more than a grain of truth in Bokros' statement. The biggest companies are financed at present by the headquarters. There is the danger of habits—habitual clients do not move. And the habitually industrial, agricultural, etc., credit lending officers will, perhaps, remain without a broader horizon and opportunity cost knowledge beyond that provided by their "habitués." In any case, the initial "mix" does not foster competition. On the other hand, and I write this reluctantly as there once was a king who advertised for a one-armed economist to avoid "on the one hand, and on the other" types of ambiguous formulations, enormous administrative difficulties could have arisen by distributing clients among these banks. The initial mix may not prove counterproductive if there are no great differences in size, the network of branches, the composition of resources which give insuperable, or so seeming, advantages to one bank over the other. Two banks, the Hungarian Credit Bank and the Countrywide Commercial and Credit Bank, have comparable balance sums, but the other three are lower by one or two orders of magnitude; the latter may take up major ventures only through syndication. The biggest balances go hand in hand with the largest number of branches, though unevenly. The second biggest bank in terms of deposits has twice as many branches as the largest, the third one significantly fewer and the two others have no branches at all. The administratively determined mix also creates major differences among banks in the deposit-coverage and the degree of Central Bank refinancing.

There will be certain problems with the regulatory role, with the constraints set by the National Bank of Hungary on money creation by commercial banks. Because of the very big differences between credit/deposit ratios, a high and differentiated cash reserve ratio may be necessary, contrary to practice in other countries. A major task will be the determination of the upper limit of refinancing, which probably will be determined as a multiplier of the banks' own capital, thereby maintaining initial differences between banks. An excessive burden will be placed on these instruments and on discounting policy in the absence of open market operations, due to a virtual absence of gilt-edged government bonds. There are both corporate and local bonds in circulation, but these are unsuitable for the task of monetary policy.

Last but not least, there is the relationship of the Central Bank to the Government. In a planned economy, the validation of monetary aspects of the planning process is of the utmost importance. There were proposals to raise the standing of the President of the Central Bank to the level of a member of the government (a Central Committee membership would be desirable, too), or to subordinate the Central Bank directly to the Parliament, so as to have a valid counterpart of, in the first case, ministers and, in the second, the Government in the Bank.

The small financial institutions mainly competed with each other on the basis of their expertise in different fields, innovations, patent, and license protection procedures, etc., as well as on their readiness to take risk through capital participation. Nowadays they have also entered major ventures through syndication. The new regulation does not exclude their later arrival at the status of banks. There is also a tendency to establish joint services for all the banks and financial institutions by joining forces, as well as to set up an interest-representing organ.

Bank reforms in Hungary are thus incomplete, but the institutional changes wrought, and the economic forces unleashed, are sufficiently different from those characterizing Hungarian banking in the past, that we must await the course of events before offering a final judgment on the correctness of the measures described in this chapter.

References

Bokros, Lajos. "The Conditions for the Emergence of Business-like Behavior in the Double-Level Banking System." *Külgazdaság*, 1986, no. 12.

Ligeti, Sándor. "The Reorganization of the Banking System." *Külgazdaság*, 1986, no. 12.

Tardos, Márton. "Question Marks in Hungarian Monetary and Fiscal Policy." *Acta Oeconomica*, vol. 33, nos. 1-2 (1985), pp. 29-52.

PART II

THE EFFICIENCY ALLOCATION OF RESOURCES— WHAT HAS REFORM ACHIEVED?

Estimates of the Output Loss
from Allocative Inefficiency

A Comparison of Hungary and West Germany

ROBERT S. WHITESELL

Introduction

It is generally believed that, relative to a market economy, the Soviet-type economic system is detrimental to an efficient allocation of resources because of a lack of meaningful market prices, improper economic incentives, and the vertical nature of the planning mechanisms, which makes the coordination of horizontal input allocations difficult. On the other hand, it can be argued that the primary deficiency of the Soviet-type planning system is in its dynamic aspects, which present impediments to technological innovation, and that it should be rather good at static resource allocation because that is the problem the system is geared to solve. This can be countered with the argument that the distribution of resources is more dependent on political than on economic considerations. In Hungary, however, substantial reform of the Soviet-type system may have improved the performance of the allocative mechanism. Attempts have been made to make prices more responsive to market forces, and direct horizontal links among firms have been strengthened. Nevertheless, much disagreement about the effectiveness of these reforms exists.

This paper attempts to measure the efficiency of resource allocation in Hungary. Two questions are addressed. First, a quantitative comparison with West Germany tests the hypothesis that the Soviet-type economic system results in a less efficient allocation of resources than a market economic system. Second, an analysis of the trend in allocative efficiency over time is presented in order to test whether the allocation mechanism improved with the institution of the New Economic Mechanism in Hungary.

The next section explains the theoretical foundation for the calculated measures of inefficiency. Section three explains the method used in calculating the measure of inefficiency, and section four discusses the data. The results are discussed in section five, and section six is the conclusion.

Theoretical analysis

The theoretical model is based on the proposition that, whenever factor marginal rates of substitution (MRS) diverge, gains can be realized through a proper reallocation of resources across sectors. Several different methods can be applied in the calculation of these potential gains: (1) factor savings, producing the initial output vector with fewer factors of production; (2) single output augmenting, producing the initial amount of n-1 different outputs and more of an arbitrarily chosen nth output; and (3) proportional output augmenting, producing equiproportional increases of each output with the initial total factor endowment. It can easily be shown that methods (1) and (3) are equivalent.[1] Since method (1) is computationally simpler, method (3) is not employed and the estimation focuses on methods (1) and (2). Since the methodology has been discussed in detail elsewhere, it will be outlined only briefly here.[2]

In the factor savings method inputs are reallocated among sectors, such that factor marginal rates of substitution are equalized while holding sectoral outputs constant. Since inputs are inefficiently allocated when factor MRSs are unequal, this reallocation of inputs allows the same levels of output to be produced with fewer inputs. A problem with this method is that there are many possible ways to reduce inputs. It is necessary to choose a particular MRS that production in each sector must meet. This problem is solved by choosing the MRS which preserves the original global capital-labor ratio. Since inputs are being reduced proportionately, a simple proportional measure of the potential gain from efficiency is

$$(1) \quad \begin{array}{c} \textit{Proportional} \\ \textit{Factor Savings} \\ \textit{Gain} \end{array} = \frac{\overline{L}}{L*} - 1 = \frac{\overline{K}}{K*} - 1.[3]$$

This measure represents both the potential increase in output achievable through an efficient reallocation of resources and the loss in output from the inefficient allocation.

A second strategy in measuring the gains from an efficient allocation is the single output augmenting approach, which involves generating the same output in all sectors except one, then allocating the savings of factors in the n-1 sectors to the nth output. The increase of output in that one sector is a measure of the gain from the proper reallocation of resources, or the loss from a misallocation. The measure of efficiency is straightforward:

$$(2) \quad \begin{array}{c} \textit{Proportional} \\ \textit{Single Output} \\ \textit{Gain} \end{array} = \frac{P_1 \overline{Y}_1 + P_2 \overline{Y}*^2}{P_1 \overline{Y}_1 + P_2 \overline{Y}_2} - 1.$$

Since the prices in which gains are measured are important in the single output augmenting approach, whereas the factor savings approach does not depend on prices, and since resources are allocated differently in the two methods, these measures will not be the same. The single output augmenting approach will also result in differing measures according to which output is expanded.

It is important to note that these are second best estimates of the true efficiency gain. The perfect estimate would entail finding a social welfare optimum. This cannot be done without knowing the output price vectors. Even if such information were available, the probability that price data represented socially optimal general equilibrium prices would be very low. The calculations are estimates of the potential gain in production from an improvement in allocative inefficiency, but no claim is made that they represent a movement toward a social welfare optimum.[4]

Econometric implementation

In order to estimate the production gain that could be achieved from an efficient reallocation of resources, aggregate production functions are estimated for various sectors of manufacturing for the period 1961-84. Several variants of the Cobb-Douglas production function are used.[5] All production functions are estimated assuming constant returns to scale. The following forms of the Cobb-Douglas production function are estimated:

(3) CDA1: $\ln y_i(t) = \ln \gamma_i + \lambda_i t + \mu_i t^2 + \alpha_i \ln k_i(t) + \varepsilon_i,$

(4) CD1: $\ln y_i(t) = \ln \gamma_i + \lambda_i t + \mu t^2 + \alpha_i \ln k_i(t) + u_i,$

(5) CDA2: $\ln y_i(t) = \ln \gamma_i + \lambda_i t + \alpha_i \ln k_i(t) + \varepsilon_i,$

(6) CD2: $\ln y_i(t) = \ln \gamma_i + \lambda_i t + \alpha_i \ln k_i(t) + u_i$

(7) CDA3: $\ln y_i(t) = \ln \gamma_i + \mu_i t^2 + \alpha_i \ln k_i(t) + \varepsilon_i,$

(8) CD3: $\ln y_i(t) = \ln \gamma_i + \mu_i t^2 + \alpha_i \ln k_i(t) + u_i,$

(9) CDA4: $\ln y_i(t) = \ln \gamma_i + \alpha_i \ln k_i(t) + \varepsilon_i,$

(10) CD4: $\ln y_i(t) = \ln \gamma_i + \alpha_i \ln k_i(t) + u_i,$

where

i = sector i
$y_i(t)$ = output-labor ratio in year t
$k_i(t)$ = capital-labor ratio in year t

γ_i = an efficiency parameter

$\lambda_i + 2\mu_i t$ = the rate of Hicks-neutral technical change

α_i = imputed output share of capital

$1 - \alpha_i$ = imputed output share of labor

u_i = an error term with zero mean and constant variance

$\varepsilon_i = u_i^t + \rho i \varepsilon_i^{t-1}$, this assumes first order autocorrelated errors.

The functions are nested and a likelihood ratio procedure used to choose a best estimate for each sector in each country.[6]

The factor savings measure of efficiency gain is calculated, for each year, by searching for a MRS* that would produce the initial bundle of outputs efficiently; i.e., forcing equalized MRSs throughout the economy, while holding the global capital-labor ratio constant. This is begun by calculating the imputed MRSs for each sector of manufacturing from the production function estimates:

$$(11) \quad MRS_i = \frac{f_L^i}{f_K^i} = \frac{1 - \alpha_i}{\alpha_i} k_i, \, i = 1,...,16.$$

As a first approximation to MRS*, a weighted average of the initial MRSs is calculated, using the sectoral shares in total output as weights. The optimal capital-labor ratio for each sector is then calculated given this new MRS* as

$$(12) \quad k_i^* = \frac{\alpha_i MRS^*}{1 - \alpha_i}.$$

Optimal labor use is then calculated from this capital-labor ratio and the predicted level of output as[7]

$$(13) \quad L_i^* = \frac{\tilde{Y}_i}{\gamma_i} e^{-\lambda_i t - \mu_i t^2} k_i^{*-\alpha_i}.$$

From (12) and (13), the optimal amount of capital is

$$(14) \quad K_i^* = k_i^* L_i^*.$$

These sectoral factor usages are then added, and the global capital-labor ratio calculated. If this new global capital-labor ratio is not equal to the original global capital-labor ratio, then a new MRS is chosen, and the process is repeated. Each new MRS is chosen as

(15) $\mathrm{MRS*} = \mathrm{MRS*}(\bar{k}/k\,*)$,

where $\bar{k}$ is the original capital-labor ratio and k^* is the most recently calculated capital-labor ratio. This process is repeated until it converges; i.e., the new capital-labor ratio is identical to the original.

The iterative procedure described above generates MRS^*, the MRS that rules in every sector. Furthermore, note that intrasectoral capital-labor ratios change, but the global capital-labor remains constant. The percentage gain in output that could be achieved by an efficient reallocation of resources is then calculated as described in equation (1) above as the Proportional Factor Savings Gain.

The single output augmenting approach is calculated similarly. As an example chemical production is used. All outputs, except chemicals, were produced efficiently given an initial MRS^*, as in equations 11 to 14. This releases some capital and labor which are then allocated to the chemical sector. The capital-labor ratio and imputed MRS for chemicals are calculated as

(16) $k_c = K_c / L_c$.

and

(17) $\mathrm{MRS_c} = [(1 - \alpha_c)k_c]/\alpha_c$,

where the c subscript represents chemicals and K_c and L_c represent the released amounts of capital and labor. If $\mathrm{MRS_c}$ is unequal to the MRS^*, then a new MRS^* is chosen and the reallocation process is repeated. This procedure is continued until the MRSs are equal in all sectors; every sector but chemicals producing the original output level, and the actually existing amounts of total capital and labor being used. The proportional gain in output that could be achieved by an efficient reallocation of inputs is calculated as the proportional increase of total output, where output is increased in only one sector. This is given in equation (2) above as the Proportional Single Output Gain.[8]

Data

The data for Hungary are gross value of output, gross value of fixed assets, and the number of hours worked for sixteen sectors of socialist industry for the period 1961-1984. Socialist industry consists of both state-owned and cooperatively owned enterprises. The sectors for Hungary are: (1) metallurgy, (2) machinery, (3) transportation equipment, (4) electrical machinery, (5) telecommunications equipment, (6) precision instruments, (7) metal products, (8) construction materials, (9) chemicals, (10) wood-working, (11) paper products, (12) printing, (13) textiles, (14) leather products, (15) clothing, (16) food processing. The data are derived from various statistical publications of the Central Statistical Office of Hungary.

The data for West Germany are gross output, value-added, gross value of fixed capital, and the number of hours worked for sixteen sectors of manufacturing for the period 1964-81 and 1984. The sectors for West Germany are the same as the Hungarian sectors except (5) is games, which includes musical instruments, sporting equipment, etc.; and (8), which is glass, stoneware, and ceramics. The sectors are not exactly equivalent, but an attempt has been made to make them as similar as possible, and at the same time, have the same number of sectors for each country. Consistent data for capital are unavailable for 1982 and 1983. The data for the value-added, capital and hours worked are derived from various issues of *Statistisches Jahrbuch für die Bundesrepublik Deutschland*. The data for gross output are from various issues of the United Nations, *Industrial Statistics Yearbook*.

It would have been preferable to have value-added data for both countries. However, sectoral data on Hungarian net material product (NMP) are unavailable for the 1960s, so a long enough series for econometric estimation using NMP was not possible. Therefore, gross output for West Germany was used in order to increase the comparability of the estimates.

Discussion of results

The results are reported in Tables 1 to 4. Table 1 represents the percentage increase in production that could be obtained from an efficient allocation of resources in Hungary using both methods of estimation. Table 2 gives the same estimates for West Germany using gross output. Tables 3 and 4 show the changes in input utilization for each sector using the factor savings method. These tables give the results for the most comparable measures. Further results are presented in the appendix. Tables A1 and A2 show the results for West Germany using value-added. Since fewer sectors were available using gross output, Table A1 gives the results using all available sectors and Table A2 gives the results using the same sectors as those available for gross output. Table A3 shows the results for Hungary using all available sectors.

The large variations in the single output augmenting calculations, especially for Hungary, can be explained easily. The procedure begins by calculating an initial imputed MRS for each sector. An optimal MRS is selected to which each sector must conform. If the optimal MRS is greater than the initial MRS, then the capital-labor ratio is increased in that sector; if the optimal MRS is less than the initial MRS, then the capital-labor ratio is decreased in that sector. The size of the inefficiency estimate will depend on two things: the magnitude of the difference between the optimal MRS and the initial imputed MRS for the sector whose output is being increased, and the size of the estimated capital and labor coefficients. For example, the largest estimate of inefficiency in Hungary is when metallurgy output is increased. The imputed MRS for metallurgy is substantially higher than the optimal MRS (see Table 3), which implies that the capital-labor ratio is much too large. Therefore, the capital-labor ratio must be decreased. The capital coefficient for metallurgy is small, 0.06, and the labor

Table 1

Percent Inefficiency, Hungary
Socialist Industry, Manufacturing Sectors
Without Chemicals, Wood, and Telecommunications

Year	Loss	Gain1	Gain2	Gain3	Gain4	Gain6	Gain7
1961	27.4	43.0	22.5	24.4	29.2	14.5	18.3
1962	27.2	42.8	22.0	24.0	28.5	14.8	18.6
1963	28.4	44.2	22.6	24.9	29.5	15.7	19.6
1964	28.5	44.7	22.6	25.1	29.6	16.3	20.2
1965	28.3	43.9	22.2	25.0	29.2	16.4	20.1
1966	30.0	45.8	23.5	26.7	31.1	17.7	21.5
1967	29.7	46.1	22.8	26.0	30.2	18.2	21.7
1968	29.6	47.4	22.4	25.5	29.7	19.1	22.3
1969	30.5	47.7	23.0	26.7	30.8	19.8	22.8
1970	30.0	46.5	22.5	26.4	30.3	19.9	22.4
1971	29.9	46.2	22.3	26.5	30.1	20.3	22.3
1972	30.5	46.8	22.6	27.2	30.8	21.1	22.7
1973	30.1	46.4	22.4	27.2	30.6	21.5	22.5
1974	30.4	47.1	22.7	27.8	31.1	22.5	22.8
1975	32.6	51.8	24.0	29.3	32.8	25.3	24.8
1976	32.9	52.3	24.3	30.0	33.4	26.3	24.9
1977	33.4	53.0	24.6	30.8	34.1	27.4	25.1
1978	32.3	51.4	23.9	30.4	33.3	27.3	24.0
1979	31.2	49.3	23.3	30.0	32.7	26.9	22.8
1980	30.3	47.5	22.8	29.9	32.2	26.7	21.7
1981	30.7	47.8	23.3	31.2	33.3	27.7	21.6
1982	31.3	47.9	24.1	32.8	34.7	28.7	21.4
1983	31.3	47.9	24.4	33.7	35.3	29.5	21.0
1984	31.4	48.5	24.8	34.7	36.2	30.7	20.8

Year	Gain8	Gain11	Gain12	Gain13	Gain14	Gain15	Gain16
1961	13.6	31.8	20.0	20.8	27.8	19.8	34.7
1962	13.2	31.1	19.6	20.1	27.0	19.3	35.9
1963	13.4	31.6	20.3	20.2	27.6	19.7	39.1
1964	13.2	31.5	20.4	19.9	27.3	19.6	41.1
1965	12.8	30.5	20.2	19.1	26.5	18.9	42.6
1966	13.3	31.6	21.6	19.7	27.7	19.5	47.0
1967	13.0	31.5	21.0	19.3	26.9	19.2	46.6
1968	12.8	32.0	20.6	19.3	26.4	19.3	46.1
1969	12.9	32.2	21.5	19.4	26.8	19.2	49.0
1970	12.5	31.4	21.2	18.7	25.9	18.5	49.0
1971	12.3	31.2	21.2	18.4	25.4	18.1	49.1
1972	12.4	31.7	21.8	18.5	25.5	18.1	50.1
1973	12.2	31.6	21.7	18.3	25.0	17.6	49.6
1974	12.3	32.3	22.1	18.5	25.0	17.6	49.6
1975	13.2	35.7	23.4	20.2	26.5	19.0	50.1
1976	13.3	36.5	23.9	20.5	26.5	18.9	49.7
1977	13.5	37.5	24.4	20.9	26.7	18.9	49.1

Table 1 (continued)

Year	Gain8	Gain11	Gain12	Gain13	Gain14	Gain15	Gain16
1978	13.0	36.9	24.0	20.3	25.6	18.0	46.5
1979	12.6	36.1	23.7	19.7	24.5	17.1	44.1
1980	12.2	35.4	23.5	19.2	23.6	16.2	41.8
1981	12.4	36.6	24.4	19.7	23.9	16.2	41.0
1982	12.7	37.6	25.5	20.2	24.2	16.0	40.5
1983	12.8	38.7	26.2	20.6	24.2	15.9	38.8
1984	13.1	40.3	26.9	21.3	24.3	15.8	36.8

coefficient is large, 0.94. This implies that decreasing capital in this sector will decrease output very little, but increasing labor will increase output substantially. Since the capital-labor ratio is much too large, a substantial increase in labor and decrease in capital is necessary. This implies a large increase in output and a large estimate of inefficiency. Since the variations in the initial imputed MRSs for Hungary are much greater than for West Germany, this also explains the greater variation in the Hungarian inefficiency estimates.

This analysis emphasizes the fact that the single output augmenting estimate only measures the ability of the system to produce more of that one good. Its ability to produce more of some goods is better than its ability to produce more of other goods. If it is assumed that the existing mix of outputs is closer to actual preferences, whether consumer or planner preferences, then the factor savings method is the preferable measure because it is equivalent to a proportional augmentation of all outputs. In this sense, the greater variability of the inefficiency estimates for Hungary is an indication that allocative inefficiency is greater in Hungary than it is in West Germany, since it reflects the fact that there is more variability in the imputed MRSs among the various sectors.

The results, comparing Tables 1 and 2, indicate that the potential output gain from an efficient reallocation of inputs, or the output loss from the existing inefficient allocation, is at least three times as large in Hungary as it is in West Germany. However, it is necessary to evaluate whether the alternative measures change this conclusion. Note the difference in the inefficiency estimates in Tables A1 and A2. It can be seen that the omission of chemicals, wood-working, and games results in a reduction of the loss from inefficiency in West Germany by about one-half. Comparing Tables 1 and A3, it can be seen that the omission of chemicals, wood-working, and telecommunications equipment results in only a very small reduction in the efficiency loss estimates.[9] The chemical sector is the primary cause of the substantial reduction in the West Germany estimates. The chemical industry is much too capital-intensive. For example, in 1975 the calculated optimal MRS is 59 and the imputed MRS for chemicals is 780, using the factor savings method. Therefore, elimination of chemicals results in a much lower estimate of inefficiency because a very inefficient sector has been eliminated. The chemical sector is also much too capital-intensive in Hungary. In 1975 the calculated optimal MRS is 203

Table 2

**Percent Inefficiency, West Germany
Manufacturing Sectors
Without Chemicals, Wood, and Games
Gross Output**

Year	FGain	Gain1	Gain2	Gain3	Gain4	Gain6	Gain9
1964	9.8	10.8	12.2	12.4	6.2	9.0	6.4
1965	9.8	10.9	11.8	12.2	6.3	8.9	6.4
1966	9.8	11.0	11.7	12.0	6.5	8.8	6.3
1967	10.0	11.2	11.8	11.9	6.8	8.9	6.4
1968	9.8	11.2	11.1	11.6	6.8	8.7	6.3
1969	9.7	11.3	10.6	11.4	6.9	8.5	6.2
1970	9.5	11.2	10.0	11.1	6.8	8.2	6.1
1971	9.4	11.2	9.7	10.8	6.9	8.0	6.0
1972	9.5	11.2	9.8	10.7	7.1	8.0	6.1
1973	9.3	11.1	9.5	10.5	7.2	7.8	6.0
1974	9.1	10.8	9.1	10.0	7.1	7.4	5.8
1975	8.3	9.7	8.2	9.0	6.6	6.7	5.3
1976	7.5	8.7	7.1	8.0	6.0	5.8	4.7
1977	7.4	8.7	7.0	7.9	6.0	5.7	4.7
1978	7.3	8.6	6.8	7.8	6.0	5.5	4.7
1979	7.1	8.4	6.4	7.5	6.0	5.3	4.6
1980	7.1	8.3	6.3	7.4	6.0	5.2	4.6
1981	6.9	8.0	6.0	7.2	5.9	4.9	4.5

Year	Gain8	Gain11	Gain12	Gain13	Gain14	Gain15	Gain16
1964	5.9	16.8	10.0	9.4	6.5	6.0	19.3
1965	6.0	17.5	9.8	9.2	6.6	5.9	19.5
1966	6.0	18.2	9.8	9.0	6.8	5.8	19.6
1967	6.0	19.2	10.2	8.7	7.2	5.7	19.9
1968	6.0	19.5	9.6	8.5	7.2	5.6	19.7
1969	6.0	20.0	9.1	8.4	7.2	5.6	19.8
1970	5.9	20.1	8.7	8.2	7.2	5.4	19.5
1971	5.9	20.6	8.5	7.9	7.2	5.3	19.4
1972	6.0	21.5	8.8	7.8	7.5	5.3	19.6
1973	5.9	21.9	8.6	7.6	7.5	5.1	19.3
1974	5.8	21.8	8.4	7.2	7.5	4.9	18.8
1975	5.3	20.5	7.8	6.4	6.9	4.4	17.0
1976	4.8	18.8	6.8	5.7	6.3	3.9	15.3
1977	4.8	19.2	6.7	5.6	6.3	3.9	15.3
1978	4.8	19.4	6.6	5.4	6.3	3.8	15.1
1979	4.8	19.3	6.3	5.3	6.2	3.7	14.7
1980	4.8	19.6	6.2	5.2	6.2	3.7	14.7
1981	4.7	19.5	6.0	5.0	6.1	3.6	14.3

and the imputed MRS for chemicals is 1869, using the factor savings method. However, its elimination does not appear to have much effect. This implies that chemicals is just one of many inefficiently supplied sectors in Hungary, whereas it is an outlier for West Germany. This further emphasizes the magnitude of the difference in inefficiency in the two economies.

This finding also indicates that the comparison of the levels of inefficiency

Table 3

Factor Reallocations
Hungary
Manufacturing Sectors
Without Chemicals, Wood, and Telecommunications
Factor Savings Method

Year	1965	1970	1975	1980	1984
Total % gain	28.3	30.0	32.6	30.3	31.4
MRS	65	83	109	140	206

MRS
KCHANG (millions of forints)
LCHANG (millions of hours worked)

	1965	1970	1975	1980	1984
METAL	2395	3590	4394	5743	10247
	−22823	−34158	−42783	−52209	−74617
	35	36	36	33	28
MACH	46	40	48	85	125
	3099	6271	8133	10136	12195
	−51	−96	−100	−78	−64
TRANS	14	26	37	58	97
	4451	5178	6763	9873	10795
	−142	−103	−98	−94	−66
ELEC	24	33	41	65	104
	1830	2521	3585	5502	6350
	−42	−43	−49	−49	−37
PREC	206	265	414	732	1200
	−1146	−1522	−3092	−6220	−8371
	9	9	12	15	13
METP	190	219	296	514	878
	−2322	−2731	−3589	−5483	−8167
	18	17	17	16	16
CONST	171	223	349	624	872
	−4482	−5713	−11005	−21398	−23961
	37	36	49	59	47
PAPER	1143	1376	2294	3879	4352
	−2784	−4150	−7321	−11674	−11524
	7	9	10	10	8
PRINT	19	23	51	68	118
	690	937	861	1831	2347
	−18	−20	−10	−16	−13

Year	1965	1970	1975	1980	1984
TEX	228	313	450	724	977
	−7796	−10326	−14499	−21194	−22207
	55	55	56	53	40
LEATH	25	32	47	82	116
	1890	2706	3361	4090	5126
	−41	−46	−41	−31	−28
CLOTH	43	57	98	182	340
	625	927	871	456	−684
	−10	−12	−7	−2	2
FOOD	5	5	6	10	14
	2894	3765	5600	9178	12117
	−202	−214	−291	−283	−258

derived by comparing Tables 1 and 2 may be biased. Since the inefficiency using value-added is about half of the inefficiency using gross output (compare Tables 2 and A1), it is possible that estimates of Hungarian inefficiency using value-added would result in losses from inefficiency that are about half as large. Using all available sectors, inefficiency using value-added for West Germany is about 10 percent. If the estimated inefficiency for Hungary using all available sectors is halved, the estimate would be reduced to the 17-18 percent range. This lowers the magnitude of difference, but does not alter the conclusion that the Hungarian economy is much more allocatively inefficient than the West Germany economy.

These results give empirical verification to the idea that the lack of horizontal links, meaningful market prices, and adequate market incentives hamper the efficiency of resource allocation in a Soviet-type planned economy. As expected, the results show a large amount of inefficiency in a market economy, but substantially less than in the Hungarian modified planned economy.

It is instructive to examine the sectoral reallocations in Tables 3 and 4. The sectoral reallocations for Hungary are consistent, regardless of which estimates are used, i.e., a sector that is too capital- (labor-) intensive is so, whether the three sectors (chemicals, telecommunications equipment, and wood-working) are included or not. For West Germany, the estimates using gross output and value-added are usually, but not always, consistent.[10] Metallurgy, construction materials (this is closest to glass, stoneware, and ceramics for West Germany), and paper goods are too capital-intensive in both countries. Metallurgy, particularly, is a problem sector. Machinery, electrical machinery, and printing are too labor-intensive in both countries. Precision instruments, metal products and textiles are too capital-intensive in Hungary and too labor-intensive in West Germany. Food processing is too labor-intensive in Hungary and too capital-intensive in West Germany. It might be thought that precision instruments and

Table 4

Factor Reallocations, West Germany
Manufacturing Sectors
Without Chemicals, Wood, and Games
Gross Output
Factor Savings Method

Year	1964	1970	1975	1980
Total				
% Gain	9.8	9.5	8.3	7.1
MRS	12	16	28	35

MRS
KCHANG (millions of deutschmarks)
LCHANG (millions of hours worked)

METAL	128	176	262	325
	−5357	−6813	−7399	−8429
	113	104	72	66
MACH	4	6	12	16
	3228	4814	5940	6934
	−468	−487	−320	−288
TRANS	23	34	64	63
	−1133	−2120	−3452	−3262
	69	89	80	69
ELEC	11	14	27	34
	43	425	100	159
	−4	−28	−4	−5
PREC	8	11	21	26
	124	178	196	278
	−13	−13	−8	−9
METP	6	10	16	22
	825	964	1408	1481
	−96	−76	−66	−53
GLASS	17	29	64	79
	−387	−754	−1463	−1713
	27	34	34	32
PAPER	13	18	36	53
	−55	−61	−134	−290
	4	4	4	7
PRINT	1	1	2	3
	1072	1598	2252	2750
	−405	−410	−316	−237

Year	1964	1970	1975	1980
LEATH	238	318	556	573
	−233	−247	−264	−236
	3	2	1	1
TEX	3	5	9	11
	1556	1826	2023	2113
	−241	−198	−126	−105
CLOTH	13	33	56	67
	−24	−207	−250	−232
	2	9	6	5
FOOD	30	46	61	80
	−1567	−2268	−2087	−2859
	81	81	50	53

metal products are high priority sectors in Hungary, so this would account for their being too capital-intensive. But this argument would imply that the machinery and electrical machinery industries should be too capital-intensive in Hungary as well. Textiles is also a peculiar case, because one would expect it to be a low priority and therefore a labor-intensive sector. There seems to be no discernible pattern here, and hence no specific conclusions can be made. The only clear pattern is that the initial imputed MRSs deviate from each other to a much greater extent, and factor reallocations are much larger for Hungary than for West Germany. This is another way of observing the fact that the Hungarian economy appears to be more allocatively inefficient.

Finally, note the trend in inefficiency in Hungary. Although it is not completely consistent across methods, the general tendency appears to be one of increasing inefficiency over time. This implies that the Hungarian economic reforms have not been effective in improving the allocation mechanism. This is further emphasized by observing that inefficiency appears to be decreasing over time in West Germany. This lends empirical support for the contention of many Hungarian and Western economists who have argued that the reform has not been radical enough to alter the fundamental deficiencies of the Soviet-type planning system. In fact, it may be that partial reforms have reduced allocative efficiency, possibly by weakening the planning mechanisms, without adequately replacing them with effective market mechanisms.

Conclusions

Cobb-Douglas production functions have been estimated for various sectors of manufacturing for Hungary and West Germany. The parameter estimates allow the calculation of imputed MRS for each sector. Two methods were used to calculate estimates of the increase in output that could have been obtained if inputs had been allocated such that MRSs were equated across sectors.

The results support the hypothesis that the Hungarian economy suffers from a substantially larger amount of allocative inefficiency than does the market economy of the Federal Republic of Germany. Furthermore, the estimates indicate that the Hungarian New Economic Mechanism has not resulted in any improvement in the resource allocation mechanism, since the degree of inefficiency appears to be increasing over time.

Notes

1. See Baretto and Whitesell (1988) for a proof of this assertion.

2. The methodology has been discussed by Desai and Martin (1983a) and Baretto and Whitesell (1988).

3. Desai and Martin (1983b) use an alternative measure. It has been shown that this measure and their measure are equivalent. See Baretto and Whitesell (1988).

4. Desai and Martin (1983b) use a fixed proportion social welfare function. Baretto and Whitesell (1988) argue that this is unnecessary and misleading. It implies a precision that is impossible.

5. Estimation of CES production functions proved troublesome. In many cases in which they did converge to a solution, the parameter estimates were unreasonable; i.e., they implied negative marginal products or a negative elasticity of substitution. Even in those cases in which marginal products and the elasticity of substitution were positive, the implied MRSs were absurd because of imputed marginal products of capital near zero. This problem is discussed in more detail in Whitesell (1986).

6. See Whitesell (1985) for a detailed description of the selection procedure.

7. Predicted output from the production function estimates was used rather than actual output. This choice is necessitated by the fact that interest is focused on allocative inefficiency. If actual output levels were used, then the measure of inefficiency would be biased upward (downward) whenever observed output was less (more) than predicted output. This is the case because the production function estimates would allow production of the observed output level with less (more) of both inputs without any reallocation among industries.

8. It must be stressed that this procedure results in sixteen different estimates of inefficiency. The estimated MRS* is different in each of the sixteen cases. The amounts of capital and labor that are reallocated are different in each case, and since they are applied to different outputs with different production functions, the effect on production is different in each case.

9. Telecommunications were deleted for Hungary to make the number of sectors equivalent with the number used with gross output in West Germany. These figures for West Germany are included in the machinery sector. For Hungary there is no comparable sector to games.

10. Exceptions are transportation equipment, leather goods, and clothing, each of which are too capital-intensive using gross output and too labor-intensive using value-added. The imputed MRSs for transportation and clothing are relatively close to the optimal MRS, and the reallocations are small, so the factor intensity reversal does not seem to imply much. The leather goods industry, however, is marginally too labor-intensive using value-added but is much too capital-intensive using gross output. This may indicate a problem with the data for this sector. Also note the weak estimates of the capital coefficient in this sector (see Tables A8 and A9). Because of this inconsistency, these sectors are not discussed in the text.

References

Baretto, Humberto and Robert S. Whitesell. "Estimation of Soviet Output Loss from Allocative Inefficiency: A Comparison of Estimates." Unpublished manuscript, April 1988.

Central Statistical Office. *Ipari Adattar*. Budapest, 1966.

Central Statistical Office. *Ipari Adattar*. Budapest, 1972.

Central Statistical Office. *Ipari Adatok*. Budapest, various issues from 1967-76.

Central Statistical Office. *Iparstatistikai Főosztály Évkönyv*, various issues for 1976-85.

Desai, Padma and Ricardo Martin. "Measuring Resource-Allocational Efficiency in Centrally Planned Economies: A Theoretical Analysis." In Padma Desai, ed. *Marxism, Central Planning and the Soviet Economy: Economic Essays in Honor of Alexander Erlich*. Cambridge: MIT Press, 1983a.

Desai, Padma. "Efficiency Loss from Resource Misallocation in Soviet Industry." *Quarterly Journal of Economics*, August 1983b, pp. 441-56.

Federal Statistical Office (FRG). *Statistisches Jahrbuch für die Bundesrepublik Deutschland*. Wiesbaden, various issues for 1964-85.

Thornton, Judith. "Differential Capital Charges and Resources Allocation in Soviet Industry," *Journal of Political Economy* 79, May/June 1971, pp. 545-61.

Toda, Yasushi. "The Imperfections in Factor Market and the Loss of Production in Centrally Planned Industry: A General Equilibrium Calculation." Paper presented to the AAASS Meeting, New Orleans, November 1986.

United Nations Statistical Office. *Yearbook of Industrial Statistics*. New York, various issues for 1967-85.

Whalley, John. "Thornton's Estimates of Efficiency Losses in Soviet Industry: Some Fixed-Point-Method Recalculations." *Journal of Political Economy* 84, Jan./Feb. 1976, pp. 153-59.

Whitesell, Robert S. "The Influence of Central Planning on the Economic Slowdown in the Soviet Union and Eastern Europe: A Comparative Production Function Analysis." *Economica* 52, May 1985, pp. 235-44.

Whitesell, Robert S. "More on the Aggregate Production Function Analysis of Soviet Economic Growth." Unpublished manuscript, July 1986.

Table A1

Percent Inefficiency, West Germany
All Sectors
Value-Added

Year	FGain	Gain1	Gain2	Gain3	Gain4	Gain6	Gain7
1964	11.0	9.5	14.8	12.1	7.8	12.8	7.4
1965	10.7	9.3	13.8	11.5	7.8	12.0	7.2
1966	10.7	9.3	13.2	11.3	8.0	11.8	7.1
1967	10.8	9.3	12.8	11.1	8.3	11.7	7.0
1968	10.7	9.3	12.3	10.8	8.4	11.1	7.0
1969	10.6	9.3	11.8	10.4	8.5	10.5	6.9
1970	10.4	9.1	11.2	9.9	8.5	9.8	6.7
1971	10.4	9.1	10.9	9.8	8.7	9.6	6.7
1972	10.6	9.2	10.9	9.8	9.1	9.6	6.7
1973	10.3	9.0	10.4	9.4	9.0	9.1	6.5
1974	10.1	8.6	10.0	9.0	8.9	8.7	6.3
1975	10.2	8.6	10.0	9.1	9.3	8.8	6.4
1976	10.4	8.8	10.2	9.1	9.6	8.6	6.6
1977	10.6	8.9	10.2	9.1	9.9	8.5	6.6
1978	10.6	8.9	10.3	9.0	10.1	8.3	6.7
1979	10.4	8.6	10.1	8.7	10.1	8.0	6.6
1980	10.2	8.4	10.0	8.5	10.0	7.6	6.5
1981	9.9	8.0	9.8	8.1	9.9	7.3	6.3
1984	9.6	7.5	10.1	7.8	10.0	6.8	6.3

Year	Gain9	Gain8	Gain10	Gain11	Gain12	Gain14	Gain13
1964	15.7	8.6	25.5	6.3	9.9	7.9	6.6
1965	16.0	8.4	24.4	6.4	9.6	7.5	6.6
1966	16.5	8.5	24.5	6.7	9.6	7.3	6.8
1967	16.9	8.5	25.2	7.0	9.6	7.1	7.2
1968	17.4	8.5	24.1	7.2	9.5	6.9	7.2
1969	17.8	8.5	22.7	7.4	9.4	6.7	7.2
1970	17.8	8.4	21.4	7.5	9.1	6.4	7.1
1971	18.1	8.4	21.3	7.8	9.1	6.3	7.3
1972	18.5	8.5	21.9	8.2	9.3	6.3	7.7
1973	18.3	8.3	21.1	8.2	9.1	6.0	7.6
1974	17.7	8.0	20.8	8.2	8.9	5.7	7.6
1975	17.9	8.1	21.7	8.6	9.1	5.6	8.0
1976	18.4	8.3	21.3	9.1	9.3	5.7	8.1
1977	18.6	8.4	21.1	9.4	9.5	5.7	8.3
1978	18.5	8.5	21.1	9.7	9.6	5.6	8.4
1979	18.0	8.3	20.3	9.8	9.4	5.5	8.3
1980	17.5	8.1	19.5	9.9	9.3	5.3	8.2
1981	16.6	7.9	19.1	9.8	9.2	5.1	8.0
1984	15.0	7.5	18.6	10.2	9.3	4.8	7.9

Year	Gain15	Gain5	Gain16
1964	6.5	13.2	16.4
1965	6.2	12.9	16.0
1966	6.1	13.0	15.9
1967	6.0	13.1	15.8
1968	5.8	12.8	15.8
1969	5.7	12.4	15.7
1970	5.5	11.9	15.3
Year	Gain15	Gain5	Gain16
1971	5.4	11.7	15.3
1972	5.4	11.7	15.4
1973	5.2	11.1	15.0
1974	5.0	10.5	14.4
1975	5.0	10.4	14.4
1976	5.1	10.1	14.8
1977	5.1	9.8	14.9
1978	5.1	9.4	14.8
1979	5.0	8.8	14.5
1980	4.9	8.1	14.1
1981	4.7	7.5	13.6
1984	4.5	6.0	12.9

Table A2

**Percent Inefficiency, West Germany
Manufacturing Sectors
Without Chemicals, Wood, and Games
Value-Added**

Year	FGain	Gain1	Gain2	Gain3	Gain4	Gain6	Gain7
1964	5.6	5.2	8.0	6.5	4.2	6.7	4.1
1965	5.3	5.1	7.4	6.1	4.2	6.2	3.9
1966	5.2	5.0	7.0	5.9	4.2	6.0	3.8
1967	5.3	5.1	6.9	5.9	4.4	6.0	3.8
1968	5.2	5.1	6.5	5.7	4.5	5.7	3.7
1969	5.2	5.1	6.3	5.6	4.6	5.4	3.7
1970	4.9	4.9	5.9	5.2	4.5	5.0	3.5
1971	4.7	4.8	5.6	4.9	4.4	4.7	3.4
1972	4.8	4.8	5.6	5.0	4.6	4.7	3.5
1973	4.6	4.6	5.2	4.6	4.5	4.4	3.3
1974	4.3	4.2	4.8	4.3	4.3	4.0	3.1
1975	4.1	4.1	4.6	4.1	4.2	3.8	2.9
1976	4.1	4.0	4.5	4.0	4.3	3.7	2.9
1977	4.2	4.0	4.5	4.0	4.4	3.6	3.0
1978	4.1	4.0	4.5	3.9	4.4	3.5	2.9
1979	4.0	3.9	4.4	3.8	4.4	3.3	2.9
1980	4.0	3.8	4.4	3.7	4.4	3.2	2.9
1981	3.9	3.6	4.3	3.6	4.4	3.1	2.8
1984	4.0	3.5	4.6	3.5	4.6	3.0	2.9

Year	Gain8	Gain11	Gain12	Gain14	Gain13	Gain15	Gain16
1964	4.7	3.4	5.3	4.4	3.5	3.6	9.1
1965	4.6	3.4	5.1	4.1	3.4	3.4	8.7
1966	4.5	3.5	5.0	3.9	3.5	3.2	8.6
1967	4.6	3.7	5.1	3.9	3.7	3.2	8.7
1968	4.6	3.9	5.0	3.8	3.7	3.2	8.6
1969	4.7	4.0	5.0	3.7	3.8	3.1	8.7
1970	4.5	3.9	4.8	3.4	3.6	2.9	8.2
1971	4.4	4.0	4.6	3.3	3.6	2.8	8.0
1972	4.4	4.2	4.7	3.3	3.8	2.8	8.1
1973	4.2	4.1	4.5	3.0	3.7	2.6	7.6
1974	4.0	4.0	4.2	2.8	3.5	2.4	7.1
1975	3.8	3.9	4.1	2.6	3.5	2.3	7.8
1976	3.8	4.0	4.1	2.6	3.5	2.3	6.7
1977	3.8	4.2	4.2	2.6	3.5	2.3	6.8
1978	3.8	4.3	4.1	2.5	3.5	2.3	6.6
1979	3.7	4.3	4.1	2.4	3.5	2.2	6.5
1980	3.7	4.3	4.1	2.4	3.5	2.2	6.4
1981	3.6	4.3	4.0	2.3	3.4	2.1	6.1
1984	3.5	4.7	4.2	2.2	3.5	2.1	6.0

Table A3

Percent Inefficiency, Socialist Industry
Manufacturing Sectors, All Sectors

Year	FGain	Gain1	Gain2	Gain3	Gain4	Gain5	Gain6
1961	29.3	44.3	25.5	28.0	33.0	14.4	15.1
1962	29.2	44.1	25.2	27.5	32.3	14.8	15.4
1963	30.4	45.3	26.2	28.5	33.4	15.7	16.3
1964	30.7	45.9	26.6	28.9	33.7	16.4	17.0
1965	30.4	44.7	26.5	28.8	33.3	16.5	17.0
1966	32.2	46.1	28.0	30.7	35.2	17.8	18.1
1967	32.0	46.3	27.8	30.1	34.4	18.3	18.6
1968	32.1	47.2	27.8	29.5	33.8	19.0	19.4
1969	32.8	46.9	28.5	30.6	34.7	19.7	19.8
1970	32.3	45.3	28.3	30.4	34.2	19.8	19.7
1971	32.4	44.8	28.6	30.7	34.3	20.2	20.1
1972	33.0	45.0	29.3	31.6	35.0	21.1	20.8
1973	32.4	44.1	29.2	31.4	34.5	21.4	20.9
1974	32.6	44.2	29.5	31.7	34.7	22.1	21.5
1975	34.1	46.9	30.7	32.4	35.4	24.0	23.4
1976	35.6	47.8	32.2	34.5	37.4	25.6	24.6
1977	36.0	48.0	32.7	35.1	37.8	26.6	25.4
1978	35.0	46.5	32.2	34.6	37.0	26.6	25.3
1979	34.9	45.1	32.4	35.5	37.5	27.0	25.3
1980	34.5	43.6	32.3	35.8	37.5	27.3	25.3
1981	34.7	43.5	32.8	36.8	38.2	28.2	25.9
1982	34.7	42.5	32.9	37.7	38.7	28.9	26.2
1983	34.6	42.1	33.2	38.3	39.1	29.6	26.7
1984	34.4	41.9	33.6	38.8	39.2	30.5	27.3

Note: FGain = factor savings gain method, and Gaini = single output augmenting method with sector i's output increasing.

Year	Gain7	Gain8	Gain9	Gain10	Gain11	Gain12	Gain13
1961	19.2	14.6	27.8	29.7	33.1	22.7	21.9
1962	19.5	14.2	28.9	29.0	32.4	23.3	21.2
1963	20.5	14.4	31.0	29.7	32.7	23.1	21.2
1964	21.2	14.2	32.7	29.8	32.7	23.4	20.9
1965	21.0	13.7	33.2	29.2	31.5	23.2	20.0
1966	22.2	14.1	35.8	30.6	32.3	24.7	20.4
1967	22.4	13.8	37.1	29.8	32.0	24.2	20.0
1968	22.9	13.6	39.1	29.3	32.4	23.7	19.9
1969	23.1	13.6	40.4	29.8	32.1	24.5	19.6
1970	22.5	13.1	40.5	29.0	31.0	24.3	18.8
1971	22.4	12.8	41.4	28.8	30.7	24.4	18.5
1972	22.6	12.9	43.0	29.2	31.0	25.1	18.5
1973	22.2	12.5	43.4	28.6	30.5	24.8	18.1
1974	22.2	12.5	44.7	28.5	30.8	25.0	18.1
1975	23.3	13.0	48.6	29.2	32.9	25.6	19.0
1976	23.8	13.4	51.1	30.5	34.0	27.1	19.6
1977	23.7	13.4	52.6	30.6	34.7	27.6	19.8

Table A3 (continued)

Year	Gain7	Gain8	Gain9	Gain10	Gain11	Gain12	Gain13
1978	22.7	13.0	52.1	29.7	34.0	27.1	19.3
1979	21.9	12.8	52.0	29.7	33.7	27.6	19.0
1980	21.0	12.5	51.5	29.3	33.3	27.8	18.7
1981	20.6	12.6	52.5	29.6	34.0	28.5	18.9
1982	20.0	12.5	52.5	29.6	34.2	29.1	18.9
1983	19.4	12.5	53.0	29.6	34.7	29.4	19.1
1984	18.8	12.5	53.5	29.5	35.5	29.7	19.4

Year	Gain14	Gain15	Gain16
1961	30.5	20.7	40.4
1962	29.7	20.3	41.9
1963	30.2	20.6	45.7
1964	30.2	20.5	48.3
1965	29.1	19.7	50.2
1966	30.2	20.1	55.3
1967	29.3	19.7	55.2
1968	28.8	19.7	54.8
1969	28.8	19.4	57.8
1970	27.8	18.5	58.1
1971	27.4	18.0	58.9
1972	27.4	17.9	60.4
1973	26.6	17.2	59.3
1974	26.3	17.0	58.8
1975	26.9	17.7	57.7
1976	27.8	17.9	59.8
1977	27.6	17.7	58.6
1978	26.5	16.9	55.5
1979	26.1	16.2	54.6
1980	25.4	15.5	52.6
1981	25.3	15.3	50.8
1982	25.0	14.8	49.0
1983	24.7	14.5	46.4
1984	24.4	14.2	43.3

Table A4

Factor Reallocations, West Germany
All Sectors
Value-Added
Factor Savings Method

Year	1964	1970	1975	1980	1984
Total % Gain	11.0	10.4	10.2	10.2	9.6
MRS*	22	32	59	70	98

MRS
KCHANG (millions of deutschmarks)
LCHANG (millions of hours worked)

METAL	123	169	252	312	471
	−4813	−6025	−6300	−7253	−8886
	83	74	48	45	38
MACH	15	23	47	63	96
	1164	1905	1871	1163	232
	−63	−70	−36	−17	−2
TRANS	13	19	35	34	42
	1421	2432	3469	6477	9815
	−86	−98	−76	−130	−141
ELEC	18	24	45	55	79
	562	1596	1954	2047	2165
	−28	−58	−38	−33	−25
PREC	4	5	9	11	20
	904	1362	1866	2507	2775
	−98	−102	−76	−84	−60
METP	10	15	25	33	37
	1331	1847	2797	2898	3971
	−90	−82	−71	−59	−64
CHEM	300	441	780	925	1157
	−8256	−13459	−19502	−22886	−26406
	79	87	71	70	62
GLASS	33	55	119	148	227
	−393	−708	−1352	−1648	−2209
	15	17	16	16	14
WOOD	0.4	1	1	1	2
	1282	1924	2606	3559	4094
	−439	−408	−346	−361	−283
PAPER	24	34	66	97	125
	−47	−20	−72	−249	−228
	2	1	1	3	2
PRINT	4	6	11	18	27
	1206	1835	2601	2693	3097
	−123	−124	−95	−73	−58
LEATH	13	17	30	31	45
	157	210	243	291	312
	−9	−9	−6	−6	−5
TEX	3	5	8	10	14
	3224	4062	4700	4743	5033
	−361	−308	−199	−165	−127

Table A4 (continued)

Year	1964	1970	1975	1980	1984
CLOTH	4	9	16	19	30
	735	872	1153	1144	1171
	−73	−48	−35	−29	−21
GAMES	3	5	9	8	15
	265	358	479	733	849
	−30	−27	−19	−28	−20
FOOD	73	109	146	193	228
	−1840	−2562	−2407	−3340	−3181
	44	41	25	28	21

Table A5

Factor Reallocations, West Germany
Without Chemicals, Wood, and Games
Value-Added
Factor Savings Method

Year	1964	1970	1975	1980	1984
Total % Gain	5.6	4.9	4.3	4.0	4.0
MRS*	18	25	37	54	75

MRS
KCHANG (millions of deutschmarks)
LCHANG (millions of hours worked)

METAL	123	169	228	312	471
	−5015	−6351	−7193	−7776	−9457
	94	85	69	54	44
MACH	15	23	35	63	96
	418	477	493	−1439	−2864
	−25	−20	−14	25	34
TRANS	13	19	32	34	42
	817	1188	933	3584	5598
	−55	−55	−27	−83	−99
ELEC	18	24	40	55	79
	−112	306	−452	−209	−527
	6	−13	12	4	7
PREC	4	5	8	11	20
	738	1070	1320	1914	2078
	−89	−92	−73	−75	−52
METP	10	15	21	33	37
	898	1100	1608	1618	2510
	−68	−56	−57	−38	−47
GLASS	33	55	96	148	227
	−539	−931	−1551	−2009	−2612
	22	24	25	22	19
PAPER	24	34	49	97	125
	−119	−132	−131	−410	−425
	6	5	3	6	4
PRINT	4	6	9	18	27
	959	1383	1788	1897	2160
	−110	−108	−93	−60	−47
LEATH	13	17	27	31	45
	87	113	95	170	178
	−6	−5	−3	−4	−3
TEX	3	5	7	10	14
	2636	3184	3433	3629	3871
	−331	−278	−199	−147	−113
CLOTH	4	9	14	19	30
	577	610	699	783	787
	−65	−38	−30	−24	−16
FOOD	73	109	131	193	228
	−1990	−2805	−2765	−3810	−3756
	51	49	37	35	27

Table A6

**Factor Reallocations, Hungary
Socialist Industry, All Sectors
Factor Savings Method**

Year	1965	1970	1975	1980	1984
Total % Gain	30.4	32.3	34.1	34.5	34.4
MRS*	105	148	203	333	479

MRS
KCHANG (millions of forints)
LCHANG (millions of hours worked)

METAL	2395	3590	4394	5743	10247
	−22572	−33710	−42051	−50837	−73025
	32	33	32	28	24
MACH	46	40	48	85	125
	4528	8724	11784	17159	20935
	−66	−116	−122	−104	−87
TRANS	14	26	37	58	97
	5167	6499	9001	14333	16274
	−150	−113	−111	−111	−81
ELEC	24	33	41	65	104
	2262	3323	4951	8390	10014
	−47	−50	−57	−60	−47
TELE	104	122	198	340	541
	9	831	188	−274	−2009
	)0.09	)6	)1	1	4
PREC	206	265	414	732	1200
	−930	−1120	−2336	−4608	−6526
	6	6	8	9	8
METP	190	219	296	514	878
	−1813	−1714	−2073	−3104	−5404
	13	9	8	7	8
CONST	171	223	349	624	872
	−3243	−3578	−7281	−13938	−15283
	24	20	27	30	24
CHEM	922	1355	1869	3723	4841
	−18082	−29903	−46495	−88806	−101341
	51	58	66	68	57
WOOD	14	24	46	80	137
	2628	3126	4906	6837	7180
	−70	−54	−52	−43	−28
PAPER	1143	1376	2294	3879	4352
	−2713	−3993	−7056	−11168	−10890
	7	8	9	8	7

Year	1965	1970	1975	1980	1984
PRINT	19	23	51	68	118
	824	1168	1233	2785	3805
	−20	−22	−13	−20	−17
TEX	228	313	450	724	977
	−6502	−8145	−11239	−15447	−15655
	41	37	37	31	23
LEATH	25	32	47	82	116
	2425	3697	5013	7153	8914
	−47	−54	−51	−43	−38
CLOTH	43	57	98	182	340
	950	1574	2086	2766	2002
	−14	−17	−15	−11	−5
FOOD	5	5	6	10	14
	3144	4179	6289	10732	14190
	−204	−218	−295	−289	−263

Table A7

Best Regression Results, Hungary Socialist Industry

Sector
R^2
LIKE
D-W

Sector					
METAL	4.7764	.0403		.0614	.5150
.9915	.5123	.0074		.1078	.1917
51.21	9.32	5.42		0.57	2.69
MACH	2.0891			.6350	.8578
.9733	.3900			.0832	.1121
41.11	5.36			7.63	7.65
TRANS	1.3693			.8012	.7877
.9935	.2224			.0454	.1344
41.43	6.16			17.64	5.86
ELEC	1.9888			.7121	.8301
.9834	.3430			.0736	.1217
37.24	5.80			9.67	6.82
TELE	2.9914	.0588		.2711	
.9967	.2044	.0053		.0641	
48.54	14.64	11.13		4.23	
1.07					
PREC	3:4694	.0622		.1405	.6322
.9964	.3830	.0111		.1258	.1733
49.72	9.06	5.59		1.12	3.65
METLP	3.5497	.0586	−.0011	.1928	
.9862	.6976	.0050	.0006	.1898	
45.02	5.09	11.65	1.97	1.02	
1.12					
CONST	2.7476		.0005	.3553	
.9938	.2147		.0002	.0488	
54.56	12.80		2.99	7.28	
1.40					
CHEM	4.0256	.0808	−.0007	.1520	.6108
.9972	.8029	.0138	.0003	.1685	.1817
51.09	5.01	5.87	2.09	0.90	3.36
WOOD	2.3749			.6088	.5170
.9953	.0689			.0169	.1868
47.69	34.46			36.06	2.77
PAPER	4.3507	.0151	.0010	.1230	
.9955	.2838	.0046	.0001	.0598	
55.57	15.33	3.27	7.64	2.06	
1.43					
PRINT	1.3409			.7669	.8100
.9835	.3032			.0620	.1280
31.79	4.42			12.37	6.33

TEX	3.6978		.0010	.2047	.6232
.9930	.4797		.0003	.1187	.1749
54.89	7.71		3.09	1.72	3.56
LEATH	2.9557			.4840	.8284
.9746	.2467			.0647	.1222
40.32	11.98			7.48	6.78
CLOTH	3.7322	.0175		.1724	
.9744	.1056	.0067		.0646	
43.48	35.33	2.63		2.67	
1.18					
FOOD	.7392	.0565	−.0032	.9628	
.9688	.5261	.0040	.0003	.1105	
46.24	1.40	11.52	9.59	8.69	
0.95					

Table A8

Best Regression Results
West Germany
Gross Output

Sector
R²
LIKE
D-W

METAL	3.8931	.0650	−.0010	.0407	
.9823	.3282	.0113	.0003	.1921	
36.13	11.86	5.74	3.07	0.21	
1.63					
MACH	3.7960			.3591	.6009
.9756	.0486			.0278	.1998
39.34	78.16			12.94	3.01
TRANS	4.0771	.0275		.1024	
.9618	.0892	.0051		.0833	
35.22	45.70	5.38		1.23	
1.39					
ELEC	3.2778	.0628	−.0007	.2033	
.9968	.0677	.0059	.0002	.0668	
46.88	48.40	10.55	4.06	3.04	
1.31					
PREC	3.7015	.0349	−.0008	.1727	
.9771	.0502	.0058	.0002	.0739	
41.84	73.67	6.02	3.39	2.34	
1.72					
METLP	3.3897	.0362		.1374	
.9804	.0190	.0093		.1272	
35.72	178.79	3.91		1.08	
0.90					
GLASS	3.3245	.0476		.0817	
.9860	.0507	.0126		.1276	
35.40	65.55	3.79		0.64	
0.66					
PAPER	4.2618	.0780	−.0009	.2030	
.9937	.1231	.0104	.0003	.1089	
36.85	34.63	7.47	3.09	1.86	
1.31					
PRINT	3.2837			.5156	
.9882	.0099			.0137	
38.08	333.29			37.75	
1.51					
LEATH	3.7363	.0296		.0039	
.9634	.0239	.0077		.1198	
37.90	156.64	3.82		0.03	
1.38					

TEX	3.2277	.0615	−.0010	.2781	
.9930	.0379	.0131	.0002	.1484	
39.72	85.10	4.68	3.81	1.87	
1.13					
CLOTH	3.3187	.0353		.0231	.5634
.9827	.0779	.0072		.0748	.2133
39.95	42.59	4.93		0.31	2.64
FOOD	4.4963	.0533	−.0006	.1003	
.9948	.1345	.0087	.0002	.1132	
48.29	33.43	6.14	3.37	0.89	
1.47					

Table A9

**Best Regression Results
West Germany
Value-Added**

Sector
R^2
LIKE
D-W

METAL .9786 35.05 1.51	2.9765 .3474 8.57	.0651 .0120 5.43	−.0011 .0003 3.19	.0423 .2034 0.21	
MACH .9940 50.10	3.4288 .0608 56.38		.0012 .0002 5.45	.1276 .0550 2.32	.7463 .1719 4.34
TRANS .9427 32.46 1.17	3.1511 .1032 30.52	.0212 .0059 3.58		.1722 .0964 1.79	
ELEC .9974 47.00 1.30	2.6977 .0671 40.21	.0789 .0059 13.38	−.0009 .0002 5.43	.1357 .0662 2.05	
PREC .9243 32.44	2.9557 .0706 41.85			.3221 .0480 6.72	.6851 .1821 3.76
METLP .9847 37.40 1.06	2.7339 .0173 157.74	.0410 .0085 4.84		.0944 .1162 0.81	
CHEM .9947 44.03 2.05	3.4466 .2158 15.97	.1022 .0100 10.17	−.0023 .0002 10.84	.0276 .1051 0.26	
GLASS .9957 47.49	2.8790 .0409 70.31	.0646 .0121 5.35	−.0008 .0003 3.05	.0452 .0934 0.48	.5402 .2249 2.40
WOOD .9422 23.31	3.1300 .0396 79.13			.5317 .0690 7.71	.5930 .2013 2.95
PAPER .9932 34.81 1.43	2.4935 .1371 18.19	.0938 .0116 8.06	−.0010 .0003 3.22	.1222 .1213 1.01	
PRINT .9912 39.34 1.28	2.9546 .0694 42.60	.0417 .0116 3.59		.1523 .1135 1.34	
LEATH .9633 37.58 1.28	2.8338 .0243 116.79	.0260 .0079 3.30		.0672 .1219 0.55	

TEX	2.2850	.0697	−.0012	.2908
.9933	.0399	.0138	.0003	.1560
38.76	57.32	5.04	4.51	1.86
1.13				
CLOTH	2.6191	.0327		.0764
.9657	.0747	.0071		.0824
33.42	35.07	4.62		0.93
0.60				
GAMES	3.1675	.0529	−.0023	.2003
.9254	.0392	.0089	.0003	.0616
35.19	80.85	5.91	7.18	3.25
1.92				
FOOD	3.5331	.0572	−.0007	.0444
.9964	.1066	.0069	.0001	.0897
52.56	33.15	8.32	5.25	0.49
1.76				

Changes in the Structure of Industrial Production and Foreign Trade in the Period of Restrictions, 1978-1986

JÁNOS GÁCS

Introduction

After 1978-79 the functioning and the performance of the Hungarian economy was directly affected by the unprecedented degree of external imbalance and the consequent restrictions applied by the central authorities. The growth of industrial production decelerated markedly in these years. As against an annual average 6-percent growth rate in 1970-78, measured in comparable prices, in 1978-86 the value of this indicator dropped to 1.4 percent. In the first period there were only two of fifty-seven industries having no growth in these eight years: coal mining, and brick and slate production. In the second period, however, in another eight-year span, production decreased in nineteen industries. A production decline of such an extent is a new and unusual phenomenon in the economic history of the past forty years.

Similarly unusual is the particularly abrupt drop in the output of several industries. The most striking example is the leather and fur industry, where production today is only two-thirds of what it used to be eight years ago. But quarry and gravel production decreased by nearly 30 percent, too, and the output of the other wood industry and of handicrafts and homecrafts by approximately 20 percent. Another sign of the slackening of general growth is the deceleration of production growth in each of the industries of the industrial sector, disaggregated to nine industries (see Table 1). A more detailed breakdown of the industrial sector shows that in forty-eight of the fifty-seven industries the second period was characterized by a lower rate of production growth than the first one, or by a decline. In one industry the fall in production was moderated and only eight industries, four of them belonging to the food industry, were able to achieve an increase in their rate of growth.

Table 1

Average Yearly Growth of Gross Production in Industry
(in comparable prices)

	1970–1978	1978–1986
Mining	2.2	–0.6
Electric power industry	7.9	2.5
Metallurgy	4.4	–0.1
Engineering industry	7.2	2.2
Building materials industry	5.2	0.9
Chemical industry	10.1	2.0
Light industry	4.8	0.7
Other industries	8.1	0.0
Food industry	4.4	2.1
Industry, total	6.0	1.4

Sources: Ipargazdasági Evkönyv 1978–1985; Ipari Zsebkönyv 1986.

Well-established knowledge about the post-1978 period of Hungarian industrial development is very narrow. Most assessments and statements contain the same logic, i.e., that in Hungarian industry the extensive slackening of growth has implied a stagnation covering all of the industries and so conserving the old industrial structure.

According to the analyses, the falling volume of industrial investment and the obstructed flow of capital have essentially impeded the restructuring of production on the capacity side. Moreover, the danger of restoring the previous industrial structure, ill-suited to this country's endowments, emerged because the allocation of investment shifted in favor of primary industries. It is generally believed that both the structure of imports for industrial use and the structure of industrial export were frozen by the lack of sufficient incentives and adequate means to support business decisions, and this is why the adjustment to world market changes was lacking.

Many of the above statements, based on impressions and partial correlations, are most probably true while others cannot be verified in this form. In the statistical analysis below I attempt to clarify, from several aspects, the directions and the rate of change of the industrial structure during the past eight years. I will show the dimensions in which the structure actually stiffened and the ones in which there was palpable shifting. Shifts for me mean either a new phenomenon characterizing the entire industry, or an evolution of new proportions in the structure of the industries. In the analysis I try to scrutinize data as disaggregated as possible. I considered this a prerequisite to reach well-established conclusions. At the same time, the results thus obtained would be more likely to directly reflect the behavior of individual companies, or groups of companies, and consequently serve as reference for future research on enterprise behavior in this period.

Owing to the incompleteness and limits of comparability of available published data, the database of this study is not fully consistent. In some sources data were found for nine aggregate industries of the industrial sector only, in others industry was represented by thirty-six more or less aggregated lines of production, or again by fifty-seven lines. Usually it was a problem to take into account the changes in the definition of certain product lines, to reconcile statistics of foreign trade with production statistics, and to overcome the lack of data at unchanged prices and of many 1986 data. I am nevertheless convinced that the problems of data inconsistency, while limiting the accuracy of the analysis, do not invalidate the evident trends.

Synthetic indicators of structural change in industry

According to production data of fifty-seven industries, measured in constant prices, the average yearly growth rate of production in these industries ranged from –2.0 to 13.6 percent in the period 1970-78, period 1, while in the period 1978-86, period 2, it fell within a zone of –5.1 to 9.1 percent. So the zone of growth rates apparently got somewhat narrower and descended: its width decreased by 1.4 percentage points, and the standard deviation of the rates of production decreased only minimally, from 3.1 to 3.0.

The above data suggest that, at variance with the general view, the degree of differentiation which industrial production underwent in the post-1978 period was nearly the same as in the preceding stage of 1970-78. Structural change, however, can be analyzed from many aspects and by a variety of methods. In this study comparative computations were made about the development of two indicators of structural change for the two periods. Alas, owing to unavailability of data we had to give up our aspiration of making computations for production data at unchanged prices, so we used current price data instead.

One indicator of structural change measures the shift in the shares of the industries in total production. The formula of this indicator is:

$$C = 0.5 \sum_{i=1}^{k} (a_{i_1} - a_{i_0})$$

where a_{i1} is the share of industry i in total production in the last year of the period under study; a_{i0} is the share of industry i in the first year of the period.[1] The value of this indicator may vary between 0 and 100.

In industrial production this indicator of structural change had the value of 9.6 in period 1 and 10.4 in period 2.

The second indicator of structural change quantifies the distance between the two multidimensional vectors formed by the production values of industries in one period and in the other. Its formula is as follows:

Table 2

The Value of Indicator T of Structural Change in Industry

	1972	1978	1980	1984	1986
	in production				
1970	14.99	22.36	31.30	35.94	33.30
1972		14.75	26.20	30.80	27.85
1978			15.56	20.09	17.01
1980				8.27	12.10
1984					9.12
	in ruble exports				
1972		11.08	14.74	14.84	13.82
1978			5.44	6.92	5.71
1980				6.80	5.68
1984					4.43
	in non-ruble exports				
1972		31.71	31.77	37.23	39.75
1978			15.91	27.66	20.95
1980				15.84	15.24
1984					15.85

Sources of data used for the computations: *Iparstatisztikai Évkönyv 1978–1985*; *Ipari Zsebkönyv 1986; Agazati Kapcsolatok Mérlege 1972, export-import elészmolasok; Statisztikai Évkönyv 1970, 1972; Külkereskedelmi Minisztérium Statisztikai Osztályának Tájékoztatja 1978–1986.*

$$T = \left\{ \frac{|A_1|}{A_1} - \frac{|A_0|}{A_0} \right\} \cdot \frac{100}{2}$$

where A_0 (A_1) is the vector of industrial production in the first (last) year of the period and $|\ |$ means the absolute value of this vector. This indicator also can have values between 0 and 100.[2]

As is shown in Table 2, structural change measured by this latter indicator was actually less between 1978 and 1986 than between 1970 and 1978: in the second period it amounts to 17.01 vs. the value of 22.36 in the first period. For the selected years all the possible indicators are included in the table; in the first column from the left the base years of the structural shifts are indicated, while the closing years are given in the upper line. The data in the table reflect slackening structural change in industry, especially in the 1980s. An interesting feature is that the shift that took place after 1984 showed some degree of reversion as compared to the changes from the 1970s to 1984.

As noted above, the two synthetic indicators were computed from production data at current prices therefore, in addition to other possible distortions, the results obtained could be influenced by price changes in the respective periods.[3] In the sixteen years, as compared to the length of the subperiods, the largest structural

Table 3

Value of Indicator C of Structural Change in Industry

	1970–1978	1978–1985
Number of employees	7.1	4.6
Gross value of fixed assets (at current prices)	10.4	5.1

	1972–1978	1978–1986
Ruble exports (at current prices)	9.6	5.7
Non-ruble exports (at current prices)	18.8	11.3

Sources: as in Table 2.

change was recorded by indicator T between 1978 and 1980, clearly reflecting, among other factors, the impact of the price revisions of 1980.

The two indicators of structural change were also computed for employment, the gross value of fixed assets, as well as for ruble and non-ruble exports, the latter three measured at current prices. These data unambiguously indicate that structural changes slowed down—although they did not cease completely (see Tables 2 and 3).

It is apparent from the data in Table 3 that even for the whole 14-year period structural change in ruble exports was insignificant compared to the changes in production and non-ruble exports. This slowness of transformation is assumed to be rooted only partly in the tardy and lagging price changes in ruble trade and to a greater extent in the institutional system of CMEA trade. As far as the structural change of non-ruble exports is concerned, it can be stated that in every subperiod it has been of the same order of magnitude but larger than the structural change in production. Even though the rate of structural change here decreased by one-third from 1972-78 to 1978-86 (37.1 and 20.95 respectively), and in these calculations period 2 is two years longer than period 1, it is nevertheless remarkable that non-ruble exports regularly, and in each subperiod (namely, 1978-80, 1980-84 and 1984-86) underwent considerable structural changes of about 16 points, but not necessarily in the same direction.

Changes in the structure of ownership and size of industrial organizations

In the first half of the 1980s significant changes took place in the distribution of ownership of industrial organizations. The previous restrictions on private activity and partnerships were eased, and a new opportunity was provided permitting partnerships of private workers to use state-owned equipment. This is partly the reason for the significant changes in the number of industrial organizations and distribution by proprietors. The number of cooperative and private small enterprises was surging after 1982, as can be seen in Table 4. Accordingly, the operations of such organizations also increased at a high rate, and even in the year 1986, when the rate of expansion of such organizations slowed down by necessity, the increase of production in this sphere was in excess of that of state industry. Measured at current prices, gross production in 1986 increased by 3.3 percent in state-owned industrial enterprises, 9.5 percent in industrial cooperatives, 9.7 percent in business sections and intrafirm business partnerships, 40.8 percent in private business partnerships, and by 9.6 percent in the shops of private artisans. Considering the low initial bench mark, the short period of unbroken rapid development, and the still restrictive and uncertain conditions of operations it stands to reason that the share of private artisans and of the so-called new type organizations in industrial production of industrial organizations did not exceed 3 percent even in 1986 (see Table 5).

Special attention should be paid to the difference shown in the 1978-1986 period between the performance of state enterprises and industrial cooperatives. Between 1978 and 1986, the expansion of the volume of gross production amounted to 12.2 percent in state industry, while cooperatives scored 27.3 percent. The difference in favor of industrial cooperatives had been manifest earlier as well, however this discrepancy has widened still further lately. While in period 1 the rate of growth of production in industrial cooperatives was only one and a half times the growth in state enterprises, after 1978 this difference became more than twofold.

The growing share of industrial cooperatives does not seem to be concentrated on one or two lines of production; on the contrary, it has expanded over a large area. There are forty industries showing an appreciable share of cooperatives in production. With respect to production data between 1978 and 1985, in current prices, the share of cooperatives increased in thirty-two production lines, and only seven production lines shifted toward the state enterprises. Strangely enough, considering the entire industrial sector, current price data indicate a growing share of the state sector. On the basis of comparable price data, the share of cooperatives increased in about as many production lines as it decreased, along with the already noted growth of the weight of the whole cooperative industry.

As regards labor productivity growth, the discrepancy existing for a longer while between the two sectors became wider, as in gross production. In 1970-1978, too, cooperative industry increased its productivity faster than state industry. However, due to the more rapid and flexible adjustment of the cooperative industry, in period 2 this difference increased and nearly reached a ratio of 2:1.[4]

In addition to, and partly in consequence of, the change in the distribution of ownership of industrial organizations, remarkable shifts took place in the size structure of organizations in the first part of the 1980s. Beside the said changes, it was of cardinal importance that, following the splitting up of several trusts and companies of nation-wide supply, the number of state-owned companies increased

Table 4

Changes in the Number of Industrial Organizations

	1975	1980	1982	1986
State enterprises	779	699	726	1,007
of this controlled by:				
ministries	543	546	573	695
councils	236	153	153	312
Industrial cooperatives	793	661	635	604[1]
Small cooperatives	—	—	80	352[1]
Industrial and service				
cooperative sections	—	—	158	968
Intrafirm business partnerships	—	—	1,634	14,069
Private business partnerships	—	—	837	3,383
Artisans	35,677	39,275	43,429	43,530
Employees of artisans (capita)	—	7,591	8,178	10,500
Persons possessing license for				
industrial activity to run				
in addition to main job	—	10,948	14,968	20,024[2]

Sources: Statisztikai Évkönyv 1986, Magyar Statisztikai Zsebkönyv 1986, Kristof (1986).

[1]Data for 1985. In 1986 the number of industrial cooperatives and small cooperatives was altogether 1,107.
[2]Data for 1985.

and the previous decline in the number of council-owned enterprises first halted then reversed (see Table 4).

Data concerning the size structure of industrial companies are shown in Table 6. It can be seen that in every company size category employing more than 100 blue-collar workers the ratio of the number of these companies, but not necessarily the number itself, decreased. With respect to share of production, however, only companies belonging to the size category of over 2,000 workers lost weight.

Dynamic and declining industries

A significant transformation of the industrial structure means nothing but having certain industries with substantially fast development, while others experience production growth slow downs, or output declines. In this context we naturally cannot speak of a general stagnation: between 1978 and 1986, too, several product lines showed faster or slower development than the average of industry, and as has been mentioned above, there was a pronounced drop of production in one-third of the production lines. Still, what were the typical features of the dynamic industries in post-1978 industrial development? Did the same ones show fast development

Table 5

Distribution of Industrial Activity among Industrial Organizations of Different Ownership

	1982	1983	1984	1985	1986
State enterprises	92.7	92.5	91.9	91.6	91.1
Industrial cooperatives	5.8	5.7	5.9	5.9	6.3
Industrial and service cooperative sections	0.1	0.3	0.6	0.7	0.8
Intrafirm business partner-ships					
Artisans	1.3	1.4	1.4	1.5	1.5
Private business partnerships	0.0	0.1	0.2	0.2	0.3
Industrial organizations, total	100.0	100.0	100.0	100.0	100.0

Sources: Iparstatisztikai Évkönyv 1985; Statisztikai Évkönyv 1986.

that had grown at exceptionally high rates at the beginning of the 1970s, in this way preserving the old structure of the industry, or did a considerable number of other production lines catch up and develop much more robustly than the average? Were they enabled to grow fast because of relatively substantial increments in fixed assets and the provision of plentiful labor or, on the contrary, were they the industries demanding less from these shrinking resources or utilizing their reserves in labor and physical capacities more economically? In the following we will try to find the answers to these questions, and to the respective ones concerning the declining industries, always having in mind that occasionally the evidence may turn out to be inconclusive.

In this analysis a line of industrial production is considered to be dynamic, average, or declining according to the elasticity of its growth rate in respect of the rate of growth in the whole industrial sector (all growth rates measured at compa-rable prices). Our classification is the following:

If the elasticity $E < 0$ declining industry
$O \leq E < 0.7$ inelastic industry
$0.7 \leq E < 1.3$ average industry
$1.3 \leq E < 1.7$ industry with medium elasticity
$1.7 \leq E$ industry with high elasticity

In the analysis, "highly elastic industries" will be considered dynamic, and the declining ones as the other characteristic extremity of structural change. The classification of the fifty-seven industries is given in Table 7, according to actual growth performance .

From the comparison of periods 1 and 2 it can be seen that the development of

Table 6

Data by Size Groups of Blue Collar Labor Employed in Companies in Socialist Industry

Blue-collar workers	Number of Companies		Value of Production	
	percentage distribution			
	1978	1986	1978	1986
–50	3.6	24.1	–0.5*	–0.1*
51–100	6.6	14.1	0.4	2.1
101–300	34.2	26.0	4.4	4.5
301–500	16.0	9.8	4.3	4.8
501–1000	15.2	11.6	12.5	15.7
1001–2000	11.7	8.5	18.5	21.0
2001–5000	9.6	4.5	34.6	30.9
5001–10000	2.1	1.0	12.9	12.5
10001–	1.0	0.4	12.9	8.5
Total	100.0	100.0	100.0	100.0

Sources: Statisztikai Évkönyv 1978, 1986.

*Negative values are due to the accounting system of some trusts, where the central headquarters manage the export activity of the whole trust.

some of the lines show a certain level of stability. Thus, for example, the highly elastic class of period 2 includes three of the four lines that had grown with high elasticity in period 1 (telecommunication industry, gas production, and pharmaceutical industry), while two declining industries of period 1 appear again in the class of declining industries of period 2. At the same time, there are considerable rearrangements, especially among the dynamic (highly elastic) lines: the group of industries qualifying for high elasticity in period 2 consists not only of the ones that used to grow with medium or high elasticity, but just as many of those that used to show average, or, what is more, inelastic growth (flax and hemp production, confectionery industry, and tobacco industry, for instance, promoted from inelastic to highly elastic lines). If the regressive lines of period 2 are considered, it is found that the lines that used to be regressive and inelastic earlier represent a higher percentage here, implying that the preceding trends were more powerful here. In some cases however, remarkable shifts took place, for example industries with medium elasticity in period 1, like handicraft and home crafts, and of high flexibility, like sawmill and sheeting, had to restrain their production in period 2.

As a next step of the analysis, it was checked whether dynamic growth or failure to grow was typical of capital-intensive or of labor-intensive lines during the past eight years.[5] Data show a slight (relative) preponderance of capital-intensive lines among industries with fast growth rate, while the declining industries were clearly dominated by labor-intensive ones.

Subsequent to the analysis of the impact of the initial capital intensity, we analyzed the role of actual expansion of fixed assets in the development of industries. According to the data, in period 2 faster growth rates were usually achieved by industries capable of increasing their respective fixed assets with a rate beyond the average; the class of dynamic lines include all the six industries that proved to be ''highly elastic'' with respect to fixed asset expansion in the industrial sector.[6] However, this correlation did not materialize with a hundred percent regularity, since in most of the dynamic lines fixed assets were increased with an average elasticity. Moreover, there were five industries increasing their production in a highly elastic manner although their fixed assets were expanded in an inelastic way. These lines are the ceramics industry, flax and hemp production, brewery production, tobacco industry, and mineral water and soft drink production, all— with one exception—being typically labor-intensive industries.

Declining industries, to some degree, behaved in a reverse manner. As expected, the cutback of production was more frequently associated with subaverage fixed asset expansion; still, three of these lines formed their fixed assets with a growth rate far above the average. At the same time, it is conspicuous that in this group of industries too, fixed assets were typically developed at average rates: nine of the eighteen declining lines expanded their fixed assets at an average rate. Only one single industry of the declining group, and also of all industry, decreased its gross fixed assets in the eight years.[7]

The degree of up-to-dateness of fixed assets used in industry, most commonly measured by the ratio net to gross value of fixed assets, showed a remarkable decrease during the past years: from 69 percent it dropped to 65 percent between 1978 and 1985. As this decrease took place in the majority of lines, forty-three out of fifty-seven, differentiation among industries can be considered here rather in terms of the rate of obsolescence than in terms of the rate of increase of up-to-dateness.[8] In fact, however, no appreciable differences could be detected; machinery in dynamic industries got obsolete at a similar, or slightly faster, rate than in declining industries.

As shown by representative surveys of the Central Statistical Office, the utilization of industrial fixed assets has been decreasing through the 1980s. Although there is no available long-range time series containing absolutely consistent and comparable data, there are indications that this decline in capacity utilization is deeper, spans a longer period of time, and is more wide-spread in the whole industry than the troughs in utilization observed before. There were also changes among the main causes of insufficient utilization, with the importance of economic reasons increasing. Among these economic reasons, the weight of material shortages increased and then stabilized at a higher level. Non-utilization of capacities due to insufficient demand increased steadily and steeply. Labor-shortage-related non-utilization kept increasing for a while, then fell back, supposedly because of

Table 7

Classification of Industries According to Growth Elasticity

1970–1978	1978–1986
	Declining lines
Coal mining	Coal mining
Brick & slate production	Crude oil production
	Iron metallurgy
	Other nonferrous metallurgy
	Iron & metal mass products
	Brick & slate production
	Quarry & gravel production
	Lime & cement industry
	Concrete panel production
	Sawmill & sheeting industry
	Architectural carpenter industry
	Other wood industries
	Cotton industry
	Rayon industry
	Leather & fur industry
	Textile clothing industry
	Handicrafts and home crafts
	Bakers' ware production
	Inelastic Lines
Iron metallurgy	Bauxite production
Other nonferrous metallurgy	Other ore production
Iron and metal mass production	Electric engineering prod.
Concrete panel production	Canned goods industry
Architectural carpenter industry	Wine production
Other wood industries	
Cotton industry	
Flax and hemp production	
Leather & fur industry	
Textile clothing industry	
Bakers' ware production	
Confectionery industry	
Tobacco industry	
Milling industry	
	Average Lines
Crude oil production	Machine & equipment production
Other ore production	Rubber industry
Machine & equipment production	Textile piece goods industry
Lime & cement industry	Knitwear industry
Building insulation industry	Meat production
Glass industry	Milling industry
Rubber industry	Sugar production
Household chemicals industry	
Paper industry	
Printing	
Wool industry	

Rayon industry
Textile piece goods industry
Knitwear industry
Shoe industry
Meat production
Poultry industry
Dairy production
Sugar production
Spirits & starch production
Wine production
Brewery production

Medium elasticity lines

Bauxite production
Electric energy industry
Aluminum metallurgy
Transport vehicle production
Electric engineering industry
Precision engineering industry
Ceramics industry
Plastics industry
Furniture industry
Handicrafts and home crafts
Edible oil production
Mineral water & soft drink production

Transport vehicle production
Furniture industry
Wool industry
Shoe industry
Dairy production

High elasticity lines

Telecommunication engineering
Gas production
Pharmaceutical industry
Sawmill & sheeting industry

Electric engineering industry
Aluminum metallurgy
Telecomm. engineering industry
Precision engineering industry
Building insulation industry
Ceramics industry
Glass industry
Gas production
Plastics industry
Pharmaceutical industry
Household chemicals industry
Paper industry
Printing
Flax and hemp production
Poultry industry
Confectionery industry
Edible oil production
Spirits and starch production
Brewery production
Mineral water & soft drink
Tobacco industry

Sources: Statisztikai Évkönyv 1970, 1978; Ipari Zsebkönyv 1986.

Note: Because of changes in the classification of industries in official statistics, we could not include analysis of the petroleum refining industry, the organic and inorganic chemicals industry, production of synthetic fertilizers and crop protection agents, and plastics and synthetic fiber production.

Table 8

Utilization of Industrial Capacities
(Utilization of calendar time-base of machines, equipment
and machine lines of major activities, and the causes
of downtime machine hours)

	1976	1979	1982	1983	1984	1985	1986
Utilization of capacities	60.4	58.4	54.5	53.4	52.5	52.8	53.1
Ratio of downtime ma- chine hours due to eco- nomic reasons (% of total machine hours)	25.9	30.7	36.3	37.0	38.4	38.4	37.7
due to lack of material	7.9	10.1	11.7	10.2	12.6	12.7	10.8
due to lack of work force	11.5	12.6	14.1	15.9	14.2	13.2	12.6
due to lack of orders	6.5	8.0	10.5	10.9	11.6	12.5	14.3

Sources: Az ipar gépi kapacitasáinak kihasználása 1979; KSH 1981; Iparstatisztikai Évkönyv 1982–1985; Ipari Zsebkönyv 1986.

Note: The ratios of downtime machine hours represent the time missed from standard working time base for the years 1976 and 1979, and the time missed from calendar working time for the other years.

the growing importance of the lack of orders (see Table 8).

Unfortunately, the data series of capacity utilization quoted above are not available for the fifty-seven lines industries, so we ourselves made calculations for the values of a well-known capacity utilization indicator.[9] This index shows the degree of utilization of the electric engines installed in the individual industries. Although the interpretation of this indicator has certain limitations, it does not seem to be less reliable than the one for which data was shown in Table 8.

Comparing the changes in the dynamic and declining lines, strangely and surprisingly, no substantial difference was found between these two groups. Industry as a whole is dominated by lines with badly declining capacity utilization, thirty out of fifty-seven can be claimed to be such, and the ratio of lines with badly declining capacity utilization is only slightly smaller among the lines with dynamic growth rates, nine out of twenty-one, and only slightly higher among the declining ones, nine out of seventeen. The distribution of other categories of capacity utilization, i.e., medium declining, average, medium increasing, highly increasing, similarly do not show differences.

As a next step of the analysis we studied the typical changes in employment of the dynamic and declining industries. In contrast to some previous parts of our analysis, characteristic differences were found here. In all industry employment decreased at an average rate of 1.7 percent yearly between 1978 and 1985. Here our analysis, just like in the previous sections, relies on the classification of

Table 9

Distribution of the Value of Hungarian Foreign Trade Turnover by Commodity Group (data in forints)

		Materials			Industrial consumer goods	Food	Total
		Energy	Parts	Machines			
Ruble exports	1978	0.6	23.5	43.1	18.6	14.2	100.0
	1980	0.5	22.5	46.0	16.9	14.1	100.0
	1984	0.7	23.6	45.1	16.7	13.9	100.0
	1986	0.6	22.5	46.0	16.7	14.2	100.0
Non-ruble exports	1978	5.6	35.6	11.7	18.1	29.0	100.0
	1980	6.9	37.8	11.2	15.4	28.7	100.0
	1984	13.2	34.8	10.6	12.2	29.2	100.0
	1986	6.5	38.2	13.6	15.6	26.1	100.0
All exports	1978	3.1	29.5	27.5	18.3	21.6	100.0
	1980	4.1	31.2	26.2	16.1	22.4	100.0
	1984	7.8	30.0	25.4	14.1	22.7	100.0
	1986	3.5	30.2	30.1	16.1	20.1	100.0
Ruble imports	1978	18.5	38.5	29.0	11.2	2.8	100.0
	1980	25.5	34.4	27.1	10.5	2.5	100.0
	1984	32.2	34.1	21.4	10.2	2.1	100.0
	1986	32.4	33.2	20.3	11.2	2.9	100.0
Non-ruble imports	1978	7.7	56.0	16.3	6.3	13.7	100.0
	1980	5.9	61.5	12.6	6.7	13.3	100.0
	1984	12.1	55.9	10.5	9.5	12.0	100.0
	1986	7.2	55.6	13.4	12.1	11.7	100.0
All imports	1978	12.6	48.1	22.0	8.5	8.8	100.0
	1980	14.8	49.2	19.2	8.4	8.4	100.0
	1984	21.5	45.7	15.6	9.9	7.3	100.0
	1986	19.4	44.8	16.7	11.7	7.4	100.0

Source: Külkereskedelmi Statisztikai Évkönyv 1979, 1980, 1986.

industries by growth elasticities, although in the case of employment speaking about the elasticity of contraction is more justified.

The analysis of employment trends in different industries showed that the majority of the dynamic lines was either capable of increasing its respective staff (there were ten lines in this category), or was less powerfully pressed to reduce its

Table 10

Major Indices of Hungarian Foreign Trade Turnover in 1986, 1978 = 100
(data in forints)

	Materials			Industrial consumer goods	Food	Total
	Energy	parts	Machines			
Ruble exports						
value	191.3	169.7	188.8	159.2	177.2	177.2
price	213.8	131.0	122.2	119.2	115.6	123.2
volume	89.5	129.6	154.6	133.5	153.2	143.7
Non-ruble exports						
value	199.4	184.3	200.9	148.3	154.7	172.0
price	111.1	137.1	138.6	137.8	106.5	124.6
volume	179.3	134.6	145.0	107.6	145.3	138.0
All exports						
value	198.6	178.5	191.4	153.8	162.2	174.6
price	120.4	134.2	126.1	128.4	109.2	123.8
volume	165.0	132.9	151.9	120.0	148.7	141.1
Ruble imports						
value	274.7	135.0	109.4	156.5	161.9	156.5
price	216.0	125.3	118.8	123.5	153.7	143.8
volume	127.2	107.8	92.0	126.7	105.3	108.7
Non-ruble imports						
value	129.1	136.7	113.1	264.3	116.5	137.5
price	191.0	147.2	139.6	132.4	111.7	140.9
volume	67.6	93.0	81.9	196.0	104.5	98.2
All imports						
value	225.9	136.0	110.9	199.9	123.0	146.1
price	219.4	138.5	126.2	126.7	117.9	142.0
volume	103.1	98.2	88.3	156.6	104.3	102.8

Sources: Külkereskedelmi Évkönyv 1979, 1980, 1986.

labor force than the average industry, five lines. At the same time, in the case of the declining group, most lines decreased the number of employees at a higher (six lines), or at a much higher (another six lines) rate than the average cut; a much higher rate of cutting employment means 3 percent or more yearly decrease.

Table 11

Export/Production Ratios in Industry (at current prices, in %)

	1972	1978	1980	1984	1986
Ruble export/production	15.34	14.15	11.24	13.14	14.41
Non-ruble export/production	10.38	11.51	12.93	13.74	11.86
Total export/production	25.72	25.66	24.17	26.88	26.27

Sources: as in Table 2.

If employment drops at a faster than average rate in the lines with declining production, and decreases at a slower than average rate, or even increases, in the dynamic industries, then one cannot unambiguously predict how labor productivity develops in dynamic and declining industries. Labor productivity, however, once again has proven to be one of the indicators, according to which salient differences were found between dynamic and declining industries. While only one of the declining lines was able to enhance productivity at a rate higher than the industrial average, most of the dynamic lines achieved higher, and a large number of them much higher, productivity growth than the average.

The above analysis touched upon the performance of industries from the point of view of production, fixed asset formation, capacity utilization, employment, and labor productivity. Taking into account the results, the following conclusions can be inferred.

In the period of sharp deceleration of industrial growth between 1978 and 1986, individual industries show a sort of polarization. One group, the dynamic industries, increased production at a relatively fast rate. In most cases, already in the preceding stages and also at the time of restrictions, they usually developed their fixed assets at higher than average rates, and at the time of a general drop of industrial employment they increased, or only slightly reduced, the number of their employees. Although these lines also suffered from the characteristic symptom of the whole industry, i.e., growing non-utilization of capacities, they could stand it relatively easily and were not forced to decrease the number of employees by the drop in utilization. This was possible, partly because in the process of a relatively dynamic growth they hoped to make fuller use of their respective capacities in the future, and they knew that this would require the existing staff. At the same time, as the rapid growth in labor productivity implies, the underutilization of labor was probably less acute in these industries than the underutilization of fixed capacities. This may give an explanation of the fact that decreasing capacity utilization here was not accompanied by a fall in employment.

The other pole of differentiation is formed by the declining industries. Although, in many of the industries that were forced to decrease their output, we cannot see

Table 12

Ratio of Non-Ruble Exports to Production

	1972	1978	1980	1984	1986
Coal mining	1.74	0.51	0.73	0.80	1.32
Crude oil & mineral gas prod.	0.26	3.73	3.36	2.03	1.03
Other mining	3.28	2.67	2.06	1.38	1.68
Electric power industry	0.32	0.30	0.48	0.00	0.05
Iron metallurgy	21.11	16.91	18.19	20.24	16.24
Aluminum metallurgy	26.87	30.46	28.09	35.93	27.97
Other nonferrous metallurgy	17.74	16.69	12.96	13.94	15.37
Machine and equipment prod.	5.14	6.57	10.20	9.26	10.76
Transport vehicle prod.	6.84	9.93	14.63	11.83	10.85
Electric engineering prod.	6.39	10.39	12.84	12.87	11.74
Telecomm. and vacuum eng.	11.56	14.69	15.89	16.15	13.02
Precision engineering	6.89	10.67	13.25	11.54	8.87
Iron & metal mass products	7.79	8.60	8.51	7.90	8.94
Brick, slate and incombust.	1.66	2.47	2.28	1.69	1.93
Concrete panel production	0.72	0.57	1.87	2.33	0.79
Ceramics industry	11.57	11.22	12.78	16.73	16.33
Glass industry	15.63	10.63	19.82	15.89	15.81
Other building materials ind.	0.79	5.20	2.15	2.61	1.15
Petroleum refining	8.35	6.92	9.44	15.10	14.31
Pharmaceutical industry	17.52	22.32	21.00	24.21	23.73
Other chemical industries	5.59	11.68	12.81	13.93	11.15
Rubber industry	9.07	15.58	23.65	22.77	22.77
Plastics industry	1.93	1.52	2.55	4.43	7.09
Wood industry	6.30	7.11	7.30	7.58	9.42
Paper industry	6.67	1.89	3.67	3.90	5.01
Printing	4.88	3.59	4.35	4.57	3.70
Textile industry	13.54	12.87	14.00	15.39	16.23
Leather and fur industry	20.24	17.21	17.79	15.52	18.49
Shoe industry	9.40	12.94	15.40	14.99	15.26
Textile clothing industry	14.96	23.46	27.95	30.65	28.73
Handicrafts and home crafts	14.67	13.25	11.22	9.39	10.29
Other industries	5.34	7.96	7.78	4.62	6.13
Meat production	27.17	18.23	24.21	31.26	21.33
Poultry and egg processing	38.78	77.38	65.30	58.96	49.40
Dairy production	2.12	2.55	5.00	5.79	3.79
Canned goods industry	16.08	19.69	15.88	18.56	20.12
Confectionary industry	3.09	2.03	1.41	2.78	2.71
Edible oil production	24.27	36.60	38.87	52.24	35.40
Spirits and starch prod.	0.75	2.77	4.96	7.23	8.42
Wine production	4.39	6.87	8.12	7.22	6.24
Other food industries	0.50	1.15	4.29	1.57	1.37
Industry, total	10.38	11.51	12.93	13.74	11.86

Sources: as in Table 2.

Table 13

Sources of Domestic Supply of Industrial Commodities

	1972	1978	1980	1984	1986
Ruble import/domestic supply	15.44	15.32	13.26	14.25	14.79
Dollar import/domestic supply	11.97	17.13	14.62	13.73	15.07
(Production − export)/domestic supply	72.59	67.56	72.12	72.02	70.14
Total	100.00	100.00	100.00	100.00	100.00

Sources: as in Table 2.
Note: Domestic supply = production + import − export

a deliberate, systematic set-back and a faithful accounting with the consequences of the unfavorable economic performance, some of the indicators already show signs of a spontaneous regression. In this group of industries the drop in capacity utilization was accompanied by lower-than-average fixed asset formation and a rapid rate of losing employment. Labor productivity growth was either slow, or negative. This latter was not a must. In the case of industries facing a shrinking market—note that two metallurgical industries and six lines supplying the construction industry belong here—it is not a necessity to restructure the production under the conditions of decreasing efficiency. Deliberate reduction of capacities and staff can be done along with updating. In these industries, however, fixed assets were seldom reduced, scrapped, or sold and, for a variety of reasons, most of the lines had no access to fixed assets necessary for an efficient reorganization of production. At the same time, although the reduction of employment was carried out at a faster than average rate in these industries, it was still not fast enough to cope with the drop in demand for the products of these industries, or with the devaluation of these products in the market.

Structural changes in industrial organizations' foreign trade

Reviews of industrial organizations' foreign trade usually establish that domestic industry failed to adjust to the changes of the external markets in the period 1978-86. Up-to-date manufactures that could have been sold with sufficient profitability have not gained ground in non-ruble exports. Under the pressure to boost exports, a surge in the export of the less processed, material-intensive type goods has taken place. The export of unprofitable and subsidy-intensive food products increased faster, both in ruble and non-ruble relations, than planned and considered to be desirable. These tendencies are reflected in the data of Tables 9 and 10.[10] The biggest item of non-ruble exports is still the group of materials, semi-finished products, and components. Although the export price index of this group increased

Table 14

Indicators of Domestic Coverage of Domestic Supply
[(Production–export)/domestic supply]

	1972	1978	1980	1984	1986
Coal mining	86.41	85.13	89.38	91.03	84.48
Crude oil & mineral gas prod.	63.44	44.58	59.62	55.97	50.25
Other mining	39.91	44.52	54.01	52.90	57.90
Electric power industry	87.76	90.55	87.89	88.60	89.08
Iron metallurgy	73.75	75.38	81.12	80.91	80.31
Aluminum metallurgy	66.11	68.97	79.21	72.13	71.45
Other nonferrous metallurgy	43.11	40.10	41.18	39.65	45.82
Machine and equipment prod.	47.14	31.42	34.08	39.62	36.87
Transport vehicle prod.	57.15	53.10	51.10	53.38	50.83
Electric engineering prod.	88.23	82.60	83.38	80.73	80.67
Telecomm. and vacuum engin.	71.92	77.46	79.19	79.34	76.59
Precision engineering	55.32	38.46	35.84	30.85	38.62
Iron & metal mass products	81.92	74.49	76.04	73.56	72.37
Brick, slate and incombust.	87.11	70.33	77.29	73.61	72.15
Glass industry	74.34	88.44	83.79	79.41	81.86
Other building materials ind.	83.42	73.95	88.48	89.68	90.16
Petroleum refinery	88.91	82.98	88.34	89.42	86.68
Pharmaceutical industry	74.54	74.34	73.39	69.31	66.64
Other chemical industries	59.40	51.04	57.40	59.55	59.25
Rubber industry	70.99	54.05	53.19	56.41	57.15
Plastic industry	79.33	67.76	76.43	80.85	80.09
Wood industry	72.38	70.15	78.03	72.12	72.63
Paper industry	56.00	58.69	57.81	62.92	62.85
Printing	90.25	91.94	92.14	93.18	92.50
Textile industry	81.61	73.33	72.33	70.42	67.75
Leather and fur industry	91.77	90.83	91.09	84.36	80.59
Shoe industry	89.82	83.56	88.19	82.18	73.31
Textile clothing industry	95.58	74.42	80.36	72.06	65.90
Other industries	98.28	90.60	92.37	89.18	83.82
Meat production	87.07	92.85	88.56	88.07	87.93
Dairy production	84.10	98.95	99.37	99.20	99.00
Canned goods industry	83.00	82.06	76.54	77.73	69.35
Confectionary industry	94.95	95.88	96.79	93.38	91.46
Edible oil production	42.50	35.71	42.62	44.38	49.48
Spirits and starch prod.	92.78	88.25	89.43	89.61	83.10
Other food industries	86.55	87.78	92.09	94.50	90.75
Industry, total	72.59	67.56	72.12	72.02	70.14

Sources: as in Table 2.

Table 15

The Extent of Intra-industry Trade in Hungarian Industry
(Intra-industry trade/all trade, in percent)

	1972	1978	1980	1984	1986
Ruble trade	54.52	63.65	58.22	53.51	52.27
Non-ruble trade	50.45	53.59	56.09	60.41	61.21
Total trade	60.52	63.33	65.78	65.55	67.76

Sources: as in Table 2.

at quite a fast rate in the reviewed period, domestic conditions did not bolster the efficient expansion of production of this commodity group, simply because this production growth was basically built on the growing consumption of imported energy and raw materials, which also had a steeply rising price index.

The export of food industry and agriculture is the other major item in non-ruble exports. Here we cannot claim that favorable domestic conditions were missing. The insignificant increase of export prices, lagging far behind the growth of costs, was due much more to the deteriorating conditions on the external markets and the slow adjustment of product structure to changing requirements. Accordingly, the divergence between costs and export prices made this export less and less efficient, while its volume grew at a very rapid rate.

As the data of Tables 9 and 10 show, the export of machinery did not drop in value or volume, nor in respective shares. However, it is a matter of fact that in value terms, both in 1978 and 1986, the non-ruble exports of the commodity groups belonging to the manufacturing industry, i.e., machinery and industrial consumer goods, did not quite amount to one-third of non-ruble exports. The other two-thirds consisted of materials and food products. These outcomes of foreign trade activity failed to fulfill the expectation, that a country with the endowments and level of development of Hungary should have substantially increased the share of manufacturing industry in its exports in the 1980s; for example, according to the Sixth Five-Year Plan, this share should have been increased from 30 to 40 percent between 1980 and 1985.[11]

In the analysis of foreign trade performance of industry, it would not be correct to stress only the unchanged character of flows that helped to maintain the existing proportions. First of all, one should refer to the fact that between 1978 and 1986 industrial production became increasingly export-oriented. As shown by Table 11, the ratio of the industrial production that goes for export has increased, even if not steadily. This is especially clear in the case of non-ruble exports.

The growth of the export ratio was not concentrated on only a few lines. Twenty-three industries increased their export-to-production ratio, and fifteen industries lowered it. In ruble exports there was a kind of balance (16:18) whereas,

Table 16

Concentration Indicators of Foreign Trade

	1972	1978	1980	1984	1986
Sectoral concentration of industrial production and trade					
Production	20.79	20.58	20.92	21.22	20.92
Total imports	24.89	25.80	25.53	25.50	26.36
Ruble imports	31.06	30.27	30.87	32.24	32.36
Non-ruble imports	31.84	30.79	31.89	31.18	29.73
Total exports	29.13	28.37	27.67	27.47	27.26
Ruble exports	28.54	32.20	33.65	33.13	33.18
Non-ruble exports	27.48	23.19	24.01	24.23	23.10
Geographic concentration of Hungarian foreign trade					
Total exports	42.04	35.72	35.44	36.30	38.37
Total imports	40.30	34.45	34.29	35.98	36.06

Sources: as in Table 2.

in the case of non-ruble exports, the majority of industrial production lines became markedly more export oriented (28:9).

One cannot evade stating here that in the 1980s the growth in export orientation of industrial organizations was not induced only by market signals and was not achieved only through the autonomous decision making of firms. But even where the role of exports increased due to administrative pressures, the new sales ratios had certain repercussions in the production and trade activity of the firms. We know of many cases when these effects were rather destructive; forced exports, for instance, typically brought about the disarrangement of subcontractor relations in the domestic market. At the same time, there are ample examples that a more intense export orientation of even this kind induced firms and cooperatives to discover and better understand their external markets, as well as to establish a more open attitude toward the world market.

If we look at Table 12 we can see that some industries increased their non-ruble export ratios more than marginally. There are eight lines, quite different in nature and weight, whose export ratios were increased in an apparently consolidated way by 5 percentage points. None of them belongs to industries receiving a disproportionally high ratio of export subsidies.[12] These industries are the following: machine and equipment production, ceramics industry, glass industry, petroleum refining, rubber industry, plastics industry, textile clothing industry, spirits and starch production. A 5 percentage point growth of the export ratio in eight years time is certainly not a spectacular rearrangement of markets, but perhaps even this rate, and the fact that several of these industries achieved dynamic production growth in this period, suggest that with sufficient incentives, pressure, and opportunities Hungarian enterprises can actively discover new markets rather than simply redirect existing trade flows, and that they are capable of producing and selling the goods demanded by those markets.

The evidence of an export drive outlined above does not mean that the operations of industry became so outward-looking that the industry would have discarded a large share of its functions to supply the domestic market by passing this task on to imports. Between 1978 and 1986 it was not only the external orientation of production that strengthened, but also import substitution; domestic production recorded a high share in local supply. The indicators in Table 13 unambiguously show that in the post-1978 period import penetration from both ruble and non-ruble relations decreased, and the part of domestic supply that was covered by domestic industry increased.[13]

It is clear that, in principle, import substitution is not necessarily a less efficient activity than production for export.[14] In the period under review, however, increased import substitution was imposed by external restrictions on imports from the ruble area and internal administrative restrictions of imports from the non-ruble area. Enterprise decisions about substitution were in most cases not made in accordance with microeconomic efficiency considerations. Even when import substitution turned out to be lucrative for a company, this kind of efficiency was mostly due to the strong protection of the domestic market. A look at the data in Table 14 suggests that, even in the case of several manufacturing and food industry commodity groups, the 70 to 90 percent domestic coverage of domestic supply could develop in Hungary by the mid-1980s only as a consequence of high protectionism.

Like enhanced export orientation, import substitution was not limited to a few lines or commodity groups. Import penetration decreased in fourteen commodity groups in the case of ruble imports and increased in twelve, and decreased in fifteen commodity groups in the case of non-ruble imports and increased in twelve. At the same time, domestic coverage of domestic supply increased in seventeen commodity groups and decreased in only nine. It must be noted that the industries where production grew at relatively high rates between 1978 and 1986, the ones called dynamic lines above, in many cases based their production growth on import substitution, however, because of slack domestic demand and a growing pressure to export this was not sufficient: these industries also had to increase their export orientation in one or both of the export relations. In terms of domestic supply, import substitution was particularly important in mining and metallurgical industries, in machine and equipment production, in most chemical industries, in the paper industry, and in edible oil production. At the same time imports reached an appreciably higher share than before only in the glass, pharmaceutical, textile, and canned goods industries.

In the period under study, foreign trade activity was characterized by central coercion to raise exports to the non-ruble area, a rather differentiated system of export incentives, as well as by a comprehensive restriction of non-ruble imports and the stiffening of external limitations on ruble imports. From all of these one could infer that in this period intra-industry trade, a progressive area of foreign trade activity, declined rather than expanded. Our computations do not verify this assumption. The values of intra-industry trade indicators reveal quite a complex picture. As can be seen from Table 15, after 1978 the share of intra-industry trade in total foreign trade continued to grow, in dollar trade showed a remarkable increase, while in the ruble trade this ratio dropped considerably.[15]

The decline in ruble intra-industry trade was most probably connected with the fact that, in the reviewed period, the opportunity to get indebted towards the Soviet Union was confined. Accordingly, Hungary could not rely on covering the increments in raw material prices in this way and was increasingly forced to pay the growing raw material bill by enhanced manufacturing and food shipments. Consequently, the importance of balancing the shipments in the same commodity group, a factor that used to contribute to the growth of intra-industry trade indicators in CMEA trade, decreased.

The growth in non-ruble intra-industry trade may have been related with the characteristic of the import restrictions and the export drive that both were relatively comprehensive, covering every industry (or else intra-industry trade would have been held back by these policies). At the same time, other reasons certainly also contributed to the steady or—in non-ruble trade—accelerating growth in intra-industry trade: such as the differentiation of domestic demand or the more responsive adjustment—in certain fields—to the sophisticated demand of external markets; the gradual relaxation of supply responsibility in companies with nation-wide influence, the extension of the institution of parallel foreign trade activity, the appearance of Far Eastern goods in the domestic market, thus breeding competition with traditional products of the domestic light industry.

When explaining the developments in intra-industry trade, we cannot exclude the possibility that central pressures exerted by the authorities to boost exports in many lines resulted in an artificial increase in the value of the intra-industry trade index but not intra-industry trade itself. One could read numerous press reports on cases when a Hungarian manufacturing firm, in order to obtain the input previously shipped by its Hungarian supplier, was forced to buy these very inputs back from the West after its producer exported them to that market. Such cases could occur, since firms that originally had quite lucrative deals with their traditional domestic buyers now were driven to achieve a better export performance by central expectations or firm specific short-term export incentives. The result was, among other things, an increase in the index of intra-industry trade, although trade was extended in such an unreasonable way that the very same products were exchanged for each other.[16]

The tendencies in the evolution of intra-industry trade outlined above were in line with the findings of Halpern-Körösi-Richter (1985). These authors made computations for the same indicator but for another population, the Hungarian manufacturing industry, for data of different aggregation level (SITC two-digit industries), and for a breakdown to somewhat different trade areas. The results obtained by them also indicate that after 1978 intra-industry trade with CMEA countries changed over from growth to decline, and in trade with OECD countries continued to expand. They had no time, however, to observe what we can already see from Table 15: that, since 1985, intra-industry trade has reached a higher level in hard currency trade than in ruble accounted trade.

In the review of structural changes of foreign trade the next point of analysis is the development of sectoral and geographic concentration of trade. The changes in concentration indicators show whether the foreign trade of a given country becomes more evenly distributed between different sectors or countries than before, or that developments make it more powerfully concentrated to a few sectors or partners. According to Michaely (1984), the indicator of sectoral concentration of export is as follows:

$$C_x = \sum_i (X_i / X)^2$$

where X_i is the export of sector i and $X = \Sigma X_i$. By analogy, this indicator can be applied to imports and to the distribution of exports and imports between countries. Its value may fall between a small positive number near zero (exactly $1/N$, where N is the number of industries or countries) and 100. 100 is the concentration value of the absolutely concentrated trade, i.e., concentrated to one industry or one country.

According to the results presented in Table 16, the sectoral concentration of foreign trade changed slowly in Hungary both before and after 1978. This corresponded to worldwide experience. The change was particularly tardy in imports, while the concentration of exports was slightly more variable. It can be stated that, after 1978, the concentration of both ruble imports and ruble exports increased. In the long run, between 1972 and 1986, there was a substantial difference between the two export relations: the already more concentrated ruble exports became even more concentrated, while exports in the dollar relation became more evenly distributed among industries.

The geographic concentration indices were computed not for industry only but for all Hungarian foreign trade and without segmenting it into ruble and non-ruble trade. The indicators clearly show that, despite the efforts to diversify trade among countries, the geographic concentration of exports as well as imports increased between 1978 and 1986. One of the explanations for this lies in the increase of the share of Hungary's trade with her biggest partner, the Soviet Union. This growth occurred in both exports and imports. For exports the ratio increased from 31.3 percent to 35.0 percent between 1972 and 1986; for imports from 28.8 to 30.8 percent. When calculated for all other countries but the Soviet Union, the indicator showed a slight drop in the case of exports, 1 percentage point, and an even smaller increase in imports, 0.6 percentage points.

Summary and conclusions

Comparisons of recent structural changes in the world economy and in the Hungarian economy justly point to the rigid structure of Hungarian industry and its foreign trade. Some basic characteristics of this economy prevented the swift structural changes that could be detected in countries usually cited as favorable examples. Here we must mention the economic and political system, based on the steadiness of hierarchical relations, and the economic policy, comprising many elements of traditional planning, that have been preoccupied with the continuous and detailed correcting of shifts and imbalances that emerged in the evolution of the economy. It would be a mistake, however, not to recognize the structural changes that evolved during this period of restrictions. Although most of these changes were modest and spontaneous ones, they are nevertheless important, because they may act as a germ of future progress.

Most synthetic indicators of structural change show a deceleration in the transformation of Hungary's industrial structure. The modification of the size and proprietary structure of industry has been accompanied by a differentiation of economic performance. This clearly indicates that, if the existing institutional obstacles to the development of non-state as well as small- and medium-sized enterprises were relaxed, this sector of the industry could help, directly or indirectly, in vitalizing all of industry.

The analysis of dynamic and declining industries revealed that a certain process of polarization has already been set off in Hungarian industry. Although this polarization is not as rapid as in many market economies, where fast adjustment is the rule, there is a possibility for this polarization to accelerate if market-type financing becomes predominant and if the paternalistic behavior of the state is increasingly confined.

In the last eight years the structure of industrial foreign trade has not improved, but rather has remained unfavorable. When compared with recent transformations in the structure of world trade, it even shows a deteriorating tendency.[17] According to our analysis, both export orientation and import substitution became more pronounced among domestic firms. However, both kinds of activity received their impetus from administrative restrictions, pressures and specific subsidies. This is why a stronger export orientation and a more intense substitution of imports many times enhanced those seemingly efficient industrial activities and trade flows that could be maintained only at enormous social costs. But we must also stress the less important, but positive, consequences of this dual orientation. The strengthening of export orientation and import substitution directed the attention of Hungarian firms to external markets, to foreign products actually or potentially competing with Hungarian ones, as well as to external prices, exchange rates, and the different forms of conducting foreign trade. This also means that industrial organizations acquired the ability to better adjust to changes in external markets in the future. This ability, however, can be utilized only if some other conditions are met. First, efficiency constraints for firms should have greater force, then possibilities of financing should become more diverse and stable, and, last but not least, the central management of the economy should determine to transform the Hungarian economy into a truly open one, on the basis of a clear-cut set of principles and objectives.[18]

Notes

In the collection of data, selection of indices, and in computation I received much assistance from my colleague, Akos Valentinyi. For all of this I owe him many thanks.

1. For the explanation of this indicator see "Changes in the structure . . ." (1981).

2. For the explanation of the indicator see Frigyes-Simon (1972).

3. Statistical data shows gross production in the industries according to the actual setup of the industrial organizations. The changes effected during this period in the organizational setup could not be filtered out from the database, at best they could be neutralized by data aggregation. Because of the cumulated nature of gross production data, value added would have been a definitely better indicator of industrial activity. However, necessary data were not available.

4. In both periods the rate of growth of fixed assets was substantially higher in the cooperative industry, but this does not give a full explanation for the indicated difference in the growth of labor productivity, since the difference between the growth rates of fixed assets in fact decreased from 1970-78 to 1978-86.

5. Irrespective of periods, those lines that, in respect of the index of fixed assets per industrial employee, unmistakably showed higher values than the whole industrial sector in the years 1978 and 1985 were classified as fixed-asset-intensive, while the industries showing clearly smaller than average values were considered labor-intensive.

6. For this analysis the yearly average rate of growth at current prices of gross fixed assets in the individual industries and the respective elasticity groups of this indicator were used.

7. It should be considered in the evaluation of the above that the declining lines were classified on the basis of comparable price data, while the growth of fixed assets was taken into account at current prices. It follows that in real terms fixed assets could actually decrease in many more lines than indicated.

8. Still, industries where the stock of fixed assets was updated can be found both in the dynamic and the declining group. Strangely, there are more such lines among the declining industries than among the dynamic ones.

9. The computations were made for the years 1978, 1980, and 1984. We chose the year 1984 instead of 1985, the last year for which data was accessible, because we assumed that the unusually harsh winter of this latter year could influence capacity utilization in different industries in an uneven and unique manner. Explanations for different indicators of capacity utilization can be found in Rimler (1986).

10. In this part of the analysis the indicators characterizing the foreign trade of the industry are not separated from data on foreign trade of other sectors, especially of agriculture.

11. Similarly, contrary to the plan, there was no growth in the share of manufacturing industry in ruble exports, although this share was already quite high by 1980.

12. This means that between 1978 and 1985 none of these industries were provided with higher than average export subsidies in more than one year.

13. The index of import penetration is given by the import/domestic supply ratio. Domestic supply is defined as the production + import – export sum, while the indigenous part of this supply is made up by the production / export difference.

The calculations on import substitution were made on foreign trade data organized according to the activity approach and not the organization approach. Only for this data could we justify the homogeneity assumption implied by the concept of these indices that import, export, and production of the same activity are interchangeable.

14. In recent years, however, less and less theoretical support is given by the literature to policies that opt for development strategies based essentially on import substitution.

15. In the computations, the so-called volume indicator of intra-industry trade (indicator B) was computed on the basis of commodity group data corresponding to 36 industrial lines. The formula of the indicator is as follows:

$$B = 1 - [\sum_i (X_i - M_i) / \sum_i (X_i + M_i)]$$

where X_i and M_i are the export and import in commodity group i. For an explanation of this indicator see Halpern-Körösi-Richter (1985).

16. I am grateful to János Deák for directing my attention to this point.

17. See, for instance, the analysis in Inotai (1986).

18. On the notion of openness and the necessary changes to make an open economy see Lányi (1986), Nagy (1986), and Gács (1986).

References

"Changes in the structure of West European Manufacturing Industry in the 1970s." In *Economic Survey of Europe in 1980*. New York: United Nations, 1981.

Frigyes, E. and N. Simon. "The Analysis of the Degree and Direction of Structural Changes" (in Hungarian). *Szigma*, no. 2 (1972).

Gács, J. "The Conditions, Chances and Predictable Consequences of Implementing a Step-by-Step Liberalization of Imports in the Hungarian Economy." *Acta Oeconomica*, vol. 36, nos. 3-4 (1986).

Halpern, L., G. Körösi, and S. Richter. "Intra-Industry Trade" (in Hungarian). *Külgazdaság*, nos. 4-5 (1985).

Inotai, A. "New Tendencies in the International Division of Labor, from a Hungarian Point of View" (in Hungarian). *Közgazdasági Szemle*, no. 9 (1986).

Kristóf, I. "The Development of Industry in the Sixth Five-Year Plan" (in Hungarian). *Statisztikai Szemle*, no. 6 (1986).

Lányi, K. "Has Our Country an Open Economy?" (in Hungarian). *Figyelő*, March 20, 1986.

Michaely, M. *Trade, Income Levels and Dependence*. Amsterdam: North Holland, 1984.

Nagy, A. "Open We Must!" *Acta Oeconomica*, vol. 37, nos. 3-4 (1986).

Rimler, J. "The Utilization of Capacities and Resources in Three European Countries" (in Hungarian). *Statisztikai Szemle*, no. 1 (1986).

Market Strategy of the Hungarian Enterprise

Sources of Inadequate Response to Environmental Challenges

PÉTER ÁKOS BOD

Introduction

Identifying and responding to environmental opportunities and threats is recognized today as being of central importance for successful management. But for those in the firm, it is often hard to identify and decipher external signals. Moreover, progress takes time; the new management styles, techniques, and concepts seeking to replace the traditional ways of making business decisions must be diffused throughout the economy in the same manner as are new products or technologies.

Corporate strategy or strategic planning, long-term business strategy, strategic management as a concept and a tool of management, took off in the 1950s and 1960s in the industrialized countries; first in the United States and Canada (Ringbakk, 1969) then in Britain at the beginning of the 1960s (Harrison, 1976), and later in other West European countries (Eppink et al., 1976; Gotcher, 1976). However, the spread of this new managerial tool was interrupted by the world-wide recession of the 1970s. The wide-spread collapse of pre-1973 business plans shook confidence in long-term corporate planning. This change in attitude was also evident in the case of planning at the national level. It is noteworthy that dynamic business corporations did not entirely stop strategic planning activities; instead, formal long-term planning evolved into the concept of adaptive strategic management.

In Hungary, the recognition of the importance of business strategy had a late start. Before the introduction of the New Economic Mechanism (NEM) in 1968, enterprises did not have sufficient business autonomy to formulate their own

Table 1

Share of European Economies in World Exports (in %)

	1973	1980	1985
Czechoslovakia	1.05	0.75	0.91
GDR	1.32	0.87	0.97
Poland	1.12	0.85	0.56
Hungary	0.76	0.46	0.42
Austria	0.93	0.88	0.89
FRG	12.04	9.70	9.53
Italy	3.90	3.89	3.87
Switzerland	1.66	1.52	1.42

Source: Kádár, 1987.

business. Under the NEM, enterprise management has been given discretionary power over short-term production and sales schedules and, to a lesser extent, as we will see, over strategic investment decisions. But one must always bear in mind that the vast majority of large-scale enterprises have until now been socially owned, with the state as a major agent in their strategic decision making. In any event, the time-orientation of management has significantly increased under the NEM, as has the attention given to market competition, quality, and technological development. However, soon after the introduction of market-oriented reform measures, the world-wide turbulence reached Hungary. The plans, programs, and other business policy documents of most Hungarian enterprises quickly turned into mere dreams; the recent take-off of autonomous strategic planning was soon followed by a forced landing. At present, the issue of long-term thinking in general, and corporate strategy in particular, is among the neglected questions.

The shortening of time horizons is all the more regrettable because one of the factors underlying the recent sluggishness of the Hungarian economy is the lack of, or vagueness of, strategic response. The external economic, social, financial, and technological environment of Hungary has changed tremendously in recent years, but the overdue adaptation of enterprises has been too cautious. The consequences are clearly seen by the rapid contraction of Hungary's share of the world market. Not much comfort can be taken from the fact that no other economy in Central Europe could retain its world share. As can be seen from Table 1, the two unreformed, centrally planned economies, the GDR and Czechoslovakia, have recorded better figures than Hungary, the country that has gone the furthest with the CMEA in transforming the institutional and management system of its economy. True, the share of the world market does not provide a full picture of the competitiveness and adaptability of the countries involved, since the world market share can be maintained, especially in centrally planned economies, by neglecting the home market or by increasing the intensity of trade with less demanding partners, such as those within the CMEA. In any event, the question arises as to why the Hungarian reform, a model for other socialist countries, has not created economic successes.

International competitiveness and economic strength at any given time are functions of various factors, including geography, history, as well as incidental elements. One of the decisive factors, however, lies in the workings and interactions of the basic institutions of society such as enterprises, special-interest lobbies, and the government (Olson, 1982). It is, therefore, appropriate to search for answers to the above question by focusing on the relationship between the enterprises and the government. This paper attempts to identify causes and factors, relying upon case studies, interviews, surveys, and empirical research conducted at the Institute for Economic Planning.

Changes and inertia in the macro-environment

Direct links between enterprises and the government

The reforms promulgated in 1968 aimed at the separation of enterprises, both state-owned and cooperatives, from state administration. Before 1968, the enterprises constituted nothing more than the lowest level of a hierarchical institutional structure. Managerial authority was reduced to the execution of tasks determined above. True, the well-documented phenomenon of "plan-bargaining" could be utilized by enterprise executives to create informal room for maneuver, but the room gained in this way remained highly uncertain and personal in nature.

Under the NEM, central planning is no longer a centrally determined flow of information between hierarchically ordered economic organizations. The disaggregation of central plan targets to enterprises, by and large, ceased. It is now up to the enterprise management to define production and sales plans as tools of short- and long-term profit-oriented management. The previous passive executive logic of plan-fulfillment should be replaced by the active logic of autonomous management, whose efficiency is measured by market success. With the passage of time, however, it has become evident that this expected logic of the market has been rather slow to evolve. As shown in the Hungarian literature (e.g., Antal, 1981), the declared goals of the reform, decentralization and indirect control, have had a rather uneven record of implementation. The enterprises' dependency on the government administration has remained essentially intact. While previously the Government issued production targets in physical terms, under the NEM it relies on monetary regulators, and direct orders have been replaced by incentives and pressure.

The indirect management system of the NEM proved to be an important improvement and a decisive factor of prosperity after its introduction. There are now market incentives for success; an enterprise unable to sell its products would quickly run into problems. Thus marketing and profitability motives begin to penetrate the motives and perspectives of managers who were previously predominantly production-oriented. The number of economists and sales experts in top management has been rising in recent years.

At the same time, under indirect macro-control important variables, such as price determination, access to hard currency, import license or export contingent within CMEA trade, tax relief; access to subsidies or "soft" government investment credits are determined by government agencies. Therefore any dynamic enterprise has a strong incentive to keep up good relations with the agencies involved in the administration of these variables. This vertical government orientation is at least as important as the horizontal market orientation, and the more radical or comprehensive is the envisaged change in business strategy, the more important the consent of the central agencies. It is not just that executives might find it easier to come to good terms with government bureaucrats than to achieve market success, especially in extremely competitive world markets. In most cases there is no other possibility, because the majority of the enterprises are truncated in their business functions. As a heritage of the reorganizations of the 1950s and 1960s, productive enterprises are generally divested of non-productive functions, such as retail, foreign trade, research and development, quality control, professional training, etc. (Inzelt, 1985).

Since 1980, reform measures have begun to lower entry and "profile" restriction which regulated activities that each enterprise could undertake, including the right to direct foreign trade (Bod, 1987b). Yet, despite the recent deregulation and organizational changes, far-reaching business decisions of strategic importance tend to be almost totally dependent on the consent or cooperation of institutions, organizations, and bureaus. Gaining this consent through horizontal channels may fail, as the involved organizations are primarily interested in their vertical links, and only to a lesser extent in horizontal cooperation. Moreover, the various organizations in the environment of each productive enterprise tend to be supervised by different government agencies; trade companies by the Ministry of Trade, foreign trade organizations by the Ministry of Foreign Trade, vocational training by the Ministry of Education or the Office of Labor and Wages, etc. Therefore any ambitious strategic initiative has a chance of being implemented only if the initiator gains the full support of the supervisory government agency. In light of this, the managers formulate their plans from the very start in a way that is perceived by them to be in line with the policy of these agencies. Less determined managers make no attempt to produce clear-cut business horizons for their organization but join the centrally inspired state development programs.[1]

The juxtaposition of corporate goals and government intentions is not in itself necessarily harmful if it results in a meaningful compromise. After all, in a socialist country the state has not only a right, but a clear responsibility to shape long-term economic processes. Yet, the intrusion of considerations peculiar to bureaucratic decision-making processes is not propitious for bold ideas. Instead, it is prone to lessen any threats to the status quo. Moreover, the responsibility for the decisions finally arrived at may get lost.

The case of Company K: an illustration

In the mid-1970s Hungarian macro-management decided to insert new dynamism into industry through the use of then cheap foreign credits. Under government inspiration, quite a few enterprises drew up ambitious plans to increase production. For example, Company K, the only producer of cables in Hungary, initiated an investment program in 1977 with the backing of state agencies and a bank loan of 3 billion forints from the Hungarian National Bank (HNB). The servicing of this huge debt, however, soon increased the costs of production. In order to maintain the company's previous profitability, the State Planning Commission raised domestic cable prices. In 1980, when the investment was 80 percent complete, it became evident that demand in the Hungarian market would increase at best by two to three percent a year as against the 10-12 percent annual growth envisaged at the start of the project, while foreign demand and export prices declined. The profit of the company further declined in 1981, so the HNB stopped granting additional credits, and later the outstanding debts had to be rescheduled.

When the project was finally concluded in 1982, capacity utilization stood at about 50 percent, weighing heavily on the overhead costs of the firm. To find additional markets, the management searched for new opportunities, but in an ill-conceived and ad hoc way. A venture in the Middle East, undertaken without sufficient business knowledge and preparation, turned into a fiasco. By 1985, the company had liabilities one billion forint in excess of its capital stock. The HNB refused any loans, and the supervising ministry ordered the financial reorganization of Company K. Being in a monopoly position, the company could avoid liquidation: it survived, but the management lost most of its autonomy—a situation that now suits neither the government, forced to finance the debts, nor the management, left to the mercy of financial authorities.

The case of Company K is by no means unique. Over a dozen large-scale manufacturing enterprises have gotten into situations where the financing of grandiose investments, inspired by growth-conscious government bodies, has become impossible under changing conditions. In this and similar cases the responsibility for decisions remain, even after the event, rather moot. To be sure, the management, under the impact of the promised incentives, entered upon a venture which it would have never undertaken on the basis of strict business calculations. The forecasts of demand were from the start grossly unrealistic, and it is no wonder that actual sales fell wide of the mark. Still, mistaken planning was partly due to the fact that the main customers of Company K had also hatched similar grandiose plans for expansion. Similarly, the participation of certain state agencies in the strategic decisions regarding the ill-fated expansion of Company K can be documented; the irresponsibility of the company's management was fuelled by similarly irresponsible state activities. The case of Company K shows striking parallels with the mistaken growth strategy of the British Steel Corporation under its ten-year development plan of 1973 (Silberton, 1982). One of the lessons that can be drawn is that the large-scale of an enterprise, its significant role in production, employment or export, and its unavoidable proximity to macro-policy shapers is not necessarily an advantage. On the one hand, as observers at smaller state enterprises or in the private sector easily notice, large-scale state enterprises have a privileged position. On the other, they are more exposed to the scrutiny and the intervention of the state. In this sector the restrictions that regulate the market entry and exit, or even the choice between home sales or export, may be de facto stronger than in the case of smaller companies.[2] To be sure, infringements on formal enterprise autonomy have been recorded by surveys and case studies on industrial units of various size and significance. Focussing on large-scale manufacturing firms is nevertheless justifiable, because these are the organizations within the Hungarian economy that, over the past few years, have come under the strongest environmental pressures, especially from changing external technological and market factors.

To correct ambiguities in rights and responsibilities, a reform of the state enterprise management system was initiated in 1985. Under the new management system, the relationship of enterprises and the state has been placed on a new footing by giving enterprises control over corporate property. Decisions on the appointment of the general director, on investment, production, marketing management, as well as organizational changes such as mergers, establishing subsidiaries, etc., are now the responsibility of the enterprises.[3]

Completed in late 1986, this reform is too recent to be evaluated from a strategic planning point of view. The strengthening of self-management, and the clear demarcation of rights and responsibilities between the organization and the state, are factors that reduce personal dependence on state agencies. Consequently, this reform is expected to create more advantageous conditions for autonomous strategic corporate planning and decision making. It is also true, however, that the self-management features of the new forms may result in all-too-strong emphasis on short-term profit and wage increases and in an inward-looking attitude.[4]

This management reform may be seen as a necessary and useful step in the evolution from state-tutored enterprises to autonomous business corporations. Yet I would personally underline its transitional character, and I envisage an organizational system under which medium- to large-scale enterprises are transformed into joint stock companies with majority or minority state participation exercised through state-owned banks and financial institutions.

Formal planning links between the state and the enterprise

The provision of ACT VII of 1972 prescribes that social sector economic organizations are obliged to compile medium-term and annual plans. The methods of planning and the content of the plans, with certain exceptions regarding defense-related issues, envisaged provision of budgetary means and foreign trade transactions determined in inter-government agreements, are established and approved by the general-manager or the general assembly in self-managed organizations. A recent modification of the National Planning Act of 1985 further increased the decision-making autonomy of economic organizations and determined the legal framework of planning within self-managed firms.

Practice has shown, however, that despite all these changes in the legal regulations, corporate planning activities have closely adhered to the methodology, time-table, and content of the national plans. Far from being an example of meaningful strategic planning, corporate medium-term planning has more often than not degenerated into bureaucratic exercises with the sole aim of fulfilling external plan-making obligations, (Mohai, 1979; Bod et al., 1987). This frequent degeneration of corporate planning is the outcome of several factors, two of which will be touched upon here. First, enterprise management may make efforts to reformulate its original ideas in order to make them fit into central development programs or current government objectives. Second, government agencies or party organs tend to look at the corporate plans from an abstract macroeconomic aspect, namely, whether or not the aggregation of the individual corporate plans in a given branch will add up precisely to the corresponding figure in the national plan. If not, then administrative pressure, mainly in the form of "consultations" with the general directors in the supervisory ministry, is applied to re-orient corporate plans and planners.

This practice has frequently been spotted by industrial researchers in the case of the medium-term (five-year) plans which, by virtue of their time horizon, tend to be of strategic importance. The practice of consultations regarding corporate plans deemed unrealistic or overambitious by government bodies has been strongly criticized in academic circles as inconsistent with the principles of the reform. Under the NEM, corporate aspirations and goals are to be influenced not through the planning system, but rather through financial regulators and other indirect economic measures. Bargaining over corporate plans destroys the value of a strategic document that should serve as a policy framework for longer term development. On the other hand, government agencies responsible for the fulfilment of the national plan, especially the branch ministries, hold the view that a comparison of aggregated corporate plans and the national plan is required to determine any discrepancies that may exist. If there is a marked discrepancy at the very start then, so goes the reasoning, an even bigger divergence will evolve by the end of the plan horizon.

It is true that, despite all the informal pressures and consultations, the sum of individual enterprise plans has systematically differed from the figures of the central plan. The difference in industry, for example, is shown in Table 2. The typical enterprise strategy suggested by the results in Table 2 is that of a factor-intensive growth trajectory. To be sure, the central plans themselves had foreseen strong economic growth until the late 1970s. But the targets of the national plans have been systematically surpassed by corporate intentions on two scores: investments and CMEA exports settled in rubles. The representative growth strategy, as it appears in formal medium-term corporate plans, aims at increasing the size and sales of the organization, mainly through exports to the less demanding CMEA markets with their high capacity for absorbing goods; and sales on the home market. Sales in competitive Western markets and exports settled in convertible currencies

Table 2

Pattern of Differences Between Aggregated Enterprise Plans and the National Plan

		1970–1975	1976–1980	1981–1985	1986–1990
Factors of production	labor	+			
	investment	+ +	+ +	+ +	
Output	production	+		+	
	ruble exports	+	+ +	+	+ +
	hard-currency exports	+	–	–	–
Efficiency	productivity	–	–	–	–
	return on investment	–	– –	–	–

Source: Bod, 1987.

Notes:
+ and + + indicate that the sum of corporate plan targets exceeds or significantly exceeds the respective central targets.
– and – – indicate that the sum of corporate plan targets are less or significantly less than the respective central targets.

are not seen as significant sources of growth for the firm's sales.

It has to be kept in mind that the information gained from the formal medium-term corporate plans is but an indirect indication of the underlying corporate strategies. Due to intensive state-enterprise interactions rather serve the plans as bargaining chips, than as true declarations of corporate strategies. In light of this, detailed research has been conducted to identify the real values, preferences, intentions, and strategic goals of managers (Papanek, 1986; Bod et al., 1987). Such strategies, of course, can only be evaluated in the context of the market structure.

On the structure of the Hungarian market

Hungary has one of the most highly concentrated industrial sectors in the world (Román, 1978; Voszka, 1980). The source of this concentration is previous concentration campaigns and the pre-1980 regulatory framework that erected barriers to the exit and entry of enterprises in the domestic product market, which was also protected from international competition. Starting in 1981, the Government began to reverse the tendency toward concentration by splitting up oversized horizontal conglomerates and by permitting existing enterprises to found subsidiaries and joint ventures, see Table 3.

This high level of concentration means that monopoly or oligopoly structures

Table 3

Number and Size of Social Sector Industrial Organizations[a]

	1960	1970	1980	1986
Number of state enterprises	1,368	812	699	1,007
Employees per firm	839	1,836	1,911	1,278
Number of cooperatives	1,251	821	661	1,207
Employees per firm	129	290	360	180

Source: Statistical Yearbook, various issues.
[a]End of the year.

are likely to characterize domestic industrial markets. Moreover, the recent aggravated balance-of-payments situation has restricted imports and, in combination with a long history of tariff and non-tariff protection from international competition, resulted in weakened competition in most market segments. Monopolistic positions, in turn, are likely to create weak responses to external signals. The Hungarian monopolies are no exceptions to this general observation.

Under Hungarian conditions, the relatively small number of industrial organizations will not necessarily imply a total lack of competition between producers. The Hungarian state enterprise or industrial cooperative is typically a multi-divisional organization consisting on the average of four to five establishments. These units, which more often than not were once autonomous firms, tend to have their own production profile and significant organizational complexity. Therefore, if the establishments were to run as strategic business units, as suggested by Dietrich (1987), the number of autonomous market agents would increase by a factor of four to five, thus increasing the probability of market competition.

The characteristics of the real market structure are important for understanding the strategic behavior of enterprises. Firms in comfortable oligopolistic, let alone monopolistic, positions can be assumed to neglect market impulses. Instead, managers recognize that their growth aspirations are best served by close ties with the authorities. If, however, there are numerous producers in a given market segment, and above marginal imports, then no firm involved in the production of this specific good will have the liberty to choose growth strategies independent of sales and profitability constraints.

To uncover the real market structure of industry, survey research is under way (Bod and Nagy, 1987). This survey, some of whose results are reported in Table 4, covers not only the shares of particular producers in selected market segments, but

Table 4

Market Structure Types in Hungarian Machinery Product Segments, 1985

Market structure types	Product segments		of which	
	nominal shares [%]	number	import surplus	export surplus
1. pure monopoly	14	34	13	15
practical monopoly	9	21	8	11
dominant producer	29	71	30	37
	[52]	[126]		
2. pure oligopoly	7	17	10	7
practical oligopoly	9	23	7	12
dominant oligopoly	21	51	25	20
	[37]	[91]		
3. atomistic market	11	28	15	13
	100	245	123	115

Source: Bod and Nagy, 1987.
Note: For a definition of market types see the Appendix. Breakdown by import or export surpluses is not complete due to lack of data in certain cases.

also other often neglected questions, as to how important is the given product within the total output of the whole multi-divisional organization, and how exports and imports affect the total supply in this market segment.[5] Pure monopoly, contrary to expectations, is rather rare, occurring in 34 product groups out of the total 245. Considering, however, the cases in which the number of producers may be high, but the market share of the biggest producer exceeds 96 percent and the next biggest is under 2 percent, then this effective monopoly can be found in twenty-one market segments, or 9 percent of all cases. Even more frequent is the market structure where one producer has over two-thirds of the total output and the rest is made up by many marginal market agents, the case of the dominant producer.

The second group is composed of those product lines that are produced under oligopoly structure. In the majority of cases there are several producers, but the total domestic output is dominated by a few firms. Finally, the third type, where a large number of producers may in principle give rise to market competition, is restricted to a mere 11 percent of the segments surveyed. Competition is also affected by the significance of imports. If imports of a given product exceed the value of exports, then even a single producer may not dominate that market segment. If a dominant market position is coupled with an export surplus, a dominant position on the domestic market is all but inevitable.

Table 4 indicates that out of the thirty-four pure monopoly cases there are fifteen markets where the producer exports more than the import to the market,

Table 5

Relative Importance of Products Measured as Share of Total Enterprise Production in Selected Product Lines

		1st producer		2nd producer		3rd producer	
number of products	producers	market share	share in total pro- duction of enterprise	market share	share in total pro- duction of enter- prise	market share	share in total pro- duction of enterprise
NC milling machines	2	77.0	1.5	21.8	0.8	0.3	0.0
steam turbine	1	100.0	3.1				
containers	20	70.3	4.0	12.1	6.7	5.3	9.4
tape recorders	2	73.2	8.7	26.7	14.6		
railroad cars	1	100.0	2.6				
electronic tubes	1	100.0	0.7				

Source: Bod and Nagy, 1987.

a sign of an extremely strong position. There is a special case that can be termed "uninterested monopoly"; the turnover of the monopolist in a given market is but a fraction, less than 10 percent of the total sale of the organization that has such a monopoly over this particular market. One can safely suppose that a diversified large-scale organization is not compelled to elaborate market strategies for a product in which it has a monopoly but which forms only a very small part of the enterprise's total business activities. Such a situation is exemplified by products shown in Table 5.

The question arises whether the recent lowering of barriers to entry and liberalization of restrictions on enterprise product lines have resulted in healthier market structures and in strengthened competition. According to our surveys, the number of market agents in industry did increase during the last two decades; in the 1970s due to the proliferation of industrial subsidiaries of agricultural cooperatives, and in the early 1980s because of the increasing number of small enterprises, small cooperatives, private work partnerships, and because of the breakup of large organizations. Thus, in 1985 hand tools were produced by 49 organizations, bolts by 80, food processing machinery by 63, industrial metal structures and forms by 144, storage tanks by 160, to name only a few products. However, the relatively small size of new market entrants prevents them from shattering the position of the big producers; the former have mainly filled market niches. Moreover, large-scale organizations have retained their hierarchical structure, which enables them to respond quickly to the desires of the authorities. Consequently, establishments and sub-divisions of large firms have not gained sufficient decision-making authority to become strategic business units and autonomous market agents. Thus, recent developments in the domestic market structure have not been strong enough to enforce a revaluation of long-standing strategies.

Influence of fiscal and monetary regulators

In the post-reform Hungarian economic system, business activities in general, and the functioning of state enterprises in particular, are to be controlled, influenced, and shaped, as a rule, through financial regulators. Conversely, the close ties created by bargaining between the state agencies and state enterprises on the one hand, and underdeveloped and distorted markets with dominantly monopolistic and oligopolistic structures on the other, render neutral and parametric state regulation unfeasible. Firms in strong bargaining positions vis-à-vis the government can make good their claims for preferential treatment, while organizations in less advantageous positions may be forced to contribute disproportionately to the overhead costs of society by being made to pay higher taxes. In any event, the rules of the game are a function of influence, sometimes of personal nature, and the rules are also volatile, thus working against long-term perspectives in economic decision making.

Contrary to conventional wisdom, the time perspective of the State, at least in the case of Hungarian regulatory agencies, is not very long. The authorities are not authorized to undertake long-term obligations. Therefore there seems to be much truth in the opinion frequently aired by corporate executives, that the short time horizon of the State contributes significantly to the general short-term orientation of enterprises.

It is also true, however, that the financial regulators are frequently blamed when regulatory agencies are, in effect, nothing but ''post offices'' in the matter. During attempts to introduce a stricter financial regime, enterprise managers interviewed often complained about ''regulators turning hard-earned profits into losses.'' To be sure, in many cases there had been a whole gamut of previous subsidies that had concealed the fact that the product or technology was obsolete, quality unsteady, or the undertaking badly prepared. Ironically, putting blame upon the regulators is not illogical, since the State is really in a position to save any enterprise, even in the case of the latter's obvious uncompetitiveness, at the expense, of course, of other firms or the taxpayer. In the long run, however, the State cannot insulate economic units from external threats, including those emanating from international competition. Therefore future-conscious executives must focus more on the hard facts of the economy, rather than on the intermediary mechanism; it is not the postman who is to blame for bad news that comes through the mail.

Market information—goals—strategies

In the light of the contraction of Hungary's share of world trade, it is interesting to obtain Hungarian corporate executives' perspectives on an evaluation of forthcoming developments that are likely to have an important impact on the efforts of their enterprises to meet the objectives contained in their strategic plans. For that reason a comprehensive survey of seventy-six industrial enterprises and cooperatives was conducted in the Summer of 1986 (Bod et al., 1987).

The best fit between an organization and its changing economic, technological, human, domestic, and international market environments can only be achieved through future-oriented management. It is extremely difficult, however, to map the real values, attitudes, goals, and perspectives of managers. Nevertheless, the results of the survey provide a solid basis for developing hypotheses about planners' and executives' perceptions, regarding the future of their organizations.

Table 6, for example, contains the objectives, reported in descending order of frequency, that executives viewed as crucial in their responses to our survey, as well as to earlier Hungarian surveys conducted in 1976 and 1981. The results are compared to a similar survey of United States executives.

The Hungarian answers depict a profile of values and objectives that is not without valuable lessons. The expansion of production, once the dominant objective, is losing importance, while the rate and the volume of profits have become more important. The emphasis given to the increase in wages, a cost element, and the objective of increases in the size of the labor force are partly explained by the labor shortage in several industrial occupations in Hungary. These results reconfirm the assumptions of the theory of the self-managed firm, namely that such a firm maximizes income per employee, unlike privately owned ones which maximize profits (Ward, 1958).[6]

The factors related to competitiveness are less clear. The importance of technological development as an objective can be explained by the strong recognition in Hungary of the widening technological gap. It is noteworthy that exports to hard currency markets are not of primary importance to managers, despite all the attention state agencies and the press pay to them. It is symptomatic of current managerial attitudes that, while several enterprises experienced sales problems causing underutilization of productive capacities at the time the survey was conducted, few planned for diversification, only four cases altogether, and a decrease of labor employed as an objective was mentioned in only three cases.

The way in which enterprise managers perceive the strategic options for their organizations is strongly determined by their assessment of the future macroeconomic environment. Table 7 presents their perception of the probable access to inputs in the five years to come. The Table reveals that the managers surveyed do not expect improving external factors, except in inter-firm relationships and in access to bank credits. Despite this, quite a few respondents declared the intention of their company to increase the share in total sales of exports to hard currency

Table 6

Declared Objectives of Hungarian and American Managers
(in descending order of importance)

United States		Hungary		
1974	1979	1976	1981	1986
1. earnings	return on investment	volume of profits	wage increases	volume of profits
2. sales	earnings	production	product development	profit-ability
3. return on capital	sales	wage increases	profitability	technological development
4. market share	market share	profitability	volume of profit	wage increases
5. capital growth	capital growth	hard currency	hard currency	productivity
6.		product development	saving on materials	product development
7.		technology development	technology development	hard currency
8.		saving on materials	organizational change	saving on materials
9.		organizational change	production	increase in labor force

Sources: Boulton et al., 1982; Papanek et al., 1986; Bod et al., 1987.

markets [see Table 8]. Similarly, an increase in the share of the CMEA exports in total sales is planned. These measures, if realized, would decrease the share of the domestic markets in enterprise sales in nearly half the cases surveyed.

To implement these structural changes, envisaged in the medium-term corporate plans, enterprises would have to demonstrate sufficient competitiveness on the markets concerned. The remarkable thing here is that the enterprises in the sample have very inadequate information on their own relative competitiveness. When questioned whether their company has analyzed the present and future competitive position of its main foreign and domestic rival[s], out of the seventy-four ratable answers forty-five managers, or 61 percent of the sample, responded in the negative; such analyses had not been made. Among those giving a negative answer, there is a fair number of Hungarian firms which must be, by any definition, exposed to competition on the market for goods, such as entertainment electronics, a fact ignored by planners when making medium-term programs for these enterprises.

The ratable answers suggest that the present level of productivity and technology of the Hungarian manufacturers in their field somewhat surpasses the average CMEA-level, but lags greatly behind their Western competitors. Compared to Third World rivals, the picture varies. The expectations of virtually all respondents

Table 7

Expected Changes in Factor Supply to 1990
(percentage distribution of answers)

	improving	unchanged	worsening	N
Labor	12	53	35	76
Credit	34	53	13	74
State subsidies	10	40	50	70
Raw materials, energy	9	63	28	76
Imports	15	28	57	71
Inter-firm cooperation	42	54	7	74

Source: Bod et al., 1987.

Table 8

Expected Changes in Sales Structure to 1990
(percentage distribution of answers)

share of sales on	will increase	will decrease	will remain unchanged
Domestic markets	10	47	43
Ruble export market	26	9	65
Hard-currency export market	37	7	56

Source: Bod et al., 1987.
Note: Increase/decrease in sales structure is reported if the expected change in the proportion of the three markets within the total sale of the firm exceeds ± 3 percent.

indicate that the advantage enjoyed by Hungarian firms within the CMEA will be reduced in the years to come, that the lag behind most highly developed countries is going to increase and that the occasionally existing competitive edge against Third World competitors will disappear.

Such a survey can only provide a general picture. Follow-up interviews and previous detailed case studies (Inzelt, 1986) have revealed that there are wide differences among Hungarian enterprises in their ability to respond to market and technological challenges, to formulate effective corporate strategies, and to implement them. The personal characteristics of the general director have been identified as the strongest factor contributing to such differences. Yet it is perhaps symptomatic that neither the domestic market, nor state regulation have proved strong enough to create an inner environment in which enterprises are, irrespective of the subjective factors involved, made to hammer out adequate strategic responses to external environmental challenges.

Conclusions

Building on data and experience gained through surveys, interviews and analyses, as well as on the available literature, this paper acknowledges the importance of the New Economic Mechanism in general, and the innovations in the status of the enterprise in particular. This acknowledgement should not conceal the ambiguities and bureaucratic tendencies in the State-enterprise interface, the significant loss in strategic autonomy of the enterprise management, and the resulting slow response to external opportunities and threats, weaknesses in environmental analyses, etc.

It must be noted that Hungarian enterprises, as government-dependent commercial organizations, face some distinctive managerial and planning problems. Enterprises are expected to promote an array of conflicting objectives, the rules of the games are frequently redefined by authorities, and the domestic market exerts inadequate pressure on, and provides ambiguous guidance for, business-minded executives. These features are by no means country-specific; government-dependent businesses tend to experience similar problems within quite different settings (Ramamarti, 1986). Private sector managerial styles and tools, including the concept of strategic planning and management, can only be applied with care and caution to business-oriented but extensively regulated enterprises under the present Hungarian system of macromanagement.

Understanding the partly general, partly particular, causes of the present situation is but the first step. What is really needed, is the identification and mobilization of factors that could help the Hungarian enterprise achieve a better "fit" to its environment. Recent years have brought about a significant increase in the role of the market, paralleled by deregulation measures (Bod, 1987b). The recently established commercial banks and the evolving capital market institutions are also factors that promise to promote market-orientation in enterprise decision making. Given the clearer demarcation of the boundaries between enterprise and the State, and the envisaged changes in the regulatory attitude of government agencies, one can expect managers to pay increased attention to effective strategies to deal with the real issues.

Notes

1. Managers of extremely strong professional or political standing may cut free from state tutelage. In industry RÁBA, in agriculture the Bábolna State Farm, in commerce SKÁLA enjoy a special position. These cases are, however, the exceptions to the rule.

2. Of the various external social influences that the corporate management has to cope with, state tutelage is only one. There also are Party supervision, territorial (council) control, trade union influence, and the ad hoc inspections of several social organizations.

3. Only the largest enterprises of national importance in defense-related industries, public utilities, and firms under restructuring are not included in the new system.

Large-scale enterprises are now run by a management council—a body of about twenty, whose members are composed partly of managers, partly of elected representatives of the workers and employees. For smaller firms with fewer than about 500 employees, the so-called management assembly form has been established. The smaller firms have all their employees serving on the assembly; in the larger firms, employees are represented by elected delegates.

4. The councils are generally against, for example, the attempts of subunits to leave the parent organization. Although such separations are supported by the government, only twenty-five units could gain business independence out of forty-five applicants in 1985; in 1986 only one subsidiary managed to become an autonomous market agent.

5. Two hundred forty-five product lines (groups) of the Hungarian machinery industry are covered by the survey, based on 1985 data.

6. Hungarian enterprises cannot be described as true self-managed firms; they share certain characteristics of both the self-managed firm and the management-dominated business corporation.

References

Antal, L. "Historical Development of the Hungarian System of Economic Control and Management." *Acta Oeconomica*, vol. 27, nos. 3-4 (1981).

Bagó, E. *Diverzifikáció az iparban* [Diversification in Industry]. Budapest: Közgazdasági és Jogi Kiadó, 1985.

Bod, P. Á. "Vállalati tervezés, stratégia, üzletpolitika" [Corporate Planning, Strategy, Business Policy]. *Társadalmi Szemle*, no. 1 (1987).

Bod, P. Á. "Proxies for Privatization: Some Lessons of the Hungarian Economic Reform." Paper presented at the Conference on New Frontiers in Economic Policy, Oct. 5-9, 1987, Warsaw.

Bod, P. Á., K. Demeter, Gy. Mohai, and Z. Nagy. "Aziparvállalati tervezés a 80-as évek közepén" [Corporate Planning in Industry in the mid-1980s]. *Tervgazdasági Közlemények*, no. 3 (1987).

Bod, P. Á. and Z. Nagy. "A gépipar piacszerkezete" [Market Structure in the Machinery Industry]. Manuscript, Institute for Economic Planning, 1987.

Boulton, W. R., S. G. Franklin, W. M. Lindsay, and L. W. Rue. "How Are Companies Planning Now?—A Survey." *Long Range Planning*, vol. 15, no. 1 (1982).

Dietrich, M. "Corporate Perspectives on the Management and Planning of Hungarian Economic Restructuring." Paper presented at the Conference on New Frontiers in Economic Policy, Oct. 5-9, 1987, Warsaw.

Eppink, J., D. Keuning, and K. De Jong. "Corporate Planning in the Netherlands." *Long Range Planning*, vol. 9, no. 3 (1976).

Gotcher, W. "Strategic Planning in European Multinationals." *Long Range Planning*, vol. 10, no. 3 (1977).

Inzelt, A. "Eltünt vállalatok, elveszett funkciók" [Lost Companies, Disappeared Functions]. *Valóság*, no. 9 (1985).

Kádár, B. "A magyar gazdaság szerkezeti alkalmazkodása—közép- európai összehasonlitásban" [Structural Adjustment—a Central European Comparison]. *Közgazdasági Szemle*, no. 1 (1987).

Mohai, Gy. "Gazdaságirányitásunk gyakorlata és a vállalati tervezés" [Practice of Our Macromanagement and Corporate Planning]. *Gazdaság és Jogtudomány*, nos. 1-2 (1979).

Olson, Jr., M. *The Rise and Decline of Nations*. New Haven and London: Yale University Press, 1982.

Papanek, G., ed. *A középtávú tervezés iparvállalatainknál* [Medium-Term Corporate Planning in Industry]. Budapest: Akadémiai Kiadó, 1986.

Ramamurti, R. "Strategic Planning in Government-dependent Business." *Long Range Planning*, vol. 19, no. 3 (1986).

Ringbakk, K. A. "Organized Planning in Major U.S. Companies." *Long Range Planning*, vol. 2, no. 1 (1986).

Román, Z. "A magyar ipar szervezeti rendszere" [Organizational Structure of Hungarian Industry]. *Gazdaság- és Jogtudományi Közlemények*, nos. 1-2 (1987).

Schweitzer, I. *A vállalatnagyság* [Enterprise Size]. Budapest: Közgazdasági és Jogi Kiadó, 1982.

Silberton, A. "Steel in a Mixed Economy." In Lord Roll of Ipsden, ed. *The Mixed Economy*. London: Macmillan, 1982.

Voszka, É. "Szerkezeti változások és a vállalati növekedés" [Organizational Changes and Corporate Growth]. *Gazdaság-és Jogtudományi Közlemények*, nos. 1-2 (1980).

Ward, B. "The Firm in Illyria: Market Syndicalism." *American Economic Review*, no. 4 (1985).

Appendix

Definitions of market types are determined as functions of the composition of total domestic output:

1.a   pure monopoly
   number of producers, n = 1
   market share, s = 100%

1.b   practical monopoly
   $n > 1$
   $s_{max} \geq 96\%$
   $s_{max-1} \leq 2\%$

1.c   dominant producer type
   $n > 1$
   $s_{max} \geq 66\%$

2.a   pure oligopoly

$$n \leq 7, \sum_{i=1}^{3} s_i \geq 96\%, s_{max} < 66\%$$

2.b   practical oligopoly

$$n > 7, \sum_{i=1}^{7} s_i \geq 96\%, s_{max} < 66\%$$

2.c   dominant oligopolistic structure

$$n > 7, \sum_{i=1}^{7} s_i < 96\%; \; 33\% < s_{max} < 66\%$$

3.   atomistic market

$$n > 7, s_{max} < 33\%, \sum_{i=1}^{3} s_i < 66\%$$

The Defense of Worktime in Hungary

Worktime and the Economic Reform

JÁNOS TIMÁR

The "defense of worktime";
worktime reduction—worktime losses

In the past several years the outlines of a comprehensive government campaign for the "defense of worktime" could be observed.[1] Measures have been taken to regulate the opening hours of shops, the time when services are furnished, and the consulting hours in offices and other state organizations to make sure that workers are able to settle their daily matters outside workhours. For the same reason, steps have been taken to schedule the bulk of "voluntary activity" outside workhours. The question of increased control of absences caused by sickness has been taken up again. There are new orders determining the minimum number of workdays in a year, the ways of allocating paid holidays, the exemption from serving the term of notice, etc.

This leads to the obvious question: Who wants to defend worktime, why, and against whom? If we look at the decrease of worktime in the course of the past two decades and at its present volume, such a "defense of worktime" is extremely justified. In Hungary the six-day, forty-eight-hour workweek and the two-week paid basic holiday became universal only after 1945. Following that, between 1968 and 1984, weekly workhours were reduced four times, while the number of paid holidays and days of rest increased.[2]

Of the 365 days of the year only 253 are workdays; more than half of the workers have a workweek of forty hours or less, the rest work forty-two hours, five days a week. The average length of paid holidays is over one month. Taking all this into account, among the socialist countries at this time, the worktime as set by law is shortest in Hungary; in the Soviet Union it is about the same; in the GDR and in Czechoslovakia about 10 percent more; and in Romania almost 19 percent more.

Table 1

Volume and Composition of All-day Absences of Workers in the Major Economic Branches in 1983 (in %)

	Industry	Building industry	Transport	State agriculture	Water mgmt.	Commerce	"Non-material" branches	Total
Absence as percent of performable work-time base	9.2	7.4	8.0	8.4	6.9	7.8	8.4	8.5
Sickness	81.3	73.2	78.9	78.7	79.5	88.2	81.0	80.0
Full-day paid leave[a]	9.8	11.6	14.8	9.8	13.8	5.8	8.2	10.0
Unpaid leave with permission	6.2	7.6	4.4	9.5	4.9	4.8	5.7	6.2
Unjustified absence	2.7	7.6	1.9	2.0	1.8	1.2	5.1	3.8
Total Absence	100.0	100.0	100.0	100.0	100.0	100.0	100.0	100.0

[a]The full-day paid leaves in this table also include exceptional shutdowns and other permitted working day losses for similar reasons. Their ratio is substantial only in water management and in the state sector of agriculture, 1.5 and 2.4 percent, respectively, whereas in the other branches it is between 0.2 and 0.7 percent.

Taking the average of the socialist sector, in 1967 the official legal worktime, taking paid holidays into consideration, was 2,320 hours, whereas in 1986 it was 1,856 hours, a decrease of 20 percent. Of course, the number of actual hours worked is lower than set by law. The difference between the two is made up of the loss caused by absences. Table 1 sums up the full-day absences of all blue-collar workers.

There are no statistics available regarding the absences of white collar workers. According to some surveys made in industrial enterprises, the volume of absences of white-collar workers due to sickness is considerably lower than that of other workers, but their volume of paid leaves of a character other than holidays is higher. Thus the volume of absences of white collar workers, at least in industrial enterprises, is not much below that of other workers.

Since the beginning of the 1970s, the full-day absence of workers has been around 8-9 percent of the performable worktime base. This causes a very high economic loss. This, however, does not mean that the ratio of absences should be interpreted as being high. Within certain limits absence is a normal phenomenon; like manufacturer's rejects it is more an expense to be reduced than an unexpected loss. It is, however, uncertain where the boundary line lies between normal absences and other worktime losses, and a situation where this phenomenon

Table 2

Breakdown of Partial Day's Absences by Cause in Manufacturing Enterprises in 1985[a] (in %)

	Blue collar	White collar
Activities	workers	
Civic duties	14.5	12.6
Voluntary work	17.3	20.4
Education	14.3	33.8
Obligatory medical check-up	4.5	1.5
Settling of private matters (council, police, court)	10.7	5.6
Other "official" matters (bank, communal management, post, etc.)	3.7	4.6
Services	8.9	2.7
Medical treatment	8.2	5.1
Family matters	17.9	13.7
Total:	100.0	100.0

[a]Based on data obtained from 109 industrial enterprises.

indicates the broken health of the economy, i.e., of the society.

According to international data, which are even vaguer than usual, among the socialist countries the ratio of absences in the GDR and in Czechoslovakia is similar to the situation in Hungary. As for the developed capitalist countries, it is much higher in Sweden, whereas it is some 15-25 percent lower in France and in the FRG. In the United States the ratio of absences is half the European level, and in Japan it is not even one-fourth of it.[3] As seen in the statistics, the ratio of absences in Hungary can be considered to be high in international terms. This explains why the annual number of per capita hours worked in industry by full-time employees is almost the same as in the economically far more developed countries of Western Europe, although in these countries the normal worktime is somewhat shorter, and the paid holiday somewhat longer than in Hungary.

As in other countries, in Hungary, too, the overwhelming majority of those absent do not work due to sickness. Some typologies will say that such absences are of an objective character.[4] However, according to all indications, the ratio of these absences is highly influenced by factors such as the system of health care and social insurance, the balance of the labor market, the safety of jobs, family conditions, the impact of national culture on identifying oneself with one's job, etc. It has also been shown by foreign surveys that absences due to sickness are greatly determined by subjective factors. The dividing line between ability and inability to work, between health and sickness, is extremely vague, enabling the worker to choose the degree of sickness under certain conditions. An important role is played here by the fact that the relation between doctor and patient is not a one-sided one where the patient passively defers to the authority of the doctor's objective diagnosis, but a reciprocal one, not to speak about the real and objective difficulties of diagnosing and the well-known problems of psychosomatic diseases. All the other components of full-day absences, such as paid leaves of a character other than holidays, unpaid leaves with permission, and, finally, unjustified absences in the aggregate do not make up for more than one-fourth of the loss due to sickness in Hungary. However, even that is a substantial loss with a rather significant and negative effect. This justifies efforts to decrease such absences, and such decreases are also easier to accomplish than those losses due to sickness.

In addition to full-day absences, those during the workday are another source of worktime losses. These include: beginning work late or finishing early, and temporary absences during the workday. Some of these are made possible by provisions of law, some are caused by voluntary work, or the settling of personal, family matters. The main reasons for these absences can be seen in Table 2.

There are statistical surveys about absences during the workday, but in this field the records of enterprises are not very reliable. According to our sample surveys, the ratio of such absences can be as high as 1.5-2 percent of the worktime, in other words roughly the same as the total of full-day absences caused by reasons other than sickness. When emphasizing the necessity and feasibility of decreasing these losses, what has been said earlier, once again, holds true: their negative impact on work performance is much higher than their ratio indicates, and their reduction is extremely necessary and practicable. In contrast to worktime losses, work outside legal workhours increases worktime performances. Such time comes partly from overtime work, partly from other sources, such as the work in VGMKs, or factory work teams.

Table 3 shows the changes in the total worktime base in the socialist sector, calculated on the basis of registered statistical data. Up to the mid-1970s the increase in the number of employees balanced the worktime base lost due to worktime decreases. This was followed later, as an inevitable consequence of demographic changes, by a decrease in this number.[5] This meant that, in spite of surplus labor from different sources, the volume of hours worked in the socialist sector decreased by 7.8 percent in the course of the last five years alone.

Of course, the above table does not show the unregistered worktime losses that I referred to earlier; neither does it show another loss, even greater than the one caused by absence, namely the loss caused by unutilized worktime. These losses are extremely difficult to measure; not even highly expensive methods, such as workday photographing, yield results that would be valid on a macroeconomical level. For this reason I tried to assess the losses of worktime utilization by applying other methods. One approach was the analysis of graphs of energy input by industrial enterprises. Their characteristics are well illustrated in Figure 1. In the case of mechanized jobs, energy input is an indirect indicator of the fluctuations in

Table 3

Changes in Worktime in the Socialist Sector, 1967–1985

Year	Average full-time labor employed		Hours worked by a full-time worker per year		Total hours worked[a]	
	1,000 persons	chain index	hours	chain index	million hours	chain index
1967	4134	100.0	2245	100.0	9897	100.0
1974	4492	108.7	2068	92.1	9964	100.7
1980	4527	100.8	2018	97.6	9842	98.8
1985	4355	96.2	1845	91.4	8986	90.8

[a]Including the hours of Enterprise Contract Work Association and part-time employers, hours worked by retired persons and other people not employed at regular jobs. The volume of this worktime has increased in the time under discussion.

worktime utilization and in the intensity of work during workhours and the week. To control the results of this method, observations of the utilization of industrial machines and equipment were made at regular intervals. According to the estimates based on such kinds of approaches, the loss of time caused by under-utilization of worktime is between 10-20 percent. As shown by workday time charts and in-depth interviews, in the case of productive workers, the major part of worktime loss is caused collectively by the shortcomings of external cooperation, as well as by the deficiency of plant and work organization, such as shortages of material and tools, failure of equipment, etc. In ancillary jobs and among white collar workers, worktime losses caused by the fault of the worker play a more important role, since in this domain the stipulation and control of work requirements is even more inadequate.

It follows from what has been shown above, as well as from the worktime systems applied, that in Hungary capital goods, equipment, and machines are under-utilized, and in the course of the last two decades, in spite of considerable worktime decreases implemented, the situation has deteriorated. The historical experiences of industrialization and international cross-section surveys clearly show the process and importance of the separation of worktime and the operating time of machinery and equipment. The decrease of worktime and the simultaneous introduction of up-to-date worktime systems render possible the increase of operating time or the maintenance of the earlier high utilization of machines, which is of special importance with regard to the rapid increase of capital intensity and cutting production costs. To sum up, we can state that as a result of full-day absences, leaves during the workday, as well as of the under-utilization of the worktime performed, at present not more than some 70-75 percent of the performable time base is utilized according to the work order; about 25-30 percent of worktime is lost.

FIGURE 1

Energy Input of a Machine Factory on Three Work-Days
(Peak consumption at 10:00 a.m. on Monday = 100)

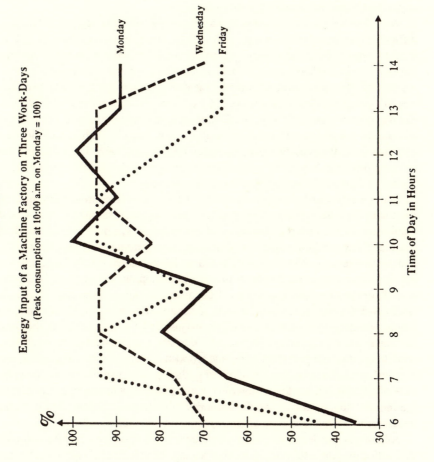

Monday

Wednesday

Friday

%

Time of Day in Hours

The operation of economic systems is inevitably accompanied by losses that belong to the normal costs of production. This is one more reason why it is advisable to refrain from a dramatization of worktime losses and, even more so, from the deceiving procedure in which the possibility of reducing worktime losses is used to prove the existence of a vast mobilizable manpower reserve. Even more deceiving is to conclude that, by doing away with worktime losses, 1 to 1.5 million people would become unneeded in our economy, and thereby raise the completely unjustified belief that unemployment is possible.

Worktime losses can be considered in part as tolerable rejects, more as a difficulty than as a fault. Another part of such losses is unquestionably due to shortcomings in the given system. But not even this limited reserve can be set free through slogans and declarations about strengthing workshop discipline, improving the attitude toward work, mobilizing the reserves, no matter how justified such measures may be. However, on the basis of domestic surveys and international experience, it is reasonable to suppose that, along with the reformation of the entire operational system of our economy, within a few years we can reduce full-day absences from the present 9-10 percent to 7-8 percent, halve leaves during the working day from 2 percent, and cut losses caused by the under-exploitation of worktime from 15-20 percent to at least 10-15 percent.

Thus we estimate the manpower reserve that can be set free through diminishing the total time loss at about 8-10 percent, realizing such saving of time would manifest itself in a quicker increase in labor productivity, which would indeed set free some half a million people and thus contribute to doing away with the overall manpower shortage and to creating a balanced labor market. It would facilitate the meeting of manpower requirements in rapidly developing branches and fields, and would contribute to the improvement of labor discipline. There are, of course, skulkers, defrauders of sickness benefits, absentees who indeed steal worktime. To defend worktime against them is by all means justified. On the other hand, the latest measures and regulations reflect that, under our specific social and economic conditions, it is also necessary to defend worktime against those state, social, and economic organizations that, as opposed to their proclaimed objectives, steal the time of citizens and workers. Moreover, some of the new measures referred to in the introduction, by restricting the authority of managers, indicate that it is also necessary to defend worktime against enterprises and their managers.

All things considered, the faults, shortcomings, malpractices, and the common inclination to yield in the domain of labor management indicate that in our economy the requirements of profitability do not yet assert themselves as required. As manifested also in the state measures taken for the defense of worktime, due to the slow and inconsistent execution of our economic reform, it is still only the Janus-faced state organs who represent the interests pertaining to the ownership of the means of production. When turning its social face to us, the state is indulgent and tolerant, ready to decrease worktime irrespective of the economic conditions. When turning its economic face to the workers, it clamors for the full exploitation of worktime, for productivity, efficiency, and profitability.

As for their attitudes toward these latter requirements expressing the proprietary interests of the society, both the leaders and their subordinates behave as wage earners, whose direct and short-range interest lies above all in the increase of wages and in the restriction of labor performance. For this reason, direct actions aiming at diminishing worktime losses can be effective only so far as they form an integral part of the process of the modernization of the entire economic system and fit into the strategy of changing the structure of the system through changes in the interest relations and the relative position of proprietors, leaders, and workers.

Total numbers of man-hours used in social reproduction and the economic reform

What has been said so far does not mean to imply that people in Hungary do not work much. Nothing is further from reality than the common belief that the time outside workhours is for leisure and, accordingly, a decrease in worktime automatically leads to an increase in leisure-time. This simplified view can often be found even in official documents dealing with worktime decreases. For instance, in the latter half of the 1960s, when the first worktime reduction was about to begin, the official view was that the reduction in workhours was "a desire manifested more and more often by the workers," since in this way "there would be more time for rest, education and training, social and family life."[6]

Industrialization has separated production from consumption, the economy from the household, both spatially and temporally. Thus worktime performed by the employees in the economy becomes distinct from the time spent on the household, which remained a dominant sector of the reproduction of manpower and human existence. Parallel to this, industrialization has limited legal self-employed small-scale production to a narrow sphere, while a special and new type of activity has evolved, wedged in somewhere between the economy and the household, an activity known as the second economy. Thus, social reproduction is taking place in three sectors which differ from one another in nature, but which are at the same time closely interrelated and consist of: the economy, i.e., the "first" economy, the "second economy,"[7] and the household economy.[8] These three economies are connected in space by transportation. It is the total time input into these sectors that I call the "time base for social reproduction."

While the optimistic, or slightly utopian, concept about the relation between worktime and leisure-time continued to be widely held, empirical studies and practice increasingly demonstrated the strict interrelation among the sectors of social reproduction and the Keynesian statement that, at a given level of living standards and earnings, the majority of people devote the time released through a reduction of workhours to increasing their income, or to lowering costs of operating their household by working outside of workhours.[9] It is precisely for this reason that I have differed slightly from many researchers, who focus on leisure-time as the time outside workhours and who center on the issues of the total time spent at work in the different sectors of social reproduction.

The fact of matter is that, when conducting studies on the efficient and intensive use of worktime, we cannot ignore the interrelations and interdependencies among the first, the second, and the household economies, including transportation and the time used by each of them. The time use shares of the sectors also indicate background conflicts. To resolve them means that it is just as necessary to improve the output capability of the economy as "it is to expand free time successfully, in other words the time spent on the overall development of the individual who as the greatest force of production will again have a reciprocal effect on the productive force or work."[10]

Figure 2 sums up the breakdown of the total number of manhours used in social reproduction by sectors in the years of worktime reduction effectuated in Hungary.[11] In the nearly twenty years under examination, there has been a negligible increase in the total time of social reproduction. But, what is particularly noteworthy is the structure of the total time use and its changes. The time released by the decline in workhours and in housework was used by the population to increase work in the second economy. Besides this, we note, on the one hand, the large amount of time spent on travel and housework and the increase of work in the second economy. The total time used for travel comes to approximately 12 percent of the total time of work. Most of that, about two-thirds, is used to get to and from work, which links it closely to worktime. Travel increases worktime, in the strict sense of the term, by about 20 percent. According to time balances, the average duration of travel to and from work is at present 70-80 minutes per workday for every economically active person. The average travel time is also increased by the fact that in Hungary 12-13 percent of people who are economically active commute.[12] In other words, the time used for travel is not only large in volume as compared to the time use of other sectors, but it is also long for the individual workers. Consequently, a further decline in the time spent on travelling would be required, since this could directly contribute to increasing leisure-time. This, however, requires measures in settlement, housing, and transport policy that are both time consuming and costly.

To anyone unaware of the time balances, the time spent working in the households may seem to be surprisingly large. Its volume is more than the worktime spent in the first economy. The numerous time-balance studies conducted in a good number of countries in the 1960s and 1970s showed similar proportions of housework. In fact, despite differences in levels of development and ways of life of countries, there are striking similarities in terms of stability and composition of housework.[13]

There is a relatively high degree of stability in the time spent on housework in the case of people of identical sex and families of similar social status. Despite this, in just one or two decades, there was some decline in the total hours of housework because of the fundamental change in the socio-employment pattern of the popu-

FIGURE 2

Time input per capita and per day of population aged 18-60 in work activity
outside the socialist sector

in minutes

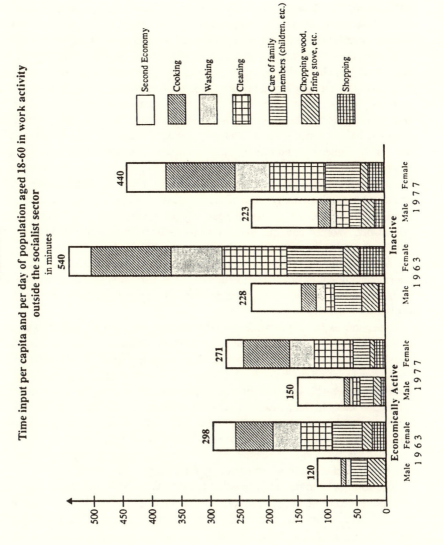

lation. The vast majority of women, who do the greater part of housework, entered into employment and now do their housework with less time input to adjust themselves to the situation of being employed. During the last decades, historically speaking in a short period of time, there have also been changes favorable to women in the development of new relations regarding the division of labor between men and women. This, however, has still not brought about any considerable decrease in the load upon women in comparison with the men, despite the fact that in Hungary nearly all the women of working age are employed in full-time work.

Studies on the volume and structure of housework show a picture that differs from what the public believes. In people's thinking the workload is not determined exclusively by the time input, and for them, beyond certain limits, this is not even a primary factor. Most people find it necessary to undertake employment in the first economy for the earnings received. For them work is just a form of external coercion and economic pressure on them, and not a source of inner satisfaction or joy. At the same time, no one measures or draws a budget of the time spent on raising children, cooking, or keeping the home tidy, etc. To the individual this is not work but activity: the former is a must, the latter just an option. However, the situation has fundamentally changed since industrialization separated the economy from the household but, as can be seen in studies, did not liberate women from housework. Women continue to carry on the bulk of housework, while industrial development and, in particular, socialist industrialization have drawn women into the economy almost to the same extent as men. It is, therefore, not so much the enormous amount of housework which deserves particular attention, but the fact that, even under conditions identical to those of men, the load carried by women is disproportionately high.

We cannot expect any rapid decline of housework or a new societal organization of the task to solve the problems stemming from this situation. Once this is so, there should be a more rational coordination of the worktime used in the economy and of the one spent on the household. Hungary's system of child care leave gives a societally acceptable solution for the period when the care for the infant, together with other tasks in the household, requires the parent's full attention and time.[14] However, amidst conditions of an advanced commodity producing economy, particularly amidst the social norms established by socialist society, it cannot be expected that women in large numbers will remain at home to care for children, or that this should or could be supported by the welfare policy of the state.

The solution is to be sought in other trends. On the one hand, social education and influence can be used to further increase male participation in housework. At the same time, efforts should be made to advance forms of employment well-known and quite successful in many countries that facilitate work coordination in the economy and the household. The most suitable methods are, above all, part-time work, work at home, and systems of flexible worktime. At present, the number of women employed in these types of work is low in Hungary. To make such methods spread, active organizational efforts will be required, both by the employers and by the potential employees. Beyond that, workers who undertake some form of part-time employment, meaning lower earnings, because they want to care for the children or for other family members advanced in years, should receive a sort of care-for-others fee to augment their earnings.

Another special and important sector of social reproduction is the second economy. As can be seen in Figure 2, its total performed time is quite significant, coming to approximately more than one-third of the total time performed in the "first" economy. A dominant role in today's second economy is played by small-scale agricultural production: of the 3.5 million households, at present 1.5 million are engaged mostly in commodity production, belonging to the second economy.[15] Its forms include household plots of members of cooperatives, plots received as a non-cash benefit by those employed by state farms, auxiliary plots of people not working in agriculture, and farms of private peasants, negligible in number.[16]

In the early 1980s small-scale agriculture produced about one-third of the gross value of agricultural production, with 3.3 billion hours of work, from which about 2 billion hours are used by the second economy, producing commodities for the market, and 1.3 billion hours are used for self-consumption, produced by the work belonging to the household activities.[17] The socialist sector produced 67 percent of the gross agricultural production in 1.5 billion hours.[18] This means that the average productivity of state farms and of cooperatives is far in excess of that of the household plots and small farms, while the average income level per hour of work in small-scale production is lower than in large-scale farming. These facts became quite obvious from the operational statistical surveys conducted by the Central Statistical Office in 1972 and 1982.[19]

Special attention should be devoted to the structural transformation of small-scale production turnover because of its interrelations with worktime. There is a decline in the time input in the traditional household plots producing for self-consumption. The elderly peasant population, which will do the work around the house almost independently of market conditions and income per unit of time, is dying out and there is a decline in traditional household farming.

In contrast to this, there has been a steady and significant increase in the time spent in work on their private plots producing commodities intensively for the market. In the last ten years alone, the share of the gross commodity production rose from 50 to 60 percent within small-scale agricultural production. The other side of the picture is that there has been an increase in the ratio of workers of "dual status," who are sometimes more interested in doing their "sideline jobs"—partly because of their capital investment in small-scale agricultural commodity production, partly because of the income that can be earned—than in doing their best in the jobs they have in the first economy.

Another important domain of work performed in the second economy is the construction and maintenance of single family homes and private flats in blocks of houses, as well as many other kinds of small-scale industrial production and services.[20] The total time used by all these industrial and other non-agricultural private sectors was more than fourfold greater in 1986 than it was two decades before, and rose over 1.3 billion hours in 1986. In spite of its considerable increase, even in 1986 the total time was very limited, and only about 40 percent of it was performed by the legal small-scale private sector (handicrafts, etc.) and 60 percent by employees of the socialist sector, outside of the worktime, in illegal but tolerated ways. The situation of all these persons who are working in the second economy, in agriculture and in other sectors of the worktime, is somewhat similar to that of women who undertake jobs but are also tied down in the household; they, too, have two shifts. In addition, it has been shown in empirical studies that the work in the second economy and the income it brings have a negative effect on complying with output requirements, as well as on the effectiveness of material incentives in the first economy.[21]

Thus relations between the widespread second economy, already socially recognized and supported and gaining strength, on the one hand, and the first economy bearing the brunt of the load of development, on the other hand, are strained, as indicated by the volume of the time base of the two, their relative ratios, and the changes within them. For the reasons given earlier, a significant improvement in economic efficiency and the dynamics of development within the first economy are required for socio-economic progress. This, however, does not mean an undervaluation of the socially useful activities of the second economy or its relegation to a less significant position, since it satisfies a social demand that large-scale enterprises of the socialist sector so far have been unable to meet. The major part of production in the second economy cannot be organized economically in the framework of large-scale industry, and it would be totally impossible to generate the enormous amount of capital and manpower this would require, primarily in agriculture. It is precisely these facts that explain why, despite the foreseeable problems, the Hungarian political leadership gave up its restriction on these activities many years ago.

However, the present situation and trend of development, evolving as a result of a liberalization of the second economy, requires further measures. Since the present Hungarian economic policy does not intend to return to restrictions and oppressions, one can break out from the vicious circle only in the other direction.[22] This means a continued support of such activities by means of credit, help given to private small-scale production by different kinds of technical and commercial assistance and, above all, the stabilization of the policy of support and the reinforcement of the atmosphere of confidence required for entrepreneurship. This support must be developed in such a way that it would lead in the direction of making intensive commodity producers independent, gradually diminishing the ratio of those in dual status involved both in the primary and in the second economy. This is also the condition for strengthening the cooperation between the first and the second economies on the basis of mutual economic interests. This trend, together with a much more balanced labor market and other conditions, would provide an incentive to the employed manpower to utilize the time spent in the first economy more intensively which would also lead to increased incomes. This would reduce the time requirement for work outside workhours and leave more time for leisure.

It may seem that we have strayed too far from the issue of the campaign to defend worktime in the socialist sector. But in every country the determinants of socio-economic development are, above all, the large up-to-date economic organizations, which are by no means to be identified with over-centralized enterprises in a monopolistic position, but which do include the modern system of banks and banking institutions, the system of research, development and education, as well as the institutions of state guidance. They concentrate the country's most up-to-date means of production and the spiritual capacities that determine development. Without the intensive, productive and economically efficient work of these institutions there can be no economic growth, no social development. It is, therefore, justified that the campaign to defend worktime focusses on the objective that the worktime base in the socialist sector should be used as completely, intensively, and efficiently as possible. However, the intensification of work in the socialist sector cannot be achieved without rationalizing and modernizing the whole operation of the interconnected and interdependent sectors and activities, in other words, without a quicker and more consistent implementation of the political and economic reform launched quite a while ago. It is only in this wider context that worktime can be defended successfully. This course will create its own problems, but societal alternatives are never between good and bad. At most they can provide the possibility of choosing the lesser of two evils.

Notes

1. By worktime I mean the period to be worked or in fact worked by employees. Accordingly, worktime is not time in the usual sense of the word being an immanent dimension of life and development. Nor is it equivalent to the time of work activities in the self-employed sector or in the household. In the developed commodity producing economy, worktime is an economic category essentially measuring the work to be done and evaluating the work of employees.

2. Between 1968 and 1974 weekly workhours decreased from forty-eight hours to forty-four hours, making every second week a five day working week. Nineteen eighty-one marked the beginning of the forty-two hour, five day week. In early 1984 industry, construction administration, and budget institutions switched over to the forty hour week.

3. Hungarian statistics have very thorough, detailed, and systematized data on population, activities, professions, etc. The system of statistical observations of worktime, however, is quite incomplete. For this reason, the determination of the volume of worktime required various supplementary calculations and estimations.

4. On this see, among others, Dodier (1982), Ishida (1980), Salowsky (1983).

5. The reason for this lies in the drop of manpower supply which occurred for demographic reasons and which, following 1986, is going to change its trend again because of the irregular age composition of the population. Thus, for some 8-9 years there will be a slight rise in the population of working age, followed later by a steady decline. For details see Timár (1987).

6. See Magyar (1969), pp. 8-10.

7. For details on the socialist "second economy" see Gábor and Galasi (1981).

8. When speaking of the first economy I mean the socialist sector employing 96 percent of Hungary's economically active population. The second economy in the socialist system includes all legal, tolerated or illegal work excluding the socialist sector. To the household-economy belong all the usual household chores, as well as the care for the children and the work related to handling family affairs. As for transport time, most of it is used when travelling to and from work, physically linking up the household with the economy.

9. That has already been shown by the first empirical sociological time research project done on commission of the National Planning Office in the early 1970s. See Miklós Szántó (1974).

10. *Complete Works of Marx and Engels*, Budapest: Kossuth Könyvkiadó, 1972, pp. 174-175.

11. I have compiled the items of the time base of social reproduction that are not within the worktime output of the socialist sector on the basis of the 1963, 1977, and 1986 household time balance surveys of the Central Statistical Office. See: *Időmérleg* [Time budget], vols. 1, 2, Central Statistical Office, 1982, p. 794, and *Időmérleg, 1977 es 1986* [Time budget 1977 and 1986], Central Statistical Office, 1987. We cannot go into details of problems pertaining to the methodology of calculations and estimations here. Let me just briefly refer to the fact that I interpolated the base data of 1963 to 1977 and then calculated the time use of 1967 and 1974. These global values seem to be quite reliable. There is much more uncertainty concerning the forecast of 1980 and 1985 since the extrapolation of the development that took place between 1963 and 1977 did not look viable. For this reason I estimated the time use for the second economy and for transportation on the basis of other analytic data sources, while for the households, based on various assumptions, I reckoned with a moderate decline in the time spent on work. The margin of error is far bigger for the estimates of these two years than for the interpolated data. Nevertheless, possible errors in estimation and calculation do not have a significant influence on the conclusions that can be drawn from the summary data.

12. See also the comparative EEC study, Scardigli (1980).

13. See Szalai (1978).

14. The system of child care leave, introduced in Hungary in 1967, enables a woman or a man with a child under the age of three to stay at home until the child turns three, while keeping the status of employment and all benefits related to it. The social insurance system pays not only a family allowance but also a more significant child care fee to the child's father or mother.

15. The Central Statistical Office qualifies household small scale farms as small scale agricultural producing units only if their activities fall within certain operative norms. Apart of the 1.5 million small farms, some 700,000 households have a garden around the house. The work on these gardens and what is produced only for self-consumption belongs to the household activities. Consequently, only the time of work for commodity production of the household plots is computed as time in the second economy.

16. The number is about 60,000.

17. In 1982 about 17 percent was done by members of agricultural cooperatives, and by employees of state farms, 24 percent by members of mixed families, 6 percent by self-employed peasants, 24 percent by employees of non-agricultural sectors, and 59 percent by economically inactive family members.

18. The total work time base was 1.9 billion hours, but we have subtracted the time output of about 400 million workhours done by agricultural cooperatives and enterprises in non-agricultural areas such as industry, building industry, etc.

19. See Oros and Schindele (1977, 1985).

20. At present in Hungary hardly more than one-fourth of the total stock of houses is

state owned. Five percent is owned by cooperatives. Single private family homes make up two-thirds, while the rest is the group of privately owned flats in blocks of houses. The composition of ownership in the case of new homes is more or less the same according to the *Pocketbook on Demography and Social Statistics, 1983*. Budapest: Central Statistical Office, 1984.

21. See Galasi (1982) and Timár (1984).

22. See *Thirteenth Congress of the Hungarian Socialist Workers' Party, 1985*. Budapest: Kossuth Könyvkiadó, 1985.

References

Dodier, N. *L'absentéisme en France*. Paris: Presses Universitaires de France, 1982.

Gábor, R. István and P. Galasi. *A második gazdaság. Tények és hypotézisek* [The Second Economy. Facts and Hypotheses]. Budapest: Közgazdasági és Jogi Könyvkiadó, 1981.

Galasi, P., ed. *A munkaerőpiac szerkezete Magyarországon* [Hungary's Labor Market Pattern]. Budapest: Közgazdasági és Könyvkiadó, 1982.

Ishida, H. "Les conditions de travail: une comparaison avec l'Europe." *Revue Française de Gestion*, September-October, 1980.

Magyar, L. *A munkaidő csökkentés elvi és gyakorlati problémái* [Theoretical and Practical Issues of Reducing Worktime]. Budapest: Közgazdasági és Jogi Könyvkiadó, 1969.

Oros, I., and M. Schindele. "Időmérleg a háztáji és kisegítő gazdaságokban" [Time Base in Household and Auxilliary Plots]. *Statistikai Szemle*, nos. 8-9 (1977).

Oros, I. "A háztáji és kisegítő gazdaságokban végzett emberi munka" [Work on Household and Auxilliary Plots]. *Statistikai Szemle*, no. 10 (1985).

Salowsky, H. *Fehlzeiten: Ein internationaler Vergleich*. Köln: Deutscher Instituts-Verlag, 1983.

Scardigli, C. *Évolution comparée des durées du travail*. Paris: CEREBE-CNRG, 1980.

Szalai, S., ed. *Idő a mérlegen* [Time on the Scales]. Budapest: Gondolat Könyvkiadó, 1978.

Szántó, M. *Munkaidő csökkentés és életmód* [Worktime Reduction and Way of Life]. Budapest: Akadémiai Kiadó, 1974.

Timár, J. "Az ingázásról" [On Commuting]. *Valosag*, no. 7 (1980).

Timár, J. "Interest Enforcement in Hungary: Possibilities and Strategies." In H. Gross, ed. *Work, Organization, Incentive Systems and Effort Bargaining in Different Social and National Contexts*. Frankfurt am Main: Institut für Sozialforschung, 1984.

Timár, J. "Employment and Employment Policies in East-European Countries." In P. Clarke, ed. *Employment Policy in East European Countries*. London: MacMillan, 1987.